THE LANGUAGE OF THE IN-BETWEEN

ILLUMINATIONS: CULTURAL FORMATIONS OF THE AMERICAS SERIES

Jorge Coronado, Editor

THE LANGUAGE OF THE IN-BETWEEN

TRAVESTIS, POST-HEGEMONY, AND WRITING IN CONTEMPORARY CHILE AND PERU

ERIKA ALMENARA

University *of* Pittsburgh Press

Published by the University of Pittsburgh Press, Pittsburgh, Pa., 15260

Manufactured in the United States of America
Printed on acid-free paper
10 9 8 7 6 5 4 3 2 1

Cataloging-in-Publication data is available from the Library of Congress

ISBN 13: 978-0-8229-4727-1
ISBN 10: 0-8229-4727-7

Cover photograph: Daniel Busato at a show, 1999–2000, Camboriú, Santa Catarina, Brasil. Photography by Carina. Courtesy of the Archivo de la Memoria Trans.

Cover design: Alex Wolfe

To Angela Paredes Montero, for her friendship, dignity, and grace

CONTENTS

ACKNOWLEDGMENTS

There are so many beings I would like to acknowledge and thank, as they have helped make this book possible. I am immensely grateful for the ideas, time, friendship, and love that many have shared with me over the past seven years, all of which have contributed to and supported the creation and completion of *The Language of the In-Between.*

First of all, my greatest thanks to Gareth Williams and Lawrence La Fountain-Stokes, who have acted as teachers, advisers, and friends patiently guiding me so that I might develop my ideas and concepts with the care and respect needed when approaching the notions of subalternity, queerness, marginalization, and oppression. I also thank María del Pilar Melgarejo, whom I met at the University of Wisconsin–Milwaukee and who shared with me a different understanding of literature and politics, but also spirituality, courage, and healing. I am also thankful to Fernando Blanco, Joseph Pierce, and Susie Porter for sharing their ideas and critiques of my work.

I am very fortunate to be part of the Department of World Languages, Literatures, and Cultures at the University of Arkansas, with wonderfully supportive colleagues and mentors. I thank them for providing me the space and conditions in which I could rehearse my ideas. I thank Fernando Riva, Violeta Lorenzo, Luis Fernando Restrepo, Linda Jones, Yajaira Padilla, Kathy Sloan, Jennifer Hoyer, Hope Christiansen, Edvan Brito, and Lía Uribe. I am grateful for the Robert C. and Sandra Connor Endowed Faculty Fellowship and the Fulbright College Humanities summer research stipend, which allowed me to complete this project. I am also grateful for the Latin American and Latino Studies Program subvention grant that covered translation and editing fees for *The Language of the In-Between.*

I have been in dialogue with many colleagues in the profession who have greatly contributed to the intellectual, historical, and affective content I present in this book. Many thanks to Talia Dajes,

Rocío Ferreira, Héctor Dominguez-Ruvalcaba, Mabel Moraña, José Antonio Mazzotti, César Ferreira, Alonso Cueto, and Susana Draper. I specially thank my colleagues Amy Olen and Erna Von Der Walde for reviewing, editing, and translating to English parts of this book with great care and generosity.

At the University of Pittsburgh Press, I want to thank Josh Shanholtzer and Jorge Coronado for believing in this project. Also, thank you to Amy Sherman for her guidance and patience through the editing process, and to Therese Malhame, the copyeditor for her careful work on the manuscript.

I have been very fortunate to have wonderful friends who have touched and illuminated the many facets of my life. Cristal del Castillo Felices, Pedro Goicochea, and Juan Ariza were a source of inspiration and courage, as was Ángela Paredes, to whom this book is dedicated. Rachel Ten Haaf, my coparent, read the first versions of the manuscript and offered suggestions and comments that made some ideas stronger. I am thankful for the good years she spent with me and for cocreating our amazing son with me.

Lastly, I want to thank my family for their love, patience, and support. Thanks to my siblings Jessica and Juan Carlos Almenara, and my niece Vanessa Almenara. Thanks to Karen Buchelli, Juliana Oxenford, Shadia Aboudayeh, Carolina Arrascue, my *comadre* Leslie Raygada, Claudia Noriega, Cinthya Placido, Verónica Olazabal, Monica Pizarro, Esther La Santa, Rocío Izquierdo, Andrés Aluma, Bruno Portillo, and Ximena Olazabal—*amigues-amores*, as Pedro Lemebel would say, who with their love and loyalty became, *en el camino*, family. Special thanks to my son Liam Alexander, the light of my life, for his beauty, for inviting me to be stronger, healthier, and happier; to my mom, Meche, Mechita, who always motivated me to learn English while living in Peru, and whom I killed in these pages in order to embrace a more real and compassionate version of her; to my *madrina* Ana Maria Chesi Leno for her unconditional love; and to Gangaji, Timido, Maria del Carmen, and Carla Williams for inhabiting an in between that allowed me to heal.

THE LANGUAGE OF THE IN-BETWEEN

INTRODUCTION

There Was Something Different in the Way That Body Danced and Sang

> There are places in this world that are neither here nor there, neither up nor down, neither real nor imaginary. These are the in-between places, difficult to find and even more challenging to sustain. Yet they are the most fruitful places of all. For in these liminal narrows a kind of life takes place that is out of the ordinary, creative, and once in a while genuinely magical.
>
> —Thomas Moore

The first time I encountered a *cuir* existence I was next to my mother, watching a performance by the Mexican artist Juan Gabriel on TV. As a ten-year-old, I could tell there was something different in the way that body danced and sang. There was something in that beautiful and attractive difference that spoke to me—in the melody that JuanGa, as my mother used to call him, was creating with his rhythm.

That evening in Lima, Peru, was perhaps when I started paying attention to bodies and rhythm. After all, we were in the middle of an internal war between the state and the Shining Path, and bodies—bleeding, destroyed, racialized bodies—were all I saw in newspapers and on TV, except during those evenings when my mother, Meche, Mechita, would turn on her VHS and play that live concert of JuanGa performing in glamorous glittered clothes, "De Mí Enamorate."[1]

As years passed and I grew into a shy teenager with low self-esteem, I encountered other *cuir* bodies, such as Ana Gabriel's, *la ronquita*. I did not know why, but I was fascinated by her body, the passion and strength in her voice and her gestures when she sang, "Simplemente amigos." It was as if she were communicating something to me that I already knew, but also did not know, especially when she said, "M*ás por* qué seguir mintiendo si no puedo engañar mi corazón, yo sé que te amo . . . ya no más mentiras si me muero de deseos." The body of my best friend would enter my mind in a communion with my own body. I imagined our bodies moving, acting, enjoying pleasure in ways I was not supposed to. That same Meche, Mechita who loved listening to and dancing with the rhythms of JuanGa's *cuir* body, once told me, "I would rather you were dead than be a lesbian." For Meche, it was ok to consume a *cuir* body for entertainment, but not to accept that her own daughter had, perhaps, one of those bodies as well.

I was never the impeccable señorita my mother wanted me to be. It is only now, at forty-three years old, that I can dare to cut my hair in a way that expresses the person I have always imagined myself to be. It might sound silly to you, but for a Miraflorina girl raised in a military family, who learned to ride horses at La Escuela Militar de Chorrillos while soldiers were killing and raping Indigenous peasants in the Peruvian Sierra and Selva, I learned to be a submissive woman who would not dare to be something different. So, when in 2001 an Indigenous *travesti* or *un cholo maricón*, as my uncles used to say, opened the door of the house where I was having my first job interview as a translator at the Asociación Civil Impacta, Salud y Educación (IMPACTA), my life was transformed forever. For the following five years I worked (and lived) in a bubble where everybody could just be: *travestis* and *maricones* could be doctors, accountants, and biologists, and I, Erikiuch, as I was baptized, could be and express all I wanted. I could even have a photo of my then girlfriend on my desk.

Friendships were made and every weekend night for the next five years, Juan, Cristal, Pedro, Alex, and Vanessa (not the doctors, accountants, or biologists, but mainly *travestis* and trans community outreach specialists and guides) and I would spend *madrugadas* dancing at *discotecas de ambiente* all over Lima and distributing condoms. It wasn't all fun and games for us, since one of our bosses loved wielding his power over us. As his assistant, which I had become after first working as a translator and later as the assistant to the program manager, I could sometimes negotiate certain freedoms for us and even financial bonuses. It was also not fun and games because in those same years it became very clear how privileged I was because I could pass as what normative discourse denominates a "woman." I was white for Peru and middle/upper class, so I did not face the exclusion or violence that my friends experienced. The IMPACTA bubble was being destroyed. My small, privileged, perfect life with my *cuir* friends was interrupted by acts of violence I witnessed, not only against my homosexual and *travesti* friends but also against my lesbian friends. Reba, for instance, an Indigenous dike who has endured insults all her life and has suffered exclusions of every sort because of her race and gender expression, was the victim of sexual abuse. Along with many others, the same happened to the Peruvian author Karen Luy de Aliaga, who gives an account of this experience in her novel *Compórtense como señoritas* (Act Like a Lady).

My (*cuir*) subjectivity was built alongside the life experiences of Indigenous and mestize effeminate male homosexuals and *travestis*, not alongside other lesbians. I say this to acknowledge the power differences between myself and them owing to my class, race, and gender privileges. I wanted to write this book to try to understand how and why the normative regime that has excluded, insulted, humiliated, and murdered my friends and many others for their race, gender and sexuality, was built and reproduced. This is not the only reason, though. I also wanted to include how these friends and many others survived and resisted this same normative regime, a regime that, sadly, has been and is reproduced in academia, where cultural critics use *cuir* existences and experiences as discursive figures or, like my mother Meche, consume them for their own benefit. This is something I hope to critique and distance myself from in the following pages. Thus, this study does not intend to be extractive and exploitative. This research does not aim to objectify Indigenous and mestize effeminate male homosexuals and *travestis*, nor to "extract" information from them only to produce a publication that serves my academic career. Also, my book does not intend to place *travesti* (or transgender) lives as metaphors, as tropological figures used to theorize and represent crises in nations, national identities, or gender norms, as has been criticized by Jay Prosser, Viviane Namaste, and Vek Lewis, among others.

During my PhD studies at the University of Michigan, Ann Arbor, I started reading literary texts and attending performances and art expositions by Peruvian and Chilean LGBT or *cuir* artists, writers, performers, intellectuals, and activists. Through these experiences, I began learning the language that would help me begin to answer my questions. These LGBT/*cuir* artists, writers, performers, intellectuals, and activists, just as my friends, were inhabiting what I understood as the "in-between." The "in-between" was not exclusive to a space "in-between" the two normatively defined gender and sexual expressions (masculine/feminine, heterosexual/homosexual), but rather they were also "in-between" races, ethnicities, and nationalities. They were mestizes, Indigenous, Black, homosexuals, bisexuals, effeminate, *travestis*, and from this same position they were resisting marginalization and oppression. My aim in this study is to signal how the experiences of a group of people who have constantly suffered marginalization, exclusion and persecution—Juan, Cristal, Pedro, Alex, and Vanessa, among others—are also experiences of the "in-between" that produce an alternative political discourse or dialectic capable of exposing and transforming the normative regime of subjectivity, as I will explain in this introduction and the chapters that follow. I hope this work will give something back to those who have inspired it.

We could say that these ideas and thoughts are already expressed in what has become known as queer theory and the notion of the queer. This book suggests a dialogue between queer theory produced in North America and knowledge around dissident genders and sexualities produced in Latin America, which we could term *cuir* theory. However, this work also considers the limits of applying North American queer theory and its corresponding notion of the queer in Latin American cases because of the multiple identities at play in the *cuir* experiences of the artists, writers, performers, intellectuals, and activists with whom my book engages, which I explain in chapter 2. As the Indigenous studies scholar Joseph Pierce explains, the works of Lohana Berkins from Argentina, and the Chilean Claudia Rodríguez, whose artistic production and life experiences I also address in this book, "have sought to unearth and shed light on forms of being and belonging that preceded the invention and institutionalization of queer theory in the US Academe" ("I Monster" 308). Likewise, a purpose of this book is to introduce and make visible the work and life experiences of *cuir* artists, writers, performers, intellectuals, and activists who, like Berkins and Rodríguez, question and point to the limitations of queer theory.

Since my first encounter with the "in-between," a concept I engage with in chapter 2, gender-based violence (*feminicidio*, *transfeminicidio*, and *travesticidio*) became dominant in Latin America, a region that is still experiencing the ongoing effects of authoritarian regimes and persistent race-, class-, and ethnicity-based inequities. More recently, the devastating effects of the COVID-19 pandemic have exposed the precariousness under which different/other subjects have historically existed. The massive toll of the pandemic has underlined the failure of several (if not all) Latin American republics to prioritize the well-being of their populations—even as many have recently commemorated the two-hundredth anniversary of their independence from colonial powers. So, what started as a reflection on my friends' life experiences as well as my own became a need for me in my role as a Latin American, *cuir*, feminist, scholar and teacher of color to discuss new ways of understanding intellectual practices within Latin American cultural and *cuir* studies. After all, these are the spaces that I now inhabit.

I find the need for this type of thinking especially urgent in the cultural and historical contexts of Peru and Chile. In my estimation, contemporary political and social issues can be traced back to the inheritance of corruption, racism, homophobia, and human rights violations stemming from the unresolved legacies of the Augusto Pinochet (1973–1990) and Alberto Fujimori (1990–2000) dictatorships.[2] For instance, in the current context of COVID-19, Peru has recorded the third-highest number of cases in the Americas, after the United States and Brazil, despite having a smaller population. The country has seen shortages of needed supplies, particularly in regions that already had weak health systems before the pandemic began, mainly those inhabited by Quechua-speaking Indigenous and peasant populations. This crisis is due in part to the deep inequalities in Peru's health system as well as the high levels of informal economic activity and government corruption. Such is the case with the failed distribution of economic aid packages favoring big enterprises and businesses instead of citizens. Peru's ex-president Martín Vizcarra and his government appear to have been replicating the corruption and marginalization exercised by the Fujimori/Montesinos mafia.

Chile, too, has been significantly affected by the pandemic. As of the writing of this introduction, it has the highest per capita infection rate of any major country, with 13,000 cases for every 1 million people. The virus is hitting hardest in the most densely populated working-class cities and towns in Chile. Chile's president, Sebastian Piñera, a conservative billionaire, declared a state of catastrophe in March 2020 and dispatched more than 74,450 military and police personnel across the country. To date, these patrols have detained 6,888 people for violating curfew, 969 for committing crimes during the curfew, and 1,255 for violating the mandated quarantine. It seems that, with COVID-19 as a cover, the military is being used to suppress the working class, which does not have the luxury of being able to work from home, just as the military dictatorship did for other reasons. This cannot be separated from the events that took place in Chile from October 2019 to June 2020 when Chile's national police (Carabineros) used excessive force in responding to massive demonstrations. As has been reported, thousands of people were injured and experienced abuses in detention, including sexual ones. Again, as we see, human rights violations, like those occurring during the Augusto Pinochet dictatorship, are still being practiced in Chile today.

Chileans Are More "White," "Masculine," and "Civilized" than Peruvians

In my personal experience, Chile and Peru have always been linked. Although my biological parents were Peruvian, my maternal grandmother, Meche's mother, was Chilean. As a child she would always talk to me about the beautiful town where she grew up, thereby seeding within me a love and respect for Chilean society despite outside voices to the contrary. Sadly, Peru and Chile's historical and political relationships maintain a negative association that was intensified by the War of the Pacific (1879–1883). Chile's victory over Peru (and Bolivia) left scars on the relations of these countries, but it also made visible some of their common anxieties, especially those related to race, ethnicity, gender and sexuality expression, and nationalism. These same anxieties were intensified and productivized during the military dictatorship in Chile and Fujimori's regime. For instance, as Ericka Beckman points out, the Chilean state's sense of nationalist superiority stemmed from the way in which it situated its role in the War of the Pacific as a righteous struggle against the supposedly "inferior" races of Peru (and also Bolivia). This assertion of Chilean racial superiority became a powerful rhetorical strategy during the 20th century that was reinforced during the dictatorship, giving birth to several discourses that sought to protect the purity of "white," "virile" and "superior" races from contamination. These narratives have continued to this day with the discourse of Chileans being more "white," "masculine," and "civilized" than their neighbors, especially "Peruvians [who] emigrated in large numbers to Chile as maids and service workers" (Beckman 84–87). In the case of Peru, the War of the Pacific also exposed ongoing problems of race and ethnicity, especially in regard to the Indigenous populations who participated in the war as rural guerrillas in the Peruvian mountains. These discourses treated the Indigenous populations as subjects that needed to be improved by others and that had to be liberated by the ruling classes, because they were viewed as incapable of liberating themselves.

In addition, during the War of the Pacific, Indigenous Peruvians were feminized and the value of the Chilean "superior race" was also measured in terms of its virility. As Beckman points out, the voice of the Chilean male was characterized as a deep voice, in contrast to the falsetto of the Peruvian. Beckman goes further and addresses this narrative of Chilean males as being more virile and masculine in a vignette published in *El Nuevo Ferrocarrilito*, titled "Una cantinera peruana." The vignette recounts how a Chilean officer who was ready to take sexual possession of a woman after kissing her, realizes that "she" was actually a "he" and kills him/her (Beckman 82). Beckman explains that Chileans also considered Peruvian criollo men as effeminate not only because of their oriental luxury and reliance on slave labor but also because they had effeminate hands (83). What we see here, then, is that the "white," "virile," and "superior" Chilean race was constituted in the nineteenth century by feminizing the Peruvian Indian "inferior" race. These constructs lead me to a question I address in this book: How do race, ethnicity, gender, and sexuality constitute each other in contemporary Chile and Peru?

In the years following the War of the Pacific, a stated desire to improve racial and ethnic tensions in Peru, and to keep and protect its purity, superiority, and virility in Chile, defined both countries, relating, moreover, race, ethnicity, and virility to a nationalist ideal. These desires were intensified by the need for modernization in both countries. The modernization of the Peruvian and Chilean nation-states, which started around 1929 and lasted until the early 1990s, was founded on the basis of a nationalist discourse that sought political dominance and hegemony via the creation (or re-creation) of a national identity that relied on the subordination/exclusion of those considered "different." Nationalism—that is, the modern process of naturalization of social and political belonging—was understood across the political spectrum almost entirely in racial and ethnic terms, and invariably as a relation to the state. Dissident gender and sexual expressions were simply not on the table for discussion in the forging of the modern social pacts between the state and the people in modern Chile and Peru. Thus, as the Canadian scholar Matthew Edwards expresses, "Queer communities throughout the Americas were relegated within the allegorical shadows of sickness, cast in opposition to the healthy, safe, and clean lifestyles associated with the heterosexual family and biological reproduction" (128) or as the trans Argentinean activist Lohana Berkins points out in her chapter of the edited volume *Un cuerpo: mil sexos; Intersexualidades* (2015), "La 'diferencia' es, en primer lugar, siempre sospechosa, desafía la homogeneización social tan cara a las y los que ejercen el poder" (95).

The Others and Me, What They Do, What I Do, What We Do

In this context, *The Language of the In-Between:* Travestis, *Post-Hegemony, and Writing in Contemporary Chile and Peru*, examines the nationalist discourse that was used as one of the main means for modernizing the Chilean and Peruvian nation-states. It explores not only how the process of modern state formation was founded on the basis of the subordination/exclusion of certain groups and populations, as other scholars have noted, but contends that literary production regarding this period consciously or unconsciously replicates or contests this same process. Thus, Peru and Chile's modernization efforts ran parallel to the aesthetic modernization exemplified in their literature.

In this, my book dialogues with the works and theoretical interventions of Licia Fiol-Matta, Jorge Salessi, Diego Falconí, and Joseph Pierce as they, in their own particular contexts of study and research, address how since the nineteenth century and especially during the twentieth century male homosexuals, effeminate men or "female masculinities" (Jack Halberstam) were categorized as threats to the social order or were subsumed by the state's deployments of "national culture" through discipline, subordination, and exclusion.

For instance, in *Médicos, Maleantes y Maricas* (1995), the Argentinean scholar Jorge Salessi reviews the politics of nation-state building in Argentina during the nineteenth century and also states how these same politics were reformulated during the modernization of the Argentinean nation-state in the first decades of the twentieth century. In his study Salessi considers how homosexuality, first denominated *sodomía*, played an important role in the modernization of Argentina, as *sodomitas* had to be eradicated to preserve the cleanness of the national body. In his review of the creation of the capital city of Buenos Aires as a symbol of the nation, Salessi studies literary texts such as *Facundo: Civilización y Barbarie*, to explain how such books played an important role in this process. In this same context, he reads Esteban Echeverría's *El matadero*, in which he finds an interesting representation of the *sodomita*. In his reading, the author shows how *sodomía*, and *sodomitas*, considered in the nineteenth century as "suspected outbreaks" (47) played an important role in the invention and organization of the city of Buenos Aires and the nation-state, as they were related to *la barbarie*.

In the second and third parts of the book, Salessi works around the figures of male homosexuals, *travestis*, *invertidos*, and *lunfardos*, still considered "subjects who belong to a different species" (158) as established by *hombres de ciencia* such as the military psychiatrist Francisco de Veyga and José Ingenieros. Both produced texts about homosexual and *travesti* community formation. The textual constructions, descriptions, and classification of sexual deviants present in the works of these two men, were extended to Argentinean intellectuals and writers during the first decades of the twentieth century, and offered particular ways of representing these so-called deviants. My book dialogues with Salessi's work when he explains the invention of a *nuevo sujeto argentino* and the ways in which sexual deviancy was considered a threat to the modern Argentinean national identity (179). This frame of thought informs my analysis of discourses of deviancy and national identity in the cases of Chile and Peru. Salessi explains, "Homosexuality was used in Argentina to define and regulate new notions of nationality . . . of the 'new race' emerging from immigration" (180), which was reflected in several literary texts produced by authors such as Carlos Octavio Bunge who portrayed the dangers that these deviants and degenerates represented for the process of modernization and creation of the new country, the new nationality.[3]

In this same context, the role that homosexuality played in nationalizing children of immigrants is striking, as it influenced how they were inculcated with notions of Argentinean identity. Immigrants were accused of threatening "the national spaces where new Argentinean subjects were produced" (Salessi 186) as it is portrayed by literary authors such as Eugenio Cambaceres in his novel *En la sangre*. In this sense, Salessi explains how initial impressions regarding the benefits of European immigration expressed by authors such as Domingo Faustino Sarmiento in the nineteenth century transformed into ideas of immigrants as potential risks of degeneration and decadency, as expressed in literary texts by Bunge. This was to be the case of Chile in its modernizing process as explained in chapter 1, in a section that takes into account the work of Salessi but also of Joseph Pierce who reads the life experience of the Bunge siblings to study Argentinean modernization, when, he explains, "The state project of normalizing culture demanded specific forms of racial identification, gender, performance, and sexuality" (*Argentine* 4).

In *A Queer Mother for the Nation* (2002), Licia Fiol-Matta studies how the figure of the Chilean schoolteacher and poet Gabriela Mistral, born Lucila Godoy, was critical to the articulation of the Chilean nationalist project. Fiol-Matta's study demonstrates how Mistral created a public discourse that supported a conservative role for women within the state in order to anchor the state's nationalist project. In this sense, Fiol-Matta reviews the Chilean state's relationship to queerness, and particularly to the queerness of women. Thus, although the Chilean state placed Mistral as a model for proper feminine conduct, she was often described as being "masculine" or simply as "queer." I see my book dialoging with Fiol-Matta's work in that both books advance research on the *cuir* experience in relation to state politics and Latin American nationalism, as well as the state's investment in nationally projected *cuirness*. Also, Fiol-Matta's book brings to the fore *cuirness* as an important presence which is little known to readers of English and rarely discussed in the Spanish-speaking world. *The Language of the In-Between* intends to do the same with its study of noncanonical artists, performers, intellectuals, and activists.

In the case of Diego Falconí's *De las cenizas al texto: Literaturas andinas de las disidencias sexuales en el siglo XX* (2016), I see a clear connection between my work and his review of literature produced in the Andean region and his proposal to "tell the literary canon in a different way, through forms that have not yet been chewed by the Andean academic tradition" (32). My book, however, proposes a dialogue between literary texts and performances produced in the Andes and, more broadly, the Southern Cone, as it works with two historically related countries, as I explained above. The reason for expanding my study beyond literary texts to also consider performances is to *re-sen-*

tir, in Falconí's words, the hegemonic place that written literature in Spanish has historically occupied, from the Spanish conquest to the present, and to "interrupt the grandiloquent tradition" of this genre that "ignore . . . specific subjectivities, cultural organizations and world views or *cosmovisiones*" (34).

While I am indebted to these works, the main thoughts and ideas of which appear in the chapters of this book, *The Language of the In-Between* differs from them by offering a new reading of *travesti* subjectivity as a body and site of contestation to hegemonic nationalist figurations in Chile and Peru. Based on the experience of homosexual, Indigenous and poor Chilean and Peruvian male *travestis* that as subaltern subjects inhabit what I earlier denominated the "in-between," my book pushes the boundaries of these figures and proposes a language, a *travesti* aesthetic as Joseph Pierce would say ("I Monster" 315), that mobilizes features of the *travesti* in the exercise of writing and performing.[4] My book locates alternate cultural productions that stake a claim for the emergence of a language capable of exposing and transforming marginalization and oppression, a language that critiques the formation of modern nation-states and modern national identity in subordination and exclusion, an act that was initiated in the nineteenth century and resumed by the military dictatorship in Chile and the presidency of Alberto Fujimori in Peru.

By language I refer to the means of expression and communication that, according to the French philosopher Jacques Derrida, does not limit itself to semantics or semiotics, and even less so to linguistics (172). Thus, communication and language designate nonsemantic movements, and both can be produced with or without words, presenting extralinguistic purposes. Following this, the language of the "in-between" that I propose in this book is a language that can be manifested or expressed through writing and performance. It is a language that, in Falconí's words, "tries to break with the binarism of Spanish and also of the academic world . . . in order to rethink language and its power of representation" (11).

The Spanish sociologist and transgender activist Miquel Miseé states that "language plays a very important role in our identity because we define ourselves, think, act and, in fact, exist through it" (106). Following this idea, the language of the "in-between" describes reality as it is experienced and negotiated by the *travestis* this book studies (El loco Moncada, La Manuela, Claudia Rodríguez, Héctor Acuña, Sofía Devenir, and Giuseppe Campuzano), figures who inhabit an "in-betweenness" of genders, sexualities, races, and ethnicities. It also constitutes the means these *travestis* use to communicate with other *travestis* and to experience themselves not only inside their communities but also inside the heterosexual, hegemonic world that excludes and marginalizes them. For instance, as I will explain in the chapters of this book, the language of the "in between" of the artists, performers, intellectuals, and activists in this study (not all of them *travestis* but all of them *cuir* and "in-between"), introduces words with specific meanings, and also gives specific meanings to words that may have a different usage in the heterosexual, hegemonic world. I argue that it is through this language that the book's *travestis* negotiate their survival and existence in nations that are not built for or with them and that have been constructed on exclusionary practices based on gender and sexual expression as well as on ethnicity and race. If "speech about marginality is integrally tied to the naturally codified character of language" (16), as Edwards explains, then the language of the "in-between"—a language that creates different ways of existing—can resist the marginality produced by language that forms and deforms *cuir* subjects. *The Language of the In-Between* looks to advance discussions around nonnormative gender, desire, embodiment, and identity in its production of a language that serves the survival, pleasure, and resistance of the *travestis* with whom this book engages.

Moreover, following the Greek sense of language as "logos," my book states that the language of the "in-between" not only expresses and communicates information and knowledge regarding the *travestis* it studies and their negotiation of reality under particular Latin American historical and political contexts, but it also constitutes an alternative political discourse or dialectic capable of exposing and transforming domination and marginalization into something that is not exclusive of *travestis*. Thus, the *travestis* this book engages with are "in-between," mediating existences that inhabit normative spaces and that relationally give sense to the center, while at the same time disrupting it. As Pierce expresses, "The normative and the queer . . . are mutually dependent on each other" (*Argentine* 5). In this light, *The Language of the In-Between* engages with the work of Claudia Salazar, Claudia Rodríguez, Sofía Devenir, Giuseppe Campuzano, José Donoso, Héctor Acuña, and Pedro Lemebel through the lens of "in-between" language to contend that these Peruvian and Chilean *cuir* artists, writers, performers, intellectuals, and activists dispute state projects of modernization and their reproduction during the Chilean military dictatorship and the governments of Alberto Fujimori. Their lives and work resist/resignify state discourses, which bear mechanisms of violence, inclusion and exclusion, visibility and invisibility, and strategies that silence subaltern voices. The *cuir* artists, writers, performers, intellectuals, and activists my book explores, inscribe several minoritarian subjects, especially *travestis*, *maricones*, *locas*, nonbinary or genderqueer people, and effeminate men, into discourse.

The Language of the In-Between also discusses the work of the Peruvian anthropologist and *indigenista* writer José María Arguedas. I study Argueda's novel *El zorro de arriba y el zorro de abajo* (*The Fox from Up Above and the Fox from Down Below*) to point out the limits of transculturation as well as the limits of Arguedas's project and the Peruvian nation-state's will to fabricate a modern national institutionalized "we." While I greatly celebrate Arguedas's love, respect, and admiration for the Indigenous culture, I also criticize his will to homogenize his own and Peruvian identity through the creation of an ideal that placed this same culture as the emblem of the Peruvian modern national identity. I contend that such a project has led to the exclusion and even resubalternization of other marginalized populations and individuals, such as women, Afro-Peruvians, and LGBT subjects. In this context, I also address the lack of a serious *cuir* critique of Arguedas's homophobia as expressed in his literary work, how this homophobia is entangled with the *indigenista* project. I also question how the transcultured and mestizo project understands gender and sexuality.

My selection of these *cuir* artists, writers, performers, intellectuals, and activists has to do with the specificities of their lived experiences and work as *cuir*, poor, Indigenous, and mestize others that shed light on but also resist the domination, persecution, and exclusion that homosexuals, *maricones*, effeminate men, nonbinary or genderqueer people, *travestis*, as well as Indigenous people, women, proletarians, and Afro-Peruvians suffered during the modernization of the Peruvian and Chilean nations-states, the Chilean military dictatorship, and the Peruvian internal armed conflict during Fujimori's governments.[5]

The Language of the In-Between is not a thorough or comprehensive history of Peruvian and Chilean *cuir* male effeminacy, *travestismo*, or *travesti* performance. Rather it is a theorization based on historical periods and events. It also has to do with my desire to bring to the field of Latin American cultural studies the work and lived experiences of noncanonical or even underground *cuir* artists, writers, performers, intellectuals, and activists such as Devenir, Acuña, and Rodríguez. I am also interested in offering a *cuir* reading of the work of canonical writers such as Arguedas and Donoso to collaborate in the development of a more panoramic scholarship of their works.

Can the *Travesti* Speak?

In an article published in 2020, Joseph Pierce explains that in Argentina, Uruguay, and Chile, *travesti* refers most frequently to "people assigned male sex at birth and who feminize their bodies, dress, and behavior; prefer feminine pronouns and forms of address; and often make significant bodily transformations by injecting silicone or taking hormonal treatments but not necessarily seek sex-reassignment surgery" ("I Monster" 306). While I agree partly with this statement, and the importance of not erasing the particular lived experience of these *travestis*, I purposely choose to recognize that the experience of each *travesti* is different and that definitions change, a reality I try to reflect in this book.[6] As Lohana Berkins explains, "It is very difficult to give a fixed definition of travesti, transexual and transgender's identities" ("Travestis" 1).

In the different interviews I conducted with *travestis*, nonbinary or genderqueer, and trans people from Peru, Chile, and the United States for the purpose of this book, I realized how varied gender and sexual expressions are, as well as "the impossibility of clearly and concisely expressing queer subjectivities" (Edwards 22). Thus, as Falconí expresses, "There are more than men and women . . . for instance there are effeminate masculinities . . . and . . . there are multiple and changing desires that do not necessarily remain under fixed paradigms" (44). For instance, while talking to Cristal del Castillo Felices, a trans woman of color from Peru, she explained to me that in the Peruvian LGBT argot certain terminologies have been normalized. *Travestis* are understood as effeminate gay men who feminize their bodies during the night but who during the mornings and afternoons, while they are working, look effeminate but are not *producidas*. When I asked Cristal if in her opinion every *travesti* prefers feminine pronouns and forms of address, she answered that not all of them do. According to her, this is related to the sphere of labor. *Muchas* or *muchos* of them, Cristal said, do not feminize their bodies completely or *se producen* as women 24/7 because they know they will not be able to find or keep a job, other than as *peluqueras* (hairdressers) or sex workers. Nevertheless, she explained to me that there are *tracas* who as sex workers face the dilemma of *producirse* completely as women or remaining as *travestis* or trans while keeping their penises. This has to do with what the person will be selling to their clients. Cristal mentioned the case of a friend who as a sex worker sometimes performs, with male clients, a feminine role and, with others, a masculine one, which is why they remain *travesti*. In the case of trans Peruvian women, Cristal told me that these are men assigned male sex at birth but who are *producidas* like women all the time, with or without bodily transformations or alterations. Trans women in Peru live and work 24/7 as women. Finally, according to Cristal, transexual women are individuals assigned male sex at birth who have gone through surgery and have a vagina. Cristal considers herself a trans woman and would not like to be a transexual woman. She considers this a very personal choice and it is how she builds and expresses her subjectivity. Cristal feels like a woman although she has a penis. She thinks each person *se construye a su manera*.

As we can see, the experience of each *travesti* is different and therefore my approach, rooted in my own positionality—without being a *travesti* myself, which is already something very delicate if not problematic—avoids pushing a specific or unique definition. I purposely chose to use the definitions of *travesti* expressed by the artists, writers, performers, intellectuals, activists, and literary and performative characters with whom my book engages. Instead of imposing my own definition or perspective on them, I hold space for this study's subjects to speak.

That said, *The Language of the In-Between* proposes the *travesti* as an "in-between" that, as Berkins expresses, "does not follow the binary standard (masculine/feminine, heterosexual/homosexual) imposed by social patriarchal conventions" ("Travestis" 2) and that is "in-between" different races, ethnicities, and in some cases geographical positions or nationalities. Thus, the *travestis* in this book are mestizes, Indigenous, Black, homosexuals, bisexuals, effeminate, and from this same position they resist marginalization and oppression. In this sense, and with Giuseppe Campuzano, I identify the *travesti* as "a full range of possibilities between the extremes of the masculine and the feminine" ("Reclaiming" 35) and not as "the quest or production of another identity for the long existing list" ("Giuseppe" 10). This is exactly why, as Salessi explains, it is so difficult for the heteronormative gaze to grasp the *travesti*'s subjectivity "as a third generic position that is not a woman, a sign, exterior, 'illusion,' or a 'man, referent, body" (342), as this gaze tries to normalize it according to one of the two binary positions.

The *Travesti* as a *Chaupi*

My conceptualization of the *travesti* and its relation or belonging to the "in-between" is inspired by the protagonist of Copi's piece *Loretta Strong* (1974).[7] The character leaves Planet Earth in search of an alternative place to live where she can harvest gold. As Edwards has explained in his analysis of this piece, because of her exile and cultural transition, but also because she exists in the margins, Loretta discovers the freedom of being "in-between," which Edwards calls "a space of her own" (43).

This conceptualization also partakes of what the Chilean scholar Fernando Blanco calls *loca travesti* as identified in the work of the Chilean writer and performer Pedro Lemebel (Blanco, "La Frida" 73). As Víctor Hugo Robles explains, Lemebel's *loca travesti* is always in transit, neither a man nor a woman, "I would not say that it is heterosexual or homosexual, either, it's another possible place . . . but it is not a fixed place" (Donoso and Robles 81). In this sense, the *loca travesti* is in dialogue with what María Mirassol defines as the "in-between," a state of fluctuation, fluidity, impermanence, inconsistency, and mutability. The *travesti* as an "in between," is also in dialogue with the figure of *la loca*. This figure, as Carl Fischer defines it, was biologically assigned as a "man" but simulates the gestures of a "woman," rejecting the binary of genders. *Loca*, "madwoman" in Spanish, means "effeminate man" or "queer," but it is also related to Spanish-language terms such as *marica*, *mariquita*, and *maricón*. As the scholar, writer, and performer Lawrence La Fountain-Stokes explains, *loca* "is a common, everyday word, used as an insult but also in some very specific contexts as a term of endearment; while potentially disparaging and at times offensive, it also used occasionally as an in-group marker of identity and recognition, and can also be a radical signifier of political consciousness" ("Translatinas/os" 240). This is the case with Lemebel, Rodríguez, and other Latin American *cuir* writers such as Reinaldo Arenas. To better understand the relationship between the *travesti* and the "in-between," in chapter 2, I fully develop the use of the term by scholars such as Homi Bhabha, Rosi Braidotti, and Santiago Silviano, among others. I also explain how my own approach to the "in-between" is indebted to these authors' definitions but is nonetheless different.

Ben. Sifuentes-Jáuregui and Vek Lewis assert that *travestis* do not intend to become an "other" (a woman), as they distort the notion of subjectivity and the idea of an "original," as defined or contemplated by the binary masculine/feminine standard imposed by patriarchal social conventions. Following these ideas, my book develops a further analysis of the ways *travestis* distort the notion of subjectivity by structuring and shaping their notion of the self from referents that are not socially accepted or recognized, or that are denied in the particular contexts of modern and contemporary Chile and Peru. Moreover, if, as Pierce states in the context of his study on Argentinean national modernization, "subjectivity is framed as part of a national project in which dissident identities and subversive desires are held up as queer responses to social marginalization" (*Argentine* 14). *The Language of the In-Between* states that *travestis* re-create this subjectivity outside the modernizing national projects of the Peruvian and Chilean nation-states by destabilizing the very foundations of such a project. Thus, the *travesti*, a figure of heterogeneity and transformation, but also of exclusion and marginalization, holds the potential to analyze and question the modernizing nationalist discourse in Peru and Chile because it denarrativizes its construction of a collective national and ethnic identity. This understanding of the *travesti* dialogues with the neologism "transloca," developed by La Fountain-Stokes, as a critical term that accounts for the intersection of geography and sexuality. *Transloca*, in La Fountain-Stokes's words, "challenges hetero-, homo-, and transnormative gender narratives" ("Translocas" 4). My notion of the *travesti* is quite similar to, albeit unlike La Fountain-Stokes's notion of *transloca* in that the *transloca*, just as the *travesti*, "must be understood as a political practice that challenges the status quo" (6).

It is this same understanding of the *travesti* that allows me to explore the *cuir*/subaltern frontiers. Besides recognizing the figure of the homosexual, Indigenous, and poor Chilean and Peruvian *travesti* as a subaltern subject, *The Language of the In-Between* ultimately proposes a historical analysis of and a resistance to the construction of a modern national identity and its repercussions in contemporary Chile and Peru, from a figure and a language that are forged in the midst of domination, exclusion, marginalization, and subordination. The lack of access to resources has created negative dynamics and consequences for *travestis*. Being confined to low-wage employment, with no opportunities to participate in public policy formulation, *trav-*

estis are forced into poverty. Transphobia also plays its role. Attitudes and opinions regarding "irregular" sexuality, identity, and above all unusual gender expression, impede the struggles of *travesti* communities against poverty. In addition, a lack of housing and health care, and the brutal violence against *travestis* and transgender people in general, put their lives in constant risk. For instance, in an article written by the Peruvian trans journalist and activist Gianna Camacho García, addressing the reality of trans lives in Peru, she explains that "trans people do not live under the same conditions as the rest of the population, we are last-class citizens" (1). She also explains that in Peru most trans people live under severe conditions of poverty.

The Language of the In-Between recuperates the figure of a "gender subaltern," the *travesti*, in order to highlight and advance discussion on the contemporary crisis of national models and cultural forms, as Gareth Williams, Alberto Moreiras, John Beverly, and others have done. My book dialogues with the work of these scholars, especially the work that Williams and Moreiras have advanced on the concept of the post-hegemonic, understanding it as "a place within the social field in which hegemonic articulations and signifying processes no longer work, in which hegemonic discourses cease to make sense" (Williams, *The Other Side* 149). Nevertheless, in this dialogue I discuss how this concept, the post-hegemonic, as well as other Latin Americanists' concepts, as Falconí points out, are "valuable but frequently blind and insufficient in the topic of gender" (24). I try to answer how the *travesti* signifies in post-hegemony studies, as well as how the *travesti* interrogates the work of post-hegemony studies. For instance, as Pierce states in the context of Argentinean modernization, which follows the same patterns as the Chilean and Peruvian cases, "Queerness attaches itself and transforms the normative, pointing out its instability, its transigent reshaping, in a moment in which the elite sought to project an image of its own splendorous sociality for those others, those deviants and degenerates who populated the dark recesses of the national imaginary" (*Argentine* 27). In this framework, I also ask how discussions and theorizations produced in the area of Latin American *cuir* studies dialogue with or advance the notion of the post-hegemonic.

The "in-between" language of the *travesti*, a subaltern language, is, as will be explained in chapter 2, post-hegemonic and grounds itself "not so much in the incorporation of subalternity as an inferior position within a hegemonic articulation but, rather, in the opening up of the political field to a certain form of unintelligibility that marks the absolute limit of the place where history is narrativized into logic" (Williams, *The Other Side* 149). Thus, the "in-between" language of the artists, writers, performers, intellectuals, and activists that this book reviews compile stories, images, spaces, praxis, and symbols that belong to dissident or subaltern communities and individuals. Their "in-between" language enacts the life experience of excluded, silenced, rejected and punished individuals and incorporates dissident genders and sexualities into the scope of citizenship, along with historically marginalized races and ethnicities. Salazar, Rodríguez, Devenir, Campuzano, Donoso, Acuña, and Lemebel propose a reconfiguration of the (modern) national identity through a language that exposes the contradictions and cracks in its discourses by questioning its hegemonic assumptions related to gender, race, class, and ethnicity.

Book Structure

Chapter 1 discusses how, similar to elsewhere in Latin America, the modern Peruvian and Chilean nation-states were founded on the basis of a nationalist discourse that sought political dominance and hegemony via the creation of a discriminatory national identity that relied on a process of subordination/exclusion to the margins of those who were considered "different" because of their gender or sexual expression, their race or ethnicity. It looks at how the construction of this identity pervaded cultural production, especially literature. To this end, the chapter explores two novels that demonstrate the limits of this national project: *El lugar sin límites* (1966) (*Hell Has No Limits*, 1999) by José Donoso, and *El zorro de arriba y el zorro de abajo* (1971) (*The Fox from Up Above and the Fox from Down Below*, 1990) by José María Arguedas. These novels look at the costs of modernization in the case of two small regional villages, Talca in Donoso's novel, and Chimbote in the work by Arguedas. The study of these texts demonstrates that the modernizing nationalist discourse of Chile and Peru purposely excluded Indigenous people, effeminate men, homosexuals, prostitutes, the mentally ill, Afro-descendants, and others, because these subjects were perceived as threats to modernity's momentum.

In the same vein, the study of these texts allows me to demonstrate that, in the case of Peru, the work of José María Arguedas reproduces the will of the Peruvian nation-state to place Indigenous subjects as emblems of modern Peruvian national identity as they were used to promote the ideology of national progress, popular incorporation, and transculturation. Moreover, in my analysis of *El zorro de arriba y el zorro de abajo*, I contend that the novel alleges that gender and sexual dissidence would never be able to be practiced in the Andean or Quechua world, and therefore dissidence is an urban vice. Because of his way of perceiving gender and sexual dissidence and its relationship or nonrelationship to the Andean or Quechua world, I explain how Arguedas reproduces not only the Peruvian nation-state effort to fabricate a modern national identity but also the colonial will to control the production of subjectivity in the Andean world, specifically with regard to gender and sexuality.

In the case of Donoso, my analysis of *El lugar sin límites* allows me to discuss how the rejection of male effeminate homosexuals during the re-creation of modern Chilean national identity has been extended to the Chilean LGBT community, where, as Claudia Rodríguez explains, *travestis* are "the most excluded" (*Cuerpos* 22) because of their indeterminacy of gender.

In chapter 2, I engage queer theory and knowledge around dissident genders and sexualities produced in Latin America (*cuir* theory) theoretical debates on the term "travesti," as a way to contextualize the main theoretical concept the book develops. In this chapter, I first explain my understanding of the *travesti* by reviewing the work of Lohana Berkins, Sofía Devenir, Marlene Wayar, and others. The chapter then presents the *travesti* as producer of a language that has the potential for resisting and questioning hegemonic discourses. To this end, I address the work of the Peruvian *travesti* performer Hector Acuña–Frau Diamanda and explain the post-hegemonic potential of the *travesti* and what I call their "in-between" language to destabilize and resist hegemonic discourses by engaging with the work of Alberto Moreiras and Gareth Williams around the post-hegemonic. This potentiality of the post-hegemonic in the *travesti* is specifically located in Acuña's performance *El estigma y la mártir* (The Stigma and the Martyr), which examines the violence and oppression inflicted against the LGBT population in Peru during the internal armed conflict between the Peruvian state and the insurgent group Shining Path (1980–2000).

Chapter 2 also reviews the work of the Chilean transgender writer, activist, and performer Claudia Rodríguez to propose a narrative that puts into action features of the *travesti*, and that I term "in-between" narrative. This narrative presents (1) a language that is different from the hegemonic language, because it does not follow orthographic or grammatical rules, (2) an "in-between" language that confuses the masculine-feminine genders, and (3) a narrative voice that is constantly being interrupted by other voices and that questions the authority of the omniscient narrator at the same time that it prevents the construction of subjectivity. Through the study of Rodríguez's *Cuerpos para odiar: Sobre nuestras muertes, las travestis, no sabemos escribir* (2013–2014), the chapter addresses the post-hegemonic potential of Rodríguez's "in-between" narrative, which, besides denouncing the general violence against *travestis* and the transgender population, transforms the historical discourses that only foster the construction and articulation of stable and firm subjectivities, since these historical discourses are produced from an ideology of homogeneity, inequality, and discrimination based on identity. The chapter ends with a recognition that the work and life experiences of Acuña and Rodríguez point to them also as producers of theoretical frames that currently are not considered or applied in the fields of Latinoamericanismo or Latin American cultural studies, a discussion that will be developed in chapters 3 and 4.

Chapter 3 reviews the work of the Chilean writer and performer Pedro Lemebel and proposes that Lemebel's "in-between" narrative questions and destabilizes the fixed and single meanings that the military dictatorship imposed on sexuality and gender to construct and elevate a heterosexual family-oriented narrative as a symbol of national identity. As the chapter explains, the military dictatorship sought to reinforce conservative societal conventions, particularly the preservation of the heterosexual family, placed as a core institution to secure the reproduction of the Chilean pure and superior race. By reviewing this dictatorship's militaristic-patriarchal discourse and its main violent actions against homosexuals, *travestis*, and effeminate men, the chapter contends that the exclusionary discourse practiced during Chile's modernization and reproduced during the military dictatorship has been questioned and contested by Pedro Lemebel. Nevertheless, and as the chapter points out, Lemebel's "in-between" narrative also criticizes the Latin American and Chilean modernizing discourses that excluded and persecuted homosexuals and effeminate men during the mid-twentieth century. To this end, the chapter works with three of Lemebel's texts. The chapter first studies *La esquina es mi corazón* (*The Corner of My Heart*) (1995) to introduce Lemebel's "in-between" narrative's post-hegemonic potentialities, and show how it gives other meanings to oppressed, invisible, and persecuted subjectivities, practices, and spaces. The chapter then reviews "Hablo por mi diferencia" (I Speak for My Difference) (1986) to propose that Lemebel's "in-between" narrative denounces and critiques the Chilean modern national identity, which through the deployment of an exclusionary discourse has marginalized and exerted violence against homosexuals, *maricones*, and effeminate men. Moreover, this section explains that "Hablo por mi diferencia" also denounces and critiques other Latin American modern discourses, such as the Cuban one, establishing a relationship between all of them and the exclusionary discourses of the Chilean right, especially that of the military dictatorship. Finally, the chapter reviews Lemebel's only novel, *Tengo miedo torero* (2001) (*My Tender Matador*, 2003), to contend that it offers suggestions as to how an alliance between those who were included under the umbrella of a national identity during the modernization of Chile—which had further repercussions in the way Chile's left conceived sexual and gender minorities—and its excluded Other might have functioned under the military dictatorship.

Turning to Lemebel's work in the chapter allows me to discuss the way that Latin American cultural critics and proponents of *cuir* critiques centered Lemebel's work as the prime example of sexual and gender dissidence in Chile in the 1990s and 2000s. I contend that Lemebel's work served as a mediator of the direct and material experiences of other sexual and gender dissidents, such as *travestis*. Thus, *cuir* critique and Latin American cultural critics had failed in addressing their experiences, work, and theorizations, repeating, in a way, the exclusion perpetuated by many of the regimes and societies criticized by these same fields. In the chapter I ask how and why certain lives, experiences, voices, and writings have become canonical within Latin American *cuir* and Latin American cultural studies, as is the case with Pedro Lemebel.

In chapter 4, I address the work of the Peruvian authors Claudia Salazar and Giuseppe Campuzano, which allows me to show how their "in-between" languages/narratives resist and redesign the Peruvian modern national identity and its exclusions of LGBT people, women, Afro-descendants, and others. This analysis leads me to consider the effects of the reproduction of such identity in the contemporary cultural and political contexts of Peru by looking at the Peruvian internal armed conflict (1980–200) and the authoritarian governments of Alberto Fujimori (1993–1995, 1995–2000, and 2000) with their brutal violence against Quechua-speaking peasant Indigenous populations, especially women. Moreover, based on my study of these authors, I propose that the place of Indigenous populations as dominated and subjugated in the construction of the Peruvian modern national identity has evolved into a desire of the Peruvian state to reduce and in some ways exterminate these populations.

The first section of the chapter focuses on the analysis of Campuzano's interactive museum-book *Museo travesti del Perú* (2008) and proposes that it reorganizes and redesigns the history of Peru and the history of its modern national identity through an "in-between" narrative structure informed by the figure of the *travesti* and *travestismo*. Campuzano's "in-between" narrative structure, I explain, implies a nonaffirmation of subjectivity, by means of a plural narrative voice in which different and diverse voices, languages, sources, and historical temporalities come together along with the use of a diverse language. While this section of the chapter focuses mainly on stating that *Museo* contests and challenges the modern national identity, the section also addresses the violence carried out on the basis of gender and sexual dissidence throughout Peruvian history but especially during the internal armed conflict.

The chapter then studies Salazar's novel *La sangre de la aurora* (2013) (*Blood of the Dawn*, 2016) and contends that through an "in-between" narrative the novel shows how the place of Indigenous populations as dominated and subjugated in the construction of Peruvian modern national identity has evolved into a desire of the state to reduce and, in some ways, exterminate these populations. Salazar's novel particularly focuses on addressing the multifaceted and brutal violence that the Peruvian state exercised against Indigenous women, but it does so by presenting them not as passive victims, which is how they have been portrayed in hegemonic discourses, but as individuals capable of agency and self-empowerment. I contend that *La sangre de la aurora* affirms the post-hegemonic potential of the "in-between" narrative.

The book ends with an Epilogue that links together the theoretical issues that the book has raised and some of the challenges for the future. Specifically, I reflect on the current and future state of the fields of *cuir*/queer studies, and Latin American literary and cultural studies. I also touch on the ways this project intersects with the fields of subaltern and post-hegemony studies, suggesting that a deeper engagement between these fields and the fields of *cuir*/queer studies could be a productive way of broadening their future impact.

CHAPTER 1

Cuiring the Birth of the *Modern(a)* Nation-State in Chile and Peru

The colonial experience of Latin America located the region on the margins of the large imperial systems. The fate of the inhabitants of this multiple and diverse space has been affected by this relationship of dependence and has had a special impact on the Indigenous populations, deemed from the start as archaic and dangerous. During the nineteenth century, models of cultural and political modernization generally became synonymous with the elimination, extermination, and violent coercion of the "barbaric" masses of Indigenous peoples by oligarchic local and national elites. Whereas this model was compromised during the processes of independence and the foundation of Latin American nations through the implementation of various republican projects, during the twentieth century a model of modernization was designed that aspired to integrate these very same populations as exceptions within the nation-state.

This was due to the fact that by the first decades of the twentieth century, Latin American economies were subordinated to centralized capitalism—dominated by the most industrialized nations—as underdeveloped countries and producers of raw materials. As the process of denationalization of the means of production gained pace, the notions of nationality and national identity were redefined and the models of government reshaped, which in turn had an impact on Indigenous peoples.[1] This situation intensified after the Great Depression of 1929 and the political instability in the region as an effect of economic transformation, which modified the productive structure and political landscape, as it demanded greater state intervention (Moraña, *Literatura* 13–14).

The different reactions of the countries in the region to this crisis and the changes that were introduced since the mid-twentieth century shaped the period of modern nation-state formation in Latin America, also known as the era of "national populism" (Tulio Halperin Donghi, Fernando Henríque Cardoso, Octavio Ianni). This era began around the time of the Great Depression and continued until the collapse of the communist bloc in the late 1980s and early 1990s, a period that would witness the violent realities of the Cold War, the political and cultural effects of the Cuban Revolution, and the violent counterreactions such as the military coup against the Chilean president Salvador Allende on September 11, 1973.

In this era, it was commonplace for nation-states to actively integrate and institutionalize the people—the common populace or the popular/subaltern sectors of society—as the originary ground from which to consider the contours of national history, national identity formations, and national modernization. This project conceived "the people" (defined broadly to include nonelite sectors) as the core of the nation, which would unite across class boundaries in a political project rooted in a shared nationalism. What was at stake in the shaping of modern Latin America, then, was the elevation of the "people" to the heart of the political life of the nation. This elevation, however, resulted in a potential hegemonic formation that aimed to synthesize all the nation's demographic and cultural differences through the re-creation of a national identity.

The process of integration and institutionalization of the "people" was carried out through the consolidation of elite-controlled populist states that strengthened the role and presence of the state in the daily life of the nation. At the same time, the "people" were imagined and ethnicized as if they constituted a natural community, having identical origins, culture, and interests. This process is what Etienne Balibar has called "fictive ethnicity." Balibar explains that the constitution of "the people" is accomplished by generating a "unity" as the basis and origin of political power. The community of people instituted by the nation-state—which would have to be rethought in the case of the modern Latin American nation-state—is what Balibar calls "fictive ethnicity." In the process of nationalization, through this "fictive ethnicity," the populations incorporated into the nation can be presented as if they had always constituted "a natural community, possessing a common identity of origins, culture and interests" (96). Some groups cannot be included within the "fictive ethnicity," since they cannot be homogenized, or cannot be incorporated into the unifying common project and destiny. As Gareth Williams points out,

> the terms of state capitalism (and of course socialist) hegemony came to be predicated on the people's ability to reproduce itself continually as a national community, as a single-willed "national-popular" community, and therefore as a constituted synthesis of multiple racial, ethnic, regional, and cultural (but rarely gendered) identities negotiated from within, and reflected directly through, the nation-state's relation to regional and national territory, as well as to the promise of national capitalist development. For this reason, the production and institutionalization of the people . . . came to be negotiated (often violently) from within populist state configurations that were considered by social elites to be the condition of possibility for the articulation of positive equivalences between diverse populations. (*The Other Side* 5)

The modern process that naturalized social and political belonging was shaped around the configuration of normative languages and identities positioned against those identities that were not considered normative, in order to set the foundations and the limits of the hegemonic field of the modern nation-state. In this regard, Mabel

Moraña notes, "The question about the elements that will constitute the continental 'identity' and the 'essence' of nationalities had been an active part of nineteenth-century thought. . . . In the 1920s and 1930s, the same essentialist strategy served the different projects co-existing in that period, as a way of rethinking the concept of 'the popular,' in an attempt to provide genetic and anthropological explanations of the origins of nationalities" (*Literatura* 6). We see a willingness to produce strongly territorialized and state-managed fixed national identities, resuming the nineteenth-century nationalism that mobilized a discourse of citizenship as a status that could be defined legally or culturally. Thus, the notion of citizenship was understood as related to identity and sought to identify the attributes of good citizens to determine which individuals could be incorporated into the notion of citizenship and which ones could not (Canaday 8).

As the political theorist Lisa J. Disch notes, "Otherness is immanent to citizenship," because citizenship helps create "internal differentiation and hierarchy" in the way some individuals are incorporated into it while highlighting their subordination or "degraded status" (Disch 382). In the Latin American case, the populations considered nonnational and "different" from the models of established national normative identities—conceived as homogeneous collectives—were subordinated and integrated into the nation as exceptions. Otherwise, they were taken as emblems of forms of belonging that were incorporated into the nation without actually being part of it, at the same time that they were taken advantage of in the pursuit of independence, unity, and progress. Rather than as classes, these populations were depicted in the modernizing process as subclasses or subaltern formations. This was the case, for example, of Indigenous populations and subjects practicing dissident genders and sexualities.[2]

This chapter discusses how the modern Peruvian and Chilean nation-states produced a nationalist discourse that sought political dominance and hegemony via the creation of a discriminatory national identity that subordinated and excluded those considered "different" because of their race, ethnicity, sexuality, or gender expression. It looks at how the construction of this identity pervaded cultural production, especially literature. To this end, the chapter explores two novels that demonstrate the limits of this national project: *El lugar sin límites* (1966) (*Hell Has No Limits*, 1999) by José Donoso, and *El zorro de arriba y el zorro de abajo* (1971) (*The Fox from Up Above and the Fox from Down Below*, 1990) by José María Arguedas. These novels look at the costs of modernization in the case of two small regional villages, Talca in Donoso's novel, and Chimbote in the work by Arguedas. The study of these texts demonstrates that the modernizing nationalist discourse in Chile and Peru purposely excluded Indigenous people, effeminate men, homosexuals, prostitutes, the mentally ill, Afro-descendants, and others, because these subjects were perceived as threats to modernity's momentum.

Reading these canonical novels is necessary now, as Chile and Peru celebrate two hundred years of independence and rethink or reaffirm their conceptualizations of the national subject and dissident genders and sexualities within such conceptualizations. As I explained in the introduction, literature has always been a privileged means for disseminating and supporting nation-state formations. Therefore, in this context, reviewing the cultural representations of dissident genders and sexualities is relevant, especially in canonical literary productions such as the novels mentioned above.

In Peru, as Antonio Cornejo Polar has pointed out, Indigenous subjects became the emblem of modern Peruvian national identity and were used to promote the ideology of national progress, popular incorporation, and transculturation. The work of José María Arguedas reproduces this will of the Peruvian nation-state. As we will see in my analysis of *El zorro de arriba y el zorro de abajo*, the novel alleges that Quechua or Andean Indigenous cultures condemn gender and sexual dissidence because it violates the ideal of harmony supported in the Andean worldview or *cosmovisión*. In this way, *El zorro de arriba y el zorro de abajo* suggests that gender and sexual dissidence would never be able to be practiced in the Andean or Quechua world, and therefore dissidence is an urban vice. Arguedas thus places the Andean or Quechua world as a reproducer of hegemonic masculinity, erasing and denying the past of the original Andean or Quechua cultures in which the practice of a nonbinary gender and sexuality was welcomed, as I will discuss further in chapter 2. Following Diego Falconí, this discussion allows me to "recontar el canon de otra manera, a través de formas aún no del todo masticadas en la tradición académica andina" (32), by suggesting that because of his way of perceiving gender and sexual dissidence and its relationship or nonrelationship to the Andean or Quechua world, Arguedas reproduces not only the Peruvian nation-state effort to fabricate a modern national identity but also the colonial will to control the production of subjectivity in the Andean world, specifically with regard to gender and sexuality.

In the case of Donoso, my analysis of *El lugar sin límites* allows me to discuss how the rejection of male effeminate homosexuals during the re-creation of modern Chilean national identity has been extended to the Chilean LGBT community, where *travestis* are, as Claudia Rodríguez explains, "the most excluded" ("Se resiste" 22) because of their indeterminacy of gender.

Finally, as we will see, the rearticulation of a national identity was understood across the political spectrum of both countries almost entirely in racial and ethnic terms; gender and sexuality were not included since heteronormative ideals were taken as the default standard. Anything that deviated from this standard was suspect. As John Beverley has observed, hegemonic nationalist discourse in twentieth-century Latin America was designed generally to suture the gaps and discontinuities within the corpus of the so-called national people rather than to allow heterogeneity and multiplicity to function as the real grounds and origins of national political life (Beverley 308). Heterogeneity, in other words, was celebrated as long as it did not disturb the nation-state's promotion of normative national identities.

The Peruvian Nation-State and Its Unfulfilled Promises

As the historian Cecilia Méndez notes, the state in Peru was ideologically based on the project of a "republic without Indians." While the independence process had enabled the criollo elite to become the dominant social group over an Indigenous majority, the first years of the republican period in the nineteenth century, immediately after the independence wars (1820–1826), did not in any way alleviate the discrimination and marginalization that the Indigenous had endured during the three centuries of Spanish colonization (Méndez 206–7). The Peruvian republic established a national identity that excluded and ignored a large mass of citizens—the Indians—who had been promised they would be included as equal under the category of "Peruvian."

At the beginning of the twentieth century, as the country's economy was relying more heavily on external markets, the Peruvian oligarchy started to address the problem of national unity and the need for the social and cultural regeneration of the country as a response to the hegemony crisis it had suffered in the decades after the War of the Pacific (1879–1883). In the midcentury, industrialization brought about the consolidation of a national bourgeoisie and other elites whose interests were closely linked to the existence of an internal market, as well as a significant increase in the migratory flow from the Sierra to the Peruvian coast. These transformations ideologically diversified the worldview of the middle sectors (Stein 51). At the same time, proletariat organizations were strong and peasant uprisings were coordinated throughout the country forcing the state to modify the institutions that channeled popular participation. In light of these processes, unity within the country became both an economic and a political problem that had to be solved in favor of "inward-oriented" development plans and the consolidation of national capitalism (Moraña, *Literatura* 39).[3]

By the time the global economic crisis erupted in 1929, as Aníbal Quijano pointed out, the Peruvian ruling class was disjointed and there was widespread popular discontent, the state depended wholly on foreign credit and was strongly under the power of economic colonization by American imperialism, and the Peruvian army had adopted the role of defender of the economic, social, and political domination of the commercial landowner bourgeoisie (271). Faced with this puzzling situation, many *criollista* and indigenista political and cultural proposals were put forward that sought to rethink Peruvian national identity as a way to promote national unity and the modernization of the country. The great intellectuals of *criollismo*, such as José de la Riva Agüero and Víctor Andrés Belaúnde, among others, addressed the Indigenous question as a vindication, albeit with a paternalistic perspective.[4]

At the same time, other proposals put forward the recuperation and dissemination of the image of the Indigenous as a way to redefine the paradigms of the national cultural. One of these proposals was that of the Peruvian Aprista Party (APRA), which postulated the concept of Indoamérica, a "country-continent" characterized by *mestizaje* and its dependent condition. APRA's anti-imperialist program focused on the interests of the middle class, which it considered to be the main victim of the dominant system.[5] In *El antiimperialismo y el APRA* (1928), for example, Victor Raul Haya de la Torre argues for a subordination of the claims of workers and peasants to the interests of a national bourgeoisie linked to foreign capital. APRA's proposals aspired to solve the issue of national disintegration, but, as it lacked a solid economic basis, it resulted mostly in an idealist and moralizing discourse.[6]

APRA's populist discourse incorporated ideas expressed by thinkers such as the former seminarian Manuel González Prada, a descendant of an aristocratic family who was one of the first to question the oligarchic system. In his famous essay "Nuestros indios" (Our Indians), González Prada argued that the Peruvian population was divided into two groups "those of mixed blood [*encastados*], who tend to dominate, and the native Indians, who are dominated" (192) and stated that Peru could not exist as a democratic republic as long as it continued to marginalize its Indigenous populations. For González Prada, "The real Peru isn't made up of the groups of American-born Spaniards and foreigners living on the strip of land situated between the Pacific and the Andes; the nation is made up of the masses of Indians living on the eastern slopes of the mountains" (49), as he mentioned in one of his other texts, "Discurso del Politeama" (1888).

The political, economic, and social situation of Peru described above, which also involved peasant mobilizations, the Indigenous question, the increasing participation of different urban sectors in Peruvian national life, as well as the influence of the Mexican Revolution and the Russian Revolution, resulted in a reconceptualization of

Peruvian Indigenous culture, traditionally regarded as "a real obstacle for progress" (Rama, "José María Arguedas" 22) or, in any case, as the definition of a prehistory buried by the impact of Spanish domination. Indigenous culture was being understood as the matrix from which to rethink Peruvian national identity as a way of promoting national unity and the modernization of the country (Moraña, *Literatura* 44). This process, however, as Gareth Williams suggests, served to "inscribe, translate, and domesticate the nation's outsider . . . into totalizing modes of representation and self-constitution" (*The Other Side* 43).

In this political and social context, cultural indigenismo became a powerful resource around which national unity was organized. The cultural production of these years, especially in the literary field, sought to affirm a new collective national identity for the country and, at the same time, the creation of a new cultural subject in Peru.[7] These cultural products showed an inclination toward the representation of dominated or marginalized social sectors and to the portrayal of social conflicts through the use of new ways of representing the national subject, who was, most of the time, male, heterosexual, and Indigenous. Antonio Cornejo Polar comments in this regard:

> In the complex and difficult process that leads to the definition of national identity; a political and intellectual operation emerges that remains in the charge of the social elites: to produce an image of the Indian, both for society and for the Indian himself . . . within this order of things national identity requires the conversion of an exclusive "we"—in which only the elites, their allies, together with their self-image, interests, and desires, fit comfortably—into a widely inclusive, almost ontological, "we." The true protagonists [the Indians] . . . are obliged to insert themselves into the process. On the way, they lose parts of their condition and mutate in order to gain access to the newly adopted ground. (*Escribir en el aire* 186)

As Williams points out in his analysis of this quote, Cornejo Polar acknowledges in these few lines the exclusions and impositions that this process has produced, resulting in what Williams calls a "transcultural fictive ethnicity" as a discourse for the reconstruction of Peruvian national identity (Williams, *The Other Side* 40). We must analyze, then, how this transculturation enabled, precisely from the cultural field and especially from the field of literature, the creation of a "fictive ethnicity," inasmuch as it responds to and is productive for the state's desires for popular incorporation, legalization, and control. In this regard we can define transculturation as an inclusive and unifying force, as an attempt to consolidate the hegemony of the nation-state in Peru throughout the twentieth century. Transculturation was part of the efforts of the creole elites "to transcend colonial history through the neutralization, idealization, and depoliticization of class and ethnic antagonisms with transcultural fictive ethnicity as its primary goal, trope, and/or rhetorical foundation" (Williams, *The Other Side* 47).

If we go back to Balibar's definition of the concept of "fictive ethnicity," we can understand how the transculturation process was a privileged vehicle to create a fictitious identity in Peru, since the formation, incorporation, and reproduction of an effectively integrated subject was sought, that is a de-indianized, mixed, or transcultural subject, as the main figure of Peruvian national identity. The term "transculturation" was first coined in the 1940s by the Cuban Fernando Ortiz. He defined transculturation as a process comprising several phenomena: deculturation (the loss of cultural elements), neoculturation (the creation of new cultural elements), and acculturation (the adoption of cultural elements from the other culture) (98).[8] For Ortiz, transculturation implies the process whereby two cultures merge, be it through peaceful conflict resolution or through the violent imposition of one culture onto another. Moreover, Ortiz explains that "the word transculturation better expresses the different phases of the process of transition from one culture to another because this does not consist merely in acquiring another culture . . . the process also necessarily involves the loss or uprooting of a previous culture, which could be defined as a deculturation" (102). As Ortiz states, the process of transculturation implies the loss of a previous culture but also the inscription of the dominated culture into the dominant one. Regardless of its promise of joining, transculturation always entails a losing party when the dominant side assimilates its Other. Transculturation implies the sublation of difference in the transcultural subject.[9]

Throughout the twentieth century, transculturation functioned as the specific cultural discourse that the ideology of modernization adopted in Latin America, incorporating and affirming the popular, the people, or the masses, but always and exclusively as a subordinate position within the articulation and construction of the national cultural market.[10] Nowhere is this clearer than in José María Arguedas's posthumous novel, *El zorro de arriba y zorro de abajo*. An analysis of this book will allow me to point out the limits of transculturation, as well as the limits of Arguedas's project and the Peruvian nation-state's will to fabricate a national institutionalized "we," where, as Antonio Cornejo Polar has signaled, the Indian was placed as the emblem of the Peruvian modern national identity and was used for the promotion of the ideology of national progress and popular incorporation. As this analysis allows me to show, the novel alleges that Quechua or Andean Indigenous cultures condemn gender and sexual dissidence because it violates the ideal of harmony supported within the Andean cultural worldview or *cosmovisión*. Arguedas thus reproduces not only the Peruvian nation-state effort to fabricate a modern national identity but also the colonial will to control the production of subjectivity in the Andean world, specifically in regard to gender and sexuality.

An "In-Between" Demon Who Speaks in Christian and in Indian

Peruvian modern national identity was negotiated and promoted actively from within literary, intellectual, and university circles. Under these circumstances, indigenismo became an essential component of the artistic, ideological, and scientific production that reflected and stimulated the social turbulences of a very conflictive period. This period constituted the political surface of a complex economic and social process marked by a fast capitalist modernization under US imperial dominance and the resulting intensification of class struggle (Cornejo Polar, "Sobre literatura" 13). Moreover, literary indigenismo worked as a highly powerful cultural machine for presenting, negotiating, and governing the symbolic terms of national unity and universal cultural difference in the Andes. Indigenismo elaborated a discourse that appeared to resist the onslaught of modernity on Indigenous culture and traditions and contributed to the project of cultural and identity recovery and reconstruction without renouncing the utopia of an egalitarian progress that could cancel the racial and class divisions brought by modernity itself.

For Ángel Rama, indigenismo capitalized on the ideological ambiguity and the very general meaning and scope of principles of social justice, and the vindication of the rights of marginal sectors to put forward an opportunistic agenda in which the Indigenous question was included as a "point of reference" but which would never manage to climb the social ladder and transcend the parameters of the lower middle class (Rama, *Writing across Cultures* 98). Rama objects to the fact that this mestizo literature "did not do justice to the true complexities of Peru's social structure" (124) with regard to present-day Indigenous culture, and rather perpetuated the perspective of the dominator on the dominated cultures.[11]

In a similar vein, José Carlos Mariátegui argued that indigenista literature could not provide a faithful version of Indigenous peoples. Rather, it tended to create an idealized and stylized rendition because, in his view, indigenista literature was still a literature written by mestizos. This is precisely why it is indigenist and not Indigenous. If an Indigenous literature finally appears, Mariátegui noted, it would be when Indigenous peoples themselves are able to produce it (274). Under this definition, the work of José María Arguedas and César Vallejo would be considered indigenista, as both of them were mestizos and not Indians writing about the value of Indigenous traditions as well as the need to redeem the Peruvian Indian.[12] Furthermore, the work of both authors was invested in the development of a national peoplehood and the fabrication of a national institutionalized "we" grounded in common cultural frameworks and languages. The problem with these literatures inserted in the indigenista project, though, was that they tried to "give a ghostly appearance" to difference and deny conflict, suggesting the existence of amalgamated identities that would enable the implementation of specific political and cultural agendas (Cornejo Polar, *Escribir en el aire* 251). It seems convenient now, to review Arguedas's work, as he was the great representative of indigenista literature in the twentieth century. Moreover, Arguedas's intellectual project developed in the context of a strong movement that sought to redeem the Peruvian Indian as well as Andean culture and traditions. This redemption, though, denied the practice of dissident genders and sexualities in these traditions and considered such practices the result of urban bad habits.

Arguedas published six novels, three collections of short stories, one short story published as a pamphlet, poems, and several anthropological studies. Even though he wrote one of his most celebrated novels, *Los ríos profundos* (1958) (*Deep Rivers*, 1978), during the period known as the "boom" of Latin American literature, he was always marginal to this group of narrators. Arguedas's work circulated along channels that were different from those of his contemporary peers.[13] We could affirm that Arguedas was a postcolonial, migrant, transculturated writer in the sense that he spent most of his childhood between two worlds, the white and the Indigenous worlds.[14] Thus, Arguedas, following Rosi Braidotti's definition, would be an "in-between" as he existed in "in-between zones" and expressed in several of his texts the sense of "nonbelonging" to either of them (Braidotti 18–19). Arguedas used to define himself as a permanent outsider (*forastero*); he experienced this condition as disturbing, since he felt as if he inhabited several worlds but belonged nowhere, always detached from a fixed place. Nevertheless, he would often point out that he considered himself to be rooted in the values and traditions of the dominated culture, which was the Indigenous culture. Because of this, he looked to reclaim this culture, always on the margins, but also considered by Arguedas as a space of resistance.

Although Arguedas recognized that he was what we could call an "in-between" subject, because as we have mentioned before and in his own words, Arguedas thought about himself as "not an acculturated man; I am a Peruvian who, like a cheerful demon, proudly speaks in

Christian and in Indian" (*Primer Encuentro* 269). He did not embrace such an "in-between" position but rather looked for a way of reconciling this "in-betweenness" by trying to homogenize his own and Peruvian identity through the creation of an ideal that placed Indian culture as the emblem of the modern Peruvian national identity.

From his first stories, included in *Agua* (1935), Arguedas addressed the question of the Indian seeking to redress the way Indigenous peoples were being represented in literary texts. In the *Primer Encuentro de Narradores Peruanos*, he stated: "I began to write when I read the first narratives about the Indians; they described them in such a false way . . . in those stories the Indian was so disfigured and so mellow and the landscape silly or so strange: 'No, I have to write it as it is, because I have enjoyed it, I have suffered it' and I wrote those first stories that were published in the little book called *Agua*" (40–41). Along with his desire to redeem the representation of the Indian in this first collection of short stories, Arguedas addressed the question of identity. In his case, though, next to the question of "Who am I?" there was the question of "To which world do I belong?" a manifestation of the diverse spaces he inhabited. Arguedas's world was a fragmented one, because in it, two opposite wor(l)ds coexisted. This implied a junction of two different societies and cultures with a long history of antagonisms.

We could consider Arguedas's literary project a long and beautiful attempt to conciliate the two worlds he inhabited. In fact, Roland Forgues states that what characterizes Arguedas's writing is his will to conciliate the Andean and the criollo world, two opposite worlds that for historical reasons, have been confused with two antagonistic social classes (307).[15] This attempt characterizes Arguedas as a "transculturador." His writing aimed at transculturating the dominated Quechua world to the dominant culture of the Western world and provide through literature the integration of both worlds (Rama, "José María Arguedas" 38). Moreover, as Cornejo Polar has pointed out, that self split between two opposite worlds, that quest, through writing, for a space where the self can dwell as one, was transformed in a potential space to forge a collective identity.

In her book *Arguedas/Vargas Llosa: Dilemas y Ensamblajes* (2013), Mabel Moraña asserts that Arguedas's work is "a cultural gesture and an ideological performance whose meaning is inseparable from the historical, social, and political contexts of each stage of his literary production" (5). That is, Arguedas's writing is also a response to or a reflection on these same contexts, which in his case support or reproduce the project of the Peruvian nation-state to create a collective national identity in which the image of the Indian will be intensified.

For Arguedas, literature is a vehicle to reinscribe the possible history of a modern Peru from a perspective that is capable of incorporating elements suppressed by official history (Moraña, *Arguedas/Vargas Llosa* 15). Nevertheless, and as I will now explain, Arguedas's project had some limitations, as it perpetuated the problems of transculturation, which, as we mentioned above, sought to conciliate the Latin American populations with the most general conditions of capitalist modernization by assimilating its Indigenous Other. In the case of Peruvian modernization, it was the Indigenous populations that, through transculturation, lost parts of their condition and mutated in order to gain access to the newly adopted ground. Moreover, and as this section will also show, those populations that could not be assimilated through transculturation were not included in Arguedas's project of a modern Peru. As we see in the analysis, Arguedas approached the question of racial and ethnic Otherness only from the place of race and ethnicity. He did not consider, and he even re-subalternized, other marginalized populations and subjects, such as women, Afro-Peruvian, and LGBT subjects, because he considered them the products of urban bad habits.

In order to contend this, I will focus on the analysis of Arguedas's posthumous and unfinished novel, *El zorro de arriba y el zorro de abajo* (hereafter referred to as *Los zorros*), because, as has been pointed out by several scholars (Antonio Cornejo Polar, Alberto Moreiras, Mabel Moraña, Ronald Forgues, Mario Vargas Llosa, and Gareth Williams), this novel draws multiple relations with all Arguedas's previous publications. As Vargas Llosa puts it, in the different texts that compose *Los zorros*, "the anxiety that Arguedas experienced towards the end of his life can be touched, an anxiety that had accumulated through a lifetime . . . in which his personal problems were entangled with the traumas and conflicts of Peruvian society" (16).

Most of Arguedas's texts, but especially *Los zorros*, express his project in which the Andean masses appear as the group from which to define the function of the national-popular subject as the agent of history and the modernization of Peru. This project considers the Indigenous tradition as having the strength to form the national collective identity that represents the future and the modernization of the country. However, this project also considers Indigenous tradition as heterosexual and gender-conforming. According to Moraña, this collective subject is a plural and heterogeneous identity, an identity of difference (*Arguedas/Vargas Llosa* 154). Difference, though, is understood by Arguedas only in ethnic and racial terms, as I mentioned before. For this reason, I disagree with Moraña when she states that "Arguedas' project, oriented towards the issue of identity, is not unaware of the dangers of essentialism and fundamentalism. . . . Arguedas avoids all reductionism and tends toward an inclusive and expansive thought, which moves from the primitive to the modern, from the mythical to the historical, from the foundational elements to its multiple historical transformations" (*Arguedas/Vargas Llosa* 156). Moreover, as Cornejo Polar has mentioned, *Los zorros* is a testimony of the unfulfillment of Arguedas's projects presented in his previous texts or the testimony of a "creator who was affected to the point of immolation by the problems of his country" (quoted in Vargas Llosa 17). In this novel, "the indigenous tradition does not survive and Peruvian society is not reorganized according to those values" (Cornejo Polar, "Hipótesis"134) because of industrial progress and the failure of transculturation.

Transculturation or the *Jardín Cielo* of Capitalism

Los zorros was published in 1971, almost two years after the death of Arguedas in December 1969. Some fragments had been published previously. A novel defined by Arguedas himself as a "contained" text, "like a body that's half-blind and deformed" (Arguedas, *The Fox* 262), *Los zorros* is a work in progress, where the narrative voice is constantly interrupted by the narrator himself, the dialogues of characters, or the omniscient narrator's reflections. Besides this, *Los zorros* presents Arguedas's suicide as an obsession that is present and has an impact on the novel. Thus, *Los zorros* alternates the fictional story and the personal diaries that Arguedas wrote between May 10, 1968, and October 22, 1969. In the letter he sent to Gonzalo Losada included in the Epilogue of the novel, Arguedas insists on affirming that *Los zorros* suffers from a "real (albeit partial) truncation" and that it is a "disconnected novel" (Arguedas, *The Fox* 261). This is important to consider because, in its form and content, this novel goes against Arguedas's writing project, produced under notions such as unity and integration when thinking about Peru and himself.

Los zorros is intimately bound to Arguedas's life and his writing project. In his words: "So if I can, I am going to try to combine it [his suicide] with the themes chosen for a novel I have finally decided to christen "The Fox from Up Above and the Fox from Down Below"; I shall also mix in all the thoughts I have had in so many instances about people and Peru, even though they may not have been specifically contained in the plan of the novel" (*The Fox* 10). As this quote testifies, *Los zorros* contains the basic logics of Arguedas's work and how it is related to Peru's realities and the hopes and desires he had for himself and the country. As Vargas Llosa contends, in *Los zorros*, "Both the work and the self-destruction of the author are viscerally linked" (298). As my analysis will show, these hopes and desires—linked to the author's self-destruction as Vargas Llosa points out—were not fulfilled and *Los zorros* attests to how this caused precisely the destruction of the author. Already the Prologue to the novel, where the author describes himself as "a modern Quechua individual" (Arguedas, *The Fox* 268), reveals the impossibility that permeated Arguedas's life as much as his writing project. He and his writing engaged in the invention of the Quechua culture as the modern horizon for Peru and Peruvian identity, but the project was probably doomed to fail and the novel is an exploration of this failure.

The main setting of *Los zorros* is Chimbote, a small and forgotten village that is suddenly transformed when it becomes an important center of fish flour production. The novel addresses the social and cultural changes that its maritime resources brought to Peru. Chimbote is an example of the miracle of national capitalism. Because of this economic boom, Chimbote has become an extremely heterogeneous place, in which men and women of different cultures live and in whose lives the weight of transnational capital dominates.[16] The novel deals with the dynamic between people from the Peruvian coast and the Andes, and uses as its background the myth *Dioses y hombres de Huarochiri*, translated from Quechua to Spanish by Arguedas himself.[17] This myth includes an episode in which two foxes run into each other in Mount Latauzaco. One of the foxes represents the Andean area of Peru and the other, the coast. These two areas are key in the novel as several Indigenous men and women from the Andean region migrate to the coastal village of Chimbote, seduced by the illusion of a better life. This is the case of one of the characters, Esteban de la Cruz, a former miner at the Cocalón mine, who tells his story of migration from the mountains: "Parobamba, little town in the Andes, there's no hope there: little pig, little sheep, tiny little vegetable plot—one or two of 'em. On big hacienda also silence, obedience, shut mouth. They eat silence up there in the high country, what we call the sierra, friend. In their highlander gut, in the blood vein of the highlander who has already tried Trojillo, Lima, Chimbote—inside his bosom there's even more silence; graveyard's all there is when they make him stay in towns up in his home country" (Arguedas, *The Fox* 157–58). As we see, Esteban, as many other Andean men (and rarely women), decides to migrate to Chimbote because he thinks his living conditions will improve there. Working in the coal mine has invaded his body; it has affected his health, and his spit is black from the coal poisoning he got while working in the mine. For Esteban, then, Chimbote represents the space where he escapes the exploitation he had endured, but also the place where he could find the cure to his illness.

It must be noted that Esteban's poisoning is related to his ethnicity and race, because, according to the novel, Indigenous men like Esteban are condemned to these same working conditions while being exploited and oppressed in the Andes. This also explains why so many people from different areas of the Andean region have found their way to Chimbote, where "the fires and the roots of the world, of the very butt-end of the earth itself, are made manifest" (Arguedas, *The Fox* 159). Chimbote is a space where social, racial, and ethnic groups from different places meet. They represent different strata of Peruvian society who, like Esteban, migrate to Chimbote hoping for a better future. In the words of Cornejo Polar, as a "cruise ship of races, social classes, cultures, Chimbote is pervaded by deep contradictions" ("Un ensayo" 296).

Chimbote is a site where transculturation takes place. We see Indigenous people from peripheral and marginal areas of Peru arriving at Chimbote, a place considered a center of modernization and progress. Through transculturation, they would be able to heal and get rid of the diseases, the exploitation, and the oppression they left behind when they migrated to Chimbote, the "jardín cielo," a place on the coast where they could live with dignity and recover the humanity they have been deprived of in the Andes.

It is worth exploring Esteban's life further to understand how transculturation works in the novel. His life, according to Cornejo Polar, "is in a way the life of the Peruvian man, a kind of sum and synthesis of what the existence in a vast, complex, and disjointed country can be" ("Un ensayo" 293). This character allows us to see that in Chimbote, "indigenous people, blacks, cholos, and zambos lose their identity and their roots and sink in an unrelenting degradation and alienation process" (Forgues 308) in what implies the process of transculturation. This is the case of Esteban's brother: "Now you take my little brother, beautiful Spanish he talks; when he was a little kid he escaped to Chimbote; now he doesn't wanna talk Quechua. . . . Beautiful Spanish he talks; looks down on his sick market-pedlar brother nowadays" (Arguedas, *The Fox* 144). As we see, Esteban's brother has embraced a new persona now that he lives in Chimbote. He does not speak Quechua, but Spanish. He represents the process of transculturation as his Andean culture has merged with the culture of the coast (Chimbote). In his case, we see the mechanisms of transculturation that Fernando Ortiz expressed, in that the process of transculturation "also necessarily involves the loss or uprooting of a previous culture, which could be defined as a deculturation" (Ortiz 19). As Ortiz states, the process of transculturation implies the loss of a previous culture but also the inscription of the dominated culture into the dominant one, as in the case of Esteban's brother who speaks Spanish and not Quechua. For transculturation to occur, and in the name of modernity, Indigenous culture must be destroyed.

Other characters from *Los zorros* undergo similar experiences, such as *el chanchero* Bazalar, who loses his Andean roots as he is incapable of thinking in Quechua, his native language. Also, don Cecilio Ramírez, who, when Maxwell plays the charango, confesses that he does not understand such melodies from the Andes although they "ease my thought and what's more, sometimes when he [Maxwell] plays with that little blind man, Crispín Antolín, it gives me a grand feelin'" (Arguedas, *The Fox* 244). What we see in the novel, then, are the workings of transculturation, which, instead of uniting the characters from different social, racial, and ethnic strata, separates and divides them, and "definitely eliminates all real possibility of forging the authentic Peruvian nationality that José María Arguedas imagined as the union of the different ethnic groups, cultures, and social classes" (Forgues 108).

Asto, another character from *Los zorros* is also a good example of what transculturation implies. Through a sexual encounter with a white Argentinean woman he can pay, Asto hopes to cease being an Indigenous man: "Me *criollo* . . . from the coast, goddamnit; me from Argentina, goddamnit. Who highlander now" (Arguedas, *The Fox* 42). The novel, then, deals with the problematic discourses of transculturation and its relation to Peruvian modernization and its connection with capitalism and imperialism. *Los zorros* embodies how the notion of transculturation implies making the changes necessary to adapt certain populations to the most general conditions of capitalist modernization, as is the case of these Andean men in Chimbote.[18] As Alberto Moreiras points out, transculturation operates as a regulative machine for the constant adaptation of backward practices and populations to the demands of a centrally driven modernization, as would be the case of the Indigenous Quechua-speaking people of Peru (186). As we see, these men are dispossessed of their essence, their spirits and their bodies have been corrupted as they have erased their Indigenous history and their language. *Los zorros* thus allows us to look at "the profound mutation that Chimbote's society is undergoing, a mutation that radically questions the ideas that [Arguedas] had formulated previously regarding mestizaje and social and cultural integration of the Indians and the marginalized sectors of society" (Forgues 314).

The infernal world of Chimbote provides a deformed image of what José María Arguedas had imagined as an ideal for his country in his previous works. This is why what Arguedas expresses in his diaries is so important to understand and, somehow, complete the narrative of the novel. Vargas Llosa even goes further by stating that "what was going to be a novel about Chimbote and fish flour turned out to be that and, simultaneously, a novel about its author and the torments he suffered as he was writing it" (301). Forgues considers that *Los zorros* is a reflection on Arguedas desperation as he sees how reality resists his aspirations and hopes for national and personal unity (309). Here we see the failure of his dream of a dynamic and deep unifying and integrative *mestizaje* or transculturation, as expressed in all his previous work.

We must remember that, generally speaking, the development of capitalist modernization shaped the modern identity of Peru and many other Latin American countries without taking into account the principles of alterity and difference. Difference was understood as "precapitalist," "feudal," "residual," or "local" (Legrás 92). For the logic of modernization, different populations, were (and are) archaic, "as real obstacles for progress" (Rama, *Writing across Cultures* 22). Becoming modern, then, meant "overcoming underdevelopment by loosening the drag of those sectors of the population that were stigmatized as 'downstream,' 'unproductive,' 'traditional,' or, to borrow a term coined by Noam Chomsky, 'unpeople'" (Franco, *Cruel Modernity* 8). *Los zorros* shows how characters such as Esteban's brother, Asto, Cecilio Ramírez, and Bazalar try to overcome their "underdevelopment" and become modern by being de-indianized or transcultured in order to be inserted and integrated into the sociopolitical, economic, and cultural plans of Chimbotes's governing capitalism, while these same men continue to be exploited, as the following quote demonstrates: "A cint for you, a cint for me; eighty for boat skipper, twinty for fishermen; mellion, cool little mellion for Peruvian foreigner gringo. Just dance, be happy! I'm a screwed-up temporary worker, factory. Eight weeks, then ass kicked outa there! You dancin' early in mornin'—whore, butterfly, scarecrow—is that what ya are?" (Arguedas, *The Fox* 51). Here we can see the payment imbalance as the fisherman, who performs the real work, makes less money. The novel thus presents the Indian as the main victim of capitalist modernization, who, as I mentioned before, by coming down to the coast with the dream of improving his life, loses his roots, his language, and his essence and continues to be exploited.

We also need to recognize that the development of capitalism and the process of becoming modern through de-indianization or transculturation addressed in *Los zorros* through the stories of the characters mentioned above, implied erasing individuals who were also victims of the capitalist modernizing process due to alterity and difference but who were not part of the emblematic population of Peruvian modern national identity, the Indigenous worker. On the one hand, the novel denounces that the bodies of these men are sick, exploited, and suffering; that their bodies have lost their Indigenous identity and roots as well as their morality. On the other hand, the novel ignores the suffering and exploited bodies of women, Afro-Peruvians, and gender and sexual dissidents. The novel's concern is to promote the ideology of national progress through the redemption of the Indian and Indigenous tradition. It promotes this ideology by emphasizing and criticizing the exploitation of the Indianas well as the loss of his roots through transculturation. However, the novel's promotion of this ideology simultaneously affirms the men's heterosexuality and gender conformity while ignoring the suffering and exploitation of these other populations.

Heterosexual Indigenous Men, Yes! Faggots and Negroes, No!

> Yo no sé las costumbres d'este lugar.
> En mi pueblo nu'hay maricas.
> Cada hombre tiene su hembra, hembra desde nacida.
> ¿Qu'es usted? Ni Dios lo sabe.
>
> —José María Arguedas

As we mentioned before, *Los zorros* is arranged by the alternation of the novel's fictional story and the personal diaries of Arguedas. The confessional chapters of the diaries are connected to the fictional portions of the novel. In the opening of the book, the author explains that his own survival and consequently the novel's existence are linked to the exploitation of the body of a young woman of color, who is not recognized as "different" or a racial Other by Arguedas or in the novel, but as a body that can be validly exploited for the sake of the author and the novel itself as it is being written because Arguedas is alive thanks to the sexual encounter with her. As he points out at the beginning of his First Diary: "For five years my writing efforts were blocked. An encounter with a plump zamba, a young prostitute, restored my 'vital tone,' as the doctors called it. The encounter with that joyful woman must have been just the subtle and very complex touch my body and soul needed in order to reforge the broken link with all the things" (Arguedas, *The Fox* 9). Arguedas opens the chapter by writing about his suicide attempts and his mental illness and relating them to an impossibility of writing. Writing then is opposed to death for Arguedas such as when he expresses that he needs to fight death by writing or when he states "because if I don't write and get published, I'll put a bullet in myself" (17). Here, Arguedas battles against death through the exploitation and consumption of the body of the plump "zamba."

Also, in the First Diary, Arguedas expresses what he thinks of effeminate men. He writes about one of his visits to Chile and narrates his experience at the Chilean "ballet." What Arguedas most notices in this spectacle is that "the huasos [Chilean cowboys] look all decked out and pansyfied (almost an insult to the huaso)" (Arguedas, *The Fox* 15). Moreover, he ties the "pansyfied huasos" with the United States of America, when he identifies "huasos *amariconados* . . . those things that are gringo fabrications for making money" (15). This is important to consider because throughout *Los zorros* the narrative places the United States as the ultimate cause and source of the exploitation of Indigenous men. Relating *maricones* to the United States means that the novel situates them in the role of the exploiter, the enemy, the opposite of Indigenous men. The latter, throughout the novel, are presented as victims of capitalism and US imperialism, but also as heterosexuals who practice gender conformity. This relation could also point to Arguedas's belief that homosexuality is something that could never occur among Indigenous people. Rather it is something typical of a foreign or urban element. Arguedas's belief, though, echoes popular notions in the 1960s and 1970s about certain cultural elements being implanted by the American empire to demoralize and corrupt the population, such as drugs or, indeed, homosexuality. Arguedas is thus claiming a certain superiority for the oppressed Indigenous people and opposing it to the immorality of the oppressors, in this case, men from the United States.

Moreover, both effeminate men or *maricones* and US capitalism have, according to Arguedas, the big goal of producing money. Thus, he expresses, "All that is for making money. And when isn't there an indispensable urgency about making money these days? What has been pansyfied in order to commercialize it will be de-pansyfied—the same thing will happen in literature, medicine, music, and even in the way women approach men" (Arguedas, *The Fox* 15). Arguedas thus confirms that for him *amariconamiento* or effeminacy is something produced by Americans that is inherent to capitalism and business. This might explain why he is so harsh when representing effeminate men in the fictional passages of *Los zorros*. In fact, the first fictional chapter begins with an expression of hegemonic/toxic masculinity that condemns the effeminacy of *maricones*:

> Chaucato put out to sea in his small trawler, Sampson I, taking his ten fishermen as crew, among them the faggot El Mudo [The Mute] and, as an extra hand on a trial basis, a violinist from the Black Cat, a nightclub where call girls served the drinks. Day is dawning. Chaucato is talking to El Mudo on the bridge: "Mudo, you son of a bitch, we' re doin' a man's work here. Havin' a dick's what makes a man different, isn't it? You were born with a dick, ya hear me, Mudo, even if it's just for screwin' yourself. When a man grabs a knife it's not so's he

> can take people spittin' at him lyin' down. To row the dory, to haul in the lead and the dragnet, to come in when the sea's rough ya gotta have a dick. Here you're either gonna end up on the ocean or else I'm gonna have' em stick a hose up your gills. (Arguedas, *The Fox* 27)

The work of fishermen, according to this example, is the work of men and not *maricones* like Mudo. Being a good fisherman implies being masculine and virile. If Mudo wants to be a good fisherman, he needs to stop being a *maricón*. Moreover, Mudo is presented as a promiscuous character as he has sex with his prostitute mother and her clients. Mudo is specially degraded because of his homosexuality and because he does not speak. He lives in unnatural ways and this is why he is portrayed in the novel as "human filth." Arguedas's position toward capitalism seems contradictory; in his First Diary he relates effeminacy to US capitalism and business. Nevertheless, in the fictional portion of *Los zorros* he relates capitalism and business to masculinity and virility. The sea, which is the source exploited, is perceived as female genitalia, "the greatest suckin' cunt in the world," that turns the *maricón* into a man: "Whoreson, faggot Mudo; out here I'm makin' a man outa ya" (Arguedas, *The Fox* 27). Also, businessmen such as Braschi, who "got more power than dynamite in his head, in his ass, in his company" (30), are viewed as very virile and their success is related to this same characteristic. In this sense, we could argue that in *Los zorros*, Chimbote is presented not only as the space where Andean men could hope for a better future through transculturation but also as the space where they could become real men and, therefore, as successful as Braschi, described by another character, Chaucato, as one of the "factory owners" who makes "every little anchovy spawn banknotes, puttin' fire to the fish with violent iron" (31). Nevertheless, Braschi is also condemned in the novel because he makes Mudo sodomize him.[19] Since Braschi, the capitalist, is meant to be a figure of contempt in the novel, the change of positions vis-à-vis the act of sodomy is particularly suggestive, with the exploiter being penetrated by the same individuals he exploits.

Hegemonic/toxic masculinity and virility are the forces behind productivity at Chimbote, extracting the products from the sea, "the big 'pussy' nowadays, the sea of Chimbote . . . the most generous, foul-smelling whore 'pussy' there is" (Arguedas, *The Fox* 45). The bay of Chimbote is the "big 'pussy,'" fornicated by virile men, and described in the novel as "the million-dollar sex" (46). This productivity is presented as positive for the economy of the country and its citizens, as Tarta says to Mudo, "Off of that 'pu-pu-pussy' you're makin' a li-li-living, fag . . . our country's li-li-living off of it" (45).[20] A parallel can be drawn here between the productivity of the feminized sea at Chimbote and the writerly productivity that Arguedas draws from the body of the young "zamba" mentioned at the beginning of the First Diary. Female genitalia, female bodies are always exploited, made productive economically and literarily.

If *Los zorros* is criticizing and denouncing the exploitation of Indigenous men, it does not do the same with the female subject or the *maricón* when dealing with notions such as productivity. These subjects are not included in what needs to be redeemed in order to establish a modern collective identity for Peru. As José Carlos Mariátegui points out, the effect of unity by virtue of which the people could appear, in everyone's eyes, as a people, that is, as the basis and origin of national and political power, could only be forged on the grounds of certain fundamental exclusions (313). *Los zorros* directly and clearly addresses and denounces the exploitation of Andean bodies. In fact, as Cornejo Polar states, "In *The Fox from Up Above and the Fox from Down Below* the Andean elements are of such magnitude and have such decisive functions that it is legitimate to think that in that novel, for the first time, Indigenous rationality is the reason driving modernity" ("Un ensayo" 303). Nevertheless, it leaves unattended the exploitation that other "different" bodies suffer.

This takes us back to what we mentioned at the beginning of this chapter about the establishment of groups and populations that were different from the normative models of national identity during the twentieth century. These groups and populations were subordinated and excluded from the modernizing project and were not considered under the same parameters as those populations that formed the national identity, that is, the heterosexual and gender-conforming Indigenous identity, in the case of Peru. They were not redeemed, protected, or elevated as emblems of national identity but damned to be excluded, and in that exclusion, exploited. As I mentioned before, the modern process of naturalization of social and political belonging was understood across the political and cultural spectrum almost entirely in racial and ethnic terms. Gender and sexuality were not on the table for discussion in the forging of the modern social pacts between the state and the "People" in modern Peru.

Loco Moncada, a Lunatic, a Faggot, a Negro!

The exclusion of women, Afro-Peruvian, homosexuals, and effeminate men from the discourse of the modern nation in Peru does not prevent these same subjects from developing an alternative political language capable of exposing marginalization and oppression—a language that serves as a critique of the formation of modern nation-states based on erasure and marginalization in the process of creating a modern national identity. In *Los zorros*, the character of Loco Moncada would be a good example of this. Not Indigenous but Black, not heterosexual but *maricón*, Moncada, "a truly Chimbotean kind of by-product" (Arguedas, *The Fox* 152) represents a different perspective on Chimbote, one that is counter to the generally accepted representation. On different occasions, we see these characters disguising themselves as fishermen, a Turkish businessmen, a pregnant women. Moncada is constantly affirming an indeterminacy of gender through *travestismo*; he is also an "in-between" subject throughout the novel, since he does not identify himself with one of the two normatively defined gender and sexual expressions (masculine/feminine, heterosexual/homosexual): "Now Moncada was acting the part of the barefooted fisherman. The previous week he had gone around all dressed up as a dandy and had preached in the center of the town. Another time he went out preaching as an Arab shopkeeper, and several months after this event some still remembered the time he had presented himself in the markets as a pregnant woman about to give birth. He had displayed his abdomen, a fake belly he had a mewling kitten shut up in, and he, Moncada the lunatic, was crying too" (Arguedas, *The Fox* 59). Besides expressing different gender roles such as the ones mentioned in this quote, Moncada represents a fragmented discourse that does not aspire to produce total or fixed meanings. This fragmented and unproductive discourse signals a profound truth or makes something visible that these same total and fixed meanings hide. According to Cornejo Polar, Moncada is a language that is "a kind of mirror in which the harbour is reflected in the only way possible: paralogically" ("Un ensayo" 297). Moncada denounces the injustices perpetrated in Chimbote by the logic of capitalism as can be seen in the following passage. Dressed as a pregnant woman, referring to the father of the fake baby they carry, Moncada says: "His father won't acknowledge him. His begetter was a trawler skipper called Anacleto Pérez Albertis. But in Chimbote the Sogesa Steel Mill workers are the only ones who acknowledge their bastards. With regular high wages, with all the legal deductions, they live in the Cuernavaca section. A real good neighborhood, officially recognized and fancy. They work the night shift and over there the wives manufacture horns better than the factory makes steel rods. Oh me, oh my!" (Arguedas, *The Fox* 59). As we can see, Moncada has a paralogic discourse because it cannot and perhaps does not desire to sustain a productive and fully iterable relation between language, reason, and collective signification. Williams defines Moncada's discourse as "pure subaltern language" (Williams, "Chimbote" 50) taking place in the streets of Chimbote. According to Moraña, this character, with this unproductive discourse, their *travestismo*, and their actions, "subverts the exploitative and disciplining logic of reproductive labor under capitalism with the ludic unproductivity of a turbulent and undisciplined perception of his/her world" (Moraña, *Arguedas/Vargas Llosa* 161). Thus, described in the novel as "a Moncada degenerated to a lower type by African blood and other viruses" (Arguedas, *The Fox* 72) "a lunatic," "quite special and original" (152), Moncada's presence is always disrupting the exploitative logic of capitalism and, compared to other characters, he more systematically resists being brought into its fold.

The novel suggests, it seems, that Afro-Peruvians and *maricones*, while excluded from the integration process of capitalist modernization, are able to observe and make visible certain problems that have deep historical roots. For instance, Moncada allows us to see that although the promise of transculturation in Chimbote announces a better future for those who migrate there, losing their roots, their difference, in order to participate in the glory of "el jardín cielo," will not even grant them a decent place to rest when they die. Through Moncada's eyes we witness how the cemetery of poor people is infringed upon and its lands appropriated by those in power:

> The madman followed the visitors to the cemetery. There he saw people bringing down crosses from high up to the dune. They were pulling the crosses up out of the sand by bending the uprights way over, and were going down the dune sinking their feet into the sand. Moncada was the only one carrying a cross in the opposite direction, going inward with a large cross at that, one with the little bag and a piece of dirty net hanging from one of the arms. The City Hall, the Beneficiencia, the police and the parish priests had ordered and persuaded the poor shanty dwellers to move their cemetery to some low-lying flatland on the other side of San Pedro's high dune. (Arguedas, *The Fox* 66)

If we recognize the discourse produced by Moncada—a colored and eccentric person who moves between genders—as a subaltern language, we need to recognize the potentiality of this same language. Moncada's subaltern language calls attention to the limits of capitalism's ability to regulate the minds and bodies of social life in Chimbote on behalf of productivity. Moreover, this language signals the historical connections between the Peruvian Republican project and the situation in Chimbote. For example, Moncada expresses, "Here, in Peru shall we say, since San Martín, Don José, there's been nothing but outsiders, foreigners giving the orders. We've been nothing but the servants of foreigners" (Arguedas, *The Fox* 59). Besides this, Moncada is a good example of a *cuir* character, one whose gaze *cuiriza* the discourse of the normalized social order.

I mentioned that Moncada, like Arguedas, is an "in-between" subject, not because of their race or ethnicity, but because of their indeterminacy of gender and their elaboration of survival strategies and strategies of selfhood that "initiate new signs of identity" (Bhabha 1). Loco Moncada, the crazed "zambo mulato," though, unlike Arguedas, embraces this "in-betweenness" and thus they see things in a different way. This gesture destabilizes the utopian project, calling into question whether Arguedas himself had doubts about its possibility. For instance, *Los zorros* shows Arguedas "in-betweenness" by exposing two styles, two genres (the diaries, the fiction), two narrators in one novel. Sadly, this "in-betweenness" is unresolved in the novel as it is unfinished, and in Arguedas's life, as he kills himself before giving the novel or his personal affairs closure. The productivity of an "in-between" position that is embraced and acknowledged will be addressed in chapters 2, 3, and 4.

Protecting Chile's Racial Purity and Superiority

According to Gabriel Salazar, there is and has only ever been one state in Chile: the state shaped by Diego Portales in the 1810–1837 foundational period. The Chilean state inaugurated by Portales is known as the "tiempo-madre" (originary period) of Chilean politics, characterized by the exaltation of authoritarianism, government arbitrariness, and the repression of civic and human rights as patriotic values. In the first half of the twentieth century, there were two presidents who played a highly significant role in perpetuating Portales's configuration of the Chilean state, Arturo Alessandri Palma (1920, 1925, 1932), nicknamed the "Lion of Tarapacá," and Carlos Ibañez del Campo (1927, 1952). Then came Augusto Pinochet, who after the 1973 military coup and the establishment of the military dictatorship explicitly announced that his regime would continue with the state form devised by Portales, which, as Salazar notes, remains untouched to this day (Salazar 15).

The continuity of the Portelian state model is clearly reflected in the way in which both Alessandri and Ibañez del Campo reacted to the great national crisis of the First Centenary (1910), in which there was a denationalization of the Chilean economy, an explosion of social misery, and the administrative corruption of the oligarchy. This crisis would later be exacerbated by the Great Depression and the collapse of the nitrate industry, which prompted constant mobilizations of nonelite sectors, forcing a dramatic expansion of the entire political system. In the face of this crisis, Chile had to be saved. One of the ways this was done was by resuming the discourse of Chilean racial superiority.

Ericka Beckman explains that the Chilean state developed a sense of nationalist superiority based on the way it interpreted its role in the War of the Pacific (1879–1883), namely, as a righteous struggle against the supposedly "inferior" races of Peru (but also Bolivia) (74). In the years following this conflict, the country was strongly defined by a desire to keep and protect racial purity and superiority, elevating race and ethnicity to a nationalist ideal. Jeffrey Klaiber has pointed out that Chile's victory in the War of the Pacific "served to confirm, strengthen and even popularize the myth of Chilean racial superiority" (27).

This assertion of Chilean racial purity and superiority became a powerful rhetorical strategy during the modernization of the Chilean nation-state, which started around 1929 and lasted until the early 1990s as a response to the economic crisis that Chile suffered, along with many other Latin American countries. As Beckman states, "Throughout the course of the twentieth century, the myth of Chilean racial superiority within Latin America would not disappear; instead, the truth claims regarding 'the Chilean race' naturalized during and after the War of the Pacific would insidiously burrow their way into official state discourse" (86), meaning that Chile became or continued being a racist state. Thus, Chile's creation (or re-creation) of a national identity relied on the subordination/exclusion to the margins of those who were considered "different" because of their race, ethnicity, gender expression, or sexuality. In turn, this drive gave birth to several discourses that sought to keep and protect the purity and superiority of its "white" race from contamination, given its elevated status as the emblem of Chilean national identity.

As Marcos Fernández Labbé points out, this national racial discourse positioned the Chilean people as endowed with a common heritage—regardless of their position in the productive system—which, together with granting it an identity, represented an asset that should be looked after, or amended when necessary, for the sake of collective well-being. As a racist state, the Chilean state governed with a hierarchy of races, where certain races were described as superior and others, in contrast, were described as inferior, separating out the groups that existed within the Latin American population but also within Chile.

For instance, during the first decades of the twentieth century, Nicolás Palacios, a widely respected turn-of-the-century Chilean intellectual and physician and the author of *Raza Chilena: Libro escrito por un chileno para los chilenos* (2012), expressed that the presence of a large number of foreigners in Chile posed the danger that foreigners would replace the Chilean people, who were being forced to emigrate or endure living conditions that were affecting their reproductive capacity and demographic growth (Barr-Melej 57).[21] He emphasized that these foreigners belonged to different races and nationalities and in the face of this situation he called for a nationalist response, as their presence would make the Chilean race disappear.[22] The pure and superior Chilean race could be contaminated by contact, or even worse, by mixing with these inferior races. On these grounds, Palacios made a call to save and protect the Chilean race. The same happened in Argentina, where immigrants were accused of threatening "national spaces for the production of the new Argentinean subject" (Salessi 186).

Carlos Ibáñez del Campo, the "general of hope," who was obsessively concerned about this threat to the race, presented himself as the sole leader capable of combating all the evils afflicting the country through nationalism. Those who supported him regarded his work as patriotic, inasmuch as it would save the country from the problems that afflicted it, steering it toward a "new Chile." Thus, calls for moralizing and depurating the country characterized the governments of Ibáñez del Campo (1927–1931/1952–1958).

Ibáñez del Campo's first administration has been classified as a dictatorship and as the first police state in Chile. He sought to achieve order and progress for the country and in the pursuit of these aims he imposed severe measures to prevent and crush dissent, which became de facto politically motivated persecutions. With the authoritarian regime of President Carlos Ibáñez del Campo, the policy of relegation, or internal exile, became a standard state recourse at the same time that all opposition was seen as subversive and contrary to the government's national reconstruction project (Rojas Flores 23).

Ibáñez del Campo was obsessed with eugenic ideas such as "depuration" and "regeneration" and he considered dissident sexualities and genders as plagues that could cause racial degeneration, affecting the purity and superiority of the Chilean race. To protect it, he adopted a number of measures to eradicate homosexuality (but also effeminacy). It must be pointed out, however, that relating effeminacy and homosexuality to racial degeneration was not an invention of Ibáñez del Campo. Around the 1930s and 1940s, these practices were defined as "asocial" and the subjects who practiced them were considered as not contributing to the country's progress. Thus, Ibáñez del Campo's moralizing and purifying crusade was in step with the definition established by the Chilean medical discourse of some social subjects as dangerous because they threatened the integrity of Chile's national unity rooted in racial purity and superiority as its key emblems. Around that time, for instance, male effeminacy and homosexuality were considered, along with alcoholism, drug addiction, and vagrancy, comparable to sexually transmitted diseases or so-called social diseases. Homosexuality was sometimes referred to as a "conduct" but homosexuals were sometimes seen as a species of its own that carried its own singular characteristics and represented a condition of degeneration of the Chilean race. In Argentina, male homosexuals, *travestis*, *invertidos*, *lunfardos*, were considered *subjects from a different species* (Salessi 158) as established by *hombres de ciencia* such as the military psychiatrist Francisco De Veyga and José Ingenieros.

As we see, these considerations around dissident gender and sexualities were not exclusive to Chile. In *Médicos, Maleantes y Maricas* (1995), the Argentinean scholar Jorge Salessi explains that homosexuality, first denominated as *sodomía*, played an important role in the modernization of Argentina, as *sodomitas* had to be eradicated to preserve the cleanliness of the national body. Salessi explains, "Homosexuality was used in Argentina in order to define and regulate new notions of nationality . . . of the 'new race' that should be the consequence of immigration" (180), which was reflected in several literary texts produced by authors such as Carlos Octavio Bunge, who portrayed the dangers that these deviants and degenerates represented for the process of modernization and creation of the new country, the new nationality. Joseph Pierce, who reads the life experience of the Bunge siblings to study Argentinean modernization, explains that "the state project of normalizing culture demanded specific forms of racial identification, gender, performance, and sexuality" (*Argentine* 4).

According to Michel Foucault, sexuality, being an eminently corporeal mode of behavior, is a matter for "individualizing disciplinary controls that take the form of permanent surveillance . . . but because it also has procreative effects, sexuality is also inscribed, takes effect, in broad biological processes that concern not the bodies of individuals but the element, the multiple unity of the population" (*The History* 251). For the Chilean state, homosexuality, deemed a debauched, perverted sexuality, was considered to have effects at the level of the Chilean population, since sexually debauched individuals were assumed to have a heredity that could degenerate the Chilean race. Moreover, as virility was seen as another important feature of the Chilean race, homosexuality and effeminacy qualified as two of its most concrete threats.

Singling out certain conducts as perversions implied that the Chilean state could expand its power and control to new areas, introducing a specific way of governing through the normalization of subjects and of the Chilean population to keep and protect the ideal of national identity rooted in racial purity and superiority. Foucault would define this style of governing the biopolitical: the Chilean state started to define biological areas of control of the Chilean population relating them to racial purity and superiority.[23] Several measures to regenerate and readapt these subjects were implemented in order to protect the country's well-being and progress. Security mechanisms, then, had to be installed around these asocial subjects so as to optimize the living conditions of the Chilean population. For instance, in 1928 and 1929, Ibáñez del Campo presented two bills to reform the Criminal Code in which sodomy, that is, the act as such, was no longer penalized, but homosexuals were criminalized because of the danger they posed. During the Ibáñez del Campo administrations, the homosexual became a morally abnormal individual, as he was considered a degenerate. The individual as a homosexual, not his sexual behavior, was thus deemed a degenerate subject who represented a threat to the Chilean population. Consequently, the homosexual had to be eliminated, but this did not always mean killing or murdering him directly, but rather indirectly. Foucault defines this kind of murder as "the fact of exposing someone to death, increasing the risk of death for some people, or, quite simply, political death, expulsion, rejection, and so on" (*Society* 256).

The Chilean state opted for the expulsion of homosexuals as a way of indirectly murdering them. An elderly Pisagua local claimed to recall a group of about fifty young men being confined in the internment camp for some months, and the contemporary gay-rights organization of Santiago has cited the persecution of gays in Pisagua as an important marker in their history of repression and struggle (Frazier 168). In this way, Pisagua was prominent less as a political prison camp than as a detention center for homosexual men, certainly during General Ibáñez del Campo's first presidency and perhaps also during his second term.

Still, little documentary evidence exists on the widely acknowledged policy of incarcerating homosexual men. An exception is a 1942 editorial debate in *El Tarapacá* that discussed the Ministry of Justice's creation of a special homosexual section in the Pisagua internment camp, where professionals, using the most advanced techniques of psychiatric and rehabilitative care, would "reform" the prisoners. The first commentary in the published debate reacted to this policy and pleaded for its reversal.

During the second government of Ibáñez del Campo, the state materialized its position toward social hygienization by issuing the 11.625

Act, known as the Antisocial States Act, promulgated on September 21, 1954, and published in the Official Gazette on October 4, 1954, aimed at sanctioning homosexual practices.[24] By separating homosexuals, the Chilean state was protecting the lives of the Chilean population and ensuring that the purity and superiority of the Chilean race could become stronger and more vigorous. As Foucault would put it when addressing the relation between race and biopolitics, the war against the homosexual was seen as a way of improving Chile's race by "eliminating" the enemy, but also as a way of regenerating one's own race, so "the race to which we belong will become all the purer" (*Society* 257).

It must be said that in the two decades between the two governments of Ibáñez del Campo, there were other presidents who maintained this relationship between race and national identity. Just a few months before the beginning of World War II in 1939, President Pedro Aguirre Cerda delivered a presidential message in which he declared the significance of fortifying the Chilean race, to "make it healthy, allow it to thrive, and provide for it the joy of life." At the same time, he confirmed the commitment of the Chilean state to invest its financial resources to fight "the plagues that degrade our race" (quoted in Fernández Labbé 178–79). In those years, the fight against the degeneration and weakening of the Chilean race was of higher significance.

One of the reasons homosexuality was considered such a menace to the Chilean population and race was its intersexual state, because the above-mentioned Chilean leaders considered intersexuality as hermaphroditism. What we see here, then, is the danger of an indeterminacy of genders, not belonging to a specific gender, "masculine" or "feminine." This is specifically what contributes to the degeneration of the Chilean race and constitutes a menace obstructing progress in the country (Prieto Millán 33). In the case of Chile, male homosexuals thus implied the existence of a sexual difference that threatened the uniformity of the Chilean national identity as it refused to comply with the expectations of its standard identity.

These considerations regarding the male effeminate homosexual are addressed in *El lugar sin límites* or *Hell Has No Limits* by José

Donoso. Besides allowing us to look at the costs of modernization in the case of a small Chilean regional village, Talca, Donoso's novel also demonstrates that Chile's modernizing nationalist discourse purposely excluded men who practiced dissident genders and sexualities (but also prostitutes) as these subjects threatened modernity's momentum. They were a menace to the establishment (or reestablishment) of a modern Chilean national identity based on the purity and superiority of its race.

In addition, the analysis of this canonical book will allow me to discuss how the rejection of male effeminate homosexuals during the re-creation of the modern Chilean national identity has been extended to the Chilean LGBT community, where *travestis*, as Claudia Rodríguez explains, "are the most excluded" ("Se resiste" 22) because of their indeterminacy of gender.

The "In-Between" against Modernization in José Donoso's *Hell Has No Limits*

José Donoso is known for his modernist literary project, which disarticulates the possibility of a realist novel capable of encompassing a vision of totality (Fornazzari 13).[25] For José Miguel Oviedo, Donoso hails from the thriving vein of Chilean realism although, as the critic maintains, Donoso enriched and modified realism by introducing forms, topics, and especially obsessions, all of which were initially foreign to the realist model (*Historia* 332). In light of this, Donoso's literary work typically yields two types of critical readings: some emphasize the realism in his work, arguing that it describes the fragility and decadence of the Chilean upper classes by using a locally rooted, transparent language (Hugo Achugar, Hernán Vidal, Antonio Cornejo Polar), while others (Philip Swanson, Sharon Magnarelli, Ana María Dopico, Adriana Valdés) adopt a modernist perspective and posit that Donoso uses radical signifying strategies, exhibits a subversive and experimental attitude toward institutions and language, and rejects totalizing narratives (Fornazzari 15). These two perspectives suggest that Donoso's writing cultivates a tension between two forms: realism and modernism.

Donoso addressed the limitations of the realist form when he mentioned that, even though his first novel *Coronación* (1957) was written in accordance with the canons of simplicity, verisimilitude, social critique, and irony, he already knew then that these features of national taste were not the only means of excellence, and that, quite the contrary, "the baroque, the twisted, the excessive could broaden the possibilities of the novel" (Donoso, "Historia personal" 32). This amounts to what, in the words of Carlos Fuentes, we could name a "desecration and contamination of a sacred rhetoric" (30), in which we can also see a desecration of the sacred national identity through the development of a literary narrative that differs from the realist mode. This is precisely what Donoso does in *El lugar sin límites*, specifically by demonstrating that Chile's modernizing nationalist discourse purposely excluded men who practiced dissident genders and sexualities. In both its contents and form, the novel resists and negates the ideal of national identity that the modern Chilean state established based on racial purity and superiority, and as threatened by homosexuality.

In the introduction to his collection of essays *José Donoso: La destrucción de un mundo* (1975), Antonio Cornejo Polar has argued that questioning identity has been a constant in Donoso's work. This trait, Cornejo Polar notes, can be seen especially in *El lugar sin límites*, "which obsessively affirms the doubt about the sense of the identity of the world and of people" (Introducción 9). In this novel, then, and as Cornejo Polar argues, "Human beings become elusive in the multiplicity of their faces, and faces are destroyed as unusable masks, oblivious to any unchanging center" (10). Therefore, besides addressing the exclusion and elimination of men who practice dissident genders and sexualities, I contend that *El lugar sin límites* also resists and negates this exclusion and elimination because the novel affirms, both in its form and content, the possibilities of gender indeterminacy that were negated and punished by the Chilean state.

The narrative center of *El lugar sin limites* is a brothel, a marginal world that traffics in flesh, where old prostitutes live, including a *travesti*, Manuela, and an unattractive girl who runs the place. Japonesita. The novel affirms gender indeterminacy both at the narrative level and through the treatment of the characters, especially Manuela, who, in the words of Severo Sarduy in his seminal essay on writing and *travestismo* ("Escritura/Travestismo"), embodies *travestismo* as inversion to its limits. Manuela, also known as Manuel González Astica, is presented as a "female" subject for some fifty pages until readers realize that Manuela is a *travesti*. This discovery occurs when the voice of Japonesita appears in the narrative, referring to Manuela as a "male" subject, calling her "father." Japonesita, then, has a problem with Manuela appearing before her as "female" and not as a father: "Last year, after that Pancho thing, his daughter bawled him out saying she was ashamed of being the daughter of an old fairy like him" (Donoso, *Hell* 57). It is worth mentioning that the narrator of the novel does not refer to Manuela as a "male" subject; when referring to them, the narrative voice always represents Manuela in terms of *travestismo* or gender indeterminacy, showing us that it is the words of others that tend to destabilize this representation of Manuel González Astica / Manuela, as suggested by the following quote: "That morning they had seen the three Farías sisters step off the train from Talca . . . two younger women also got off, and a man, if you could call him that. The women, watching from a careful distance, discussed what he might be: skinny as a broomstick, with long hair, his eyes were made up almost as much as the Farías sisters" (74). Cornejo Polar has pointed out that *El lugar sin límites* has an unequivocally open and ambiguous verbal structure (Introducción 10), especially in regard to the voice of the narrator. At the beginning of the novel, we encounter a traditional third-person narrator who very quickly, and inconspicuously, paves the way for the characters' direct expression, thus becoming the vehicle for many voices. The narrator is interrupted by the voices of several narrator-characters, as we note in the following example in which the narrative voice allows Manuela's voice to take over: "She ran her tongue over her toothless gums: hot sawdust, and breath like rotten eggs. From drinking so much new wine to hurry the men out and close early. She gave a start—of course!—she opened her eyes and sat up in bed: Pancho Vega was in town . . . last year the beast got it into his head that she had to dance flamenco. . . . You bet! Big brute!

Think I'd dance for you, just look at you! I do that for gentlemen, for my friends" (Donoso, *Hell* 7–8). In the following passage, the voice of the narrator is interrupted by the voice of Japonesita: "La Manuela took hold of Japonesita's lank hair, squinted both eyes and looked at her, you have to try to look pretty, and began to untangle it—what good it is being a woman if you're not a flirt, that's what men like, silly, that's what they come here for, to forget the scarecrows they're married to, and with your hair this way, look, this is how you do it, now it looks nice . . . and la Manuela untangles it for her and here they put a ribbon, don't you have a pretty ribbon?" (55). These examples show that, in the novel, expression is always ambiguous and this makes it difficult to identify whether the narrator or one of the characters is speaking. The narrator does not reproduce the character's words, but rather takes their perspective. These alternating perspectives work in the novel as an interruption, producing the effect of a text with shared authorship. This assembly of voices and narrative consciousness is delivered in a fluid language with hardly any punctuation or pauses, collaborating with the mingling of voices and consciousnesses interrupting each other in the narration. In the following quotation we can see how difficult it is to know who is speaking or to determine the reliability of what is spoken: "Because the moon's out Japonesita said to herself, or maybe said out loud, or maybe Don Céspedes . . ." (158). Thus, the narrative voice is deliberately denying any certainty about the words, whether or not they have been spoken, and if so by whom.

Another instance of textual (and sexual) fluidity can be seen in the passage in which Big Japonesa, after making a bet with Alejandro Cruz, seduces la Manuela, an encounter in which they engender Japonesita. In this passage we see the agglutination of narrative voices and consciousnesses as they are narrating and being narrated with a fluid language. The voice of Manuela is interrupted by that of Big J aponesa:

> She likes to do what she's doing here on the sheets with me. She's pleased that I can't: not with anybody, tell me, pretty

> Manuela, tell me not with any other woman before me; pretty Manuela, tell me I'm the first, the only, so I can have you all to myself my pretty little girl, my love, Manuelita I'm going to have you, I like your terrified body and all your fears and I want to destroy your fears, no, don't be afraid Manuela, no, not destroy them but gently smooth them away to reach a part of me that she, poor Big Japonesa, thought existed but doesn't exist and never has, it never has existed despite your touching and caressing me and murmuring. (Donoso, *Hell* 125)

At the same time, though, this fluid language complicates and erases binary genders and identities, transforming them into what Sarduy in the above-mentioned essay equates with *travestismo*. In Sarduy's words, "Transvestism, as practiced in Donoso's novel, may well be the best metaphor for writing: what Manuela makes us see is not a woman who might be hiding a man *beneath her appearance* . . . but the very fact of transvestism itself" (Sarduy "Escritura/Travestismo" 37). In the following passage, the language of Big Japonesa's narrative voice, a fluid and ambiguous language in which more than one narrative consciousness intervenes, becomes a vehicle for gender performativity as Manuel González Astica becomes la Manuela and enjoys the sexual encounter as Manuela. This passage suggests that gender identity is performative and is being constructed through language (John Austin, Judith Butler), inasmuch as the voices, engaged in an ambiguous and mobile language, undo la Manuela's biological gender:

> No honey, Manuela, as if we were two women, look, see, our legs wound together, sex in sex, two identical sexes, Manuela, don't be afraid of my thighs moving, my hips, my mouth in yours, like two women . . . no, no you're the woman, Manuela, I'm the man, look how I'm taking off your panties and loosening your brassiere so your breasts will be bare and I can play with them, yes you have them Manuela, don't cry, you do have breasts, tiny like a little girl's, but you have them and that's why I love you. You talk and caress me and suddenly you tell

> me, now Darling Manuela, now you can . . . I dreamed about my breasts being caressed and something happened while she was saying, yes little girl . . . and I feel her heat devouring me, me, a me that doesn't exist, and she helps me, laughing with me. . . . I stay, sleeping over her, and she says into my ear; as if in a dream: my sweet girl, my sweet boy, her words muffled in the pillow . . . because what I'm needing so much now no longer exists, that you and that me I'd like so desperately to call to from this corner. (Donoso, *Hell* 126–27)

In this passage we see how language is seeking to erase gender distinctions between the gender binary, not only for la Manuela but also for Big Japonesa. The narrative destabilizes any identitarian consciousness that may lead us to a recognition of the self as "masculine" or "feminine." As we have already pointed out, Donoso's novel, in addition to including a character who is gender fluid—Manuela—is also written from that same perspective.

So far, we have seen how *El lugar sin límites* addresses the exclusion and persecution of homosexuals by the Chilean state through a disarticulation of language and gender barriers. In what follows, I will also delve into the ways gender politics are linked to a critique of caudillismo and the modernization process, especially through the character of Don Alejandro Cruz, the man who dares Big Japonesa to seduce Manuela. He is a hacendado, owner of the vineyards surrounding the little village of Estación El Olivo, and a congressman for Talca. Cruz is described as follows: "He's like God here in town. He does whatever he wants. They're all afraid of him. Don't you know he owns all the vineyards, all of them, as far as the eye can see? And he's so good that when someone offends him, like the guy who was bothering you, he immediately forgives and forgets. He is either a very good man or else he doesn't have time to worry about people like us" (Donoso, *Hell* 86). For Cruz, the whole village is an economic entity, his economic entity: "Projects, always projects. Now he's selling us land here in Estación, but I know him and I haven't fallen for it yet. According to him, everything's on its way up. Next year he's going to parcel out a block of his land and he's going to make a town out of it, he's going to sell model homes, he says, with easy payments, and when he's sold all the lots he's going to have electricity brought to town and then we'll be riding high for sure" (86). As Fernando Moreno Turner argues, Cruz's economic power is immense, it is the generator, not only of space but also of human life because, as highlighted in the novel, "They said he was Don Alejo's son. But then they'd say that about everybody, Miss Lila, Japonesita, and God knows who else, every blue-eyed peon for miles around but not me" (41). Cruz's political power is compounded by his political ambitions to become a congressman, for which he also conquers the people's votes through his promises of development (electricity):

> He has a wife, of course, a pretty blond, very ladylike, distinguished I'd say, and another woman in Talca and who knows how many more in the capital. And all of them working like dogs for him during election . . . and on election day he even came with a truck and anyone who didn't want to vote was thrown in by forcé and let's go my friend, to San Alfonso to vote for me, and he gave them money and they were so happy with the whole thing that later on they went around asking when there were going to be more elections. (Donoso, *Hell* 86–87)

As a paternalistic figure, the night he wins the election and Manuela is invited to perform at the celebration party, Cruz, along with other men of the village mock and humiliate Manuela when they "prove" that they are a *travesti*:

> The crowd broke into applauses as la Manuela dropped panting in the chair next to Don Alejo.
>
> Let's dance, sweetie. . . ."
>
> . . .
>
> La Manuela, head thrown back and body arched, pinned herself to Don Alejo and together they danced a few steps

> surrounded by the cheering men forming a circle around them. The postmaster came forward and snatched la Manuela from Don Alejo. They managed one turn around the floor before the mayor took her away from him and more and more came from the circle that closed in on la Manuela. Someone stroked her while she was dancing, another rubbed her leg. The vineyard boss of a neighboring estate tucked up the skirt, and when they saw that, the men grouped around her, trying to carry her off, helped raise the skirt over her head, binding her arms as if in a strait jacket. Embarrassed and choking with laughter, they felt her skinny, hairy legs and lank backside.
>
> "She's hot."
>
> "She's steaming."
>
> "Let's throw her in the canal."
>
> Don Alejo stood up.
>
> "Let's go."
>
> "We've got to cool her off."
>
> . . .
>
> And they pitched la Manuela into the water. The men who were watching her from above, standing between the blackberries and the canal, doubled over with laughter, pointing at the figure that struck poses and danced waist deep in water with her dress floating around her like a wide stain singing "El Relicario." (Donoso, *Hell* 91–92).

Don Alejo participates in this humiliation in which power and those who hold it undo the performativity of Manuela, especially, as the narration indicates, at that moment in which her flamenco dancer dress, a crucial garment in her process of *travestismo*, becomes a stain. These subjects, who represent the Chilean state, seem to need fixed and immovable gender identities—male/female—as can be seen in their efforts to reveal that Manuela is in fact biologically a man.

This hypothesis is supported, moreover, by Cruz's bet that Big Japonesa will not be able to seduce Manuela to have sex with her.

Cruz promises Big Japonesa that if she manages to do so, he will hand over to her the property deeds of the house where she runs the brothel, which she rents from him: "I can excite la Manuela no matter how queer he is, there wasn't one who wouldn't have given anything to be in la Manuela's place . . . just try and get that queer hot for you. If you manage to excite him and he performs like a man, fine, I'll give you whatever you ask for. But it has to be with us watching, and put some action into it" (Donoso, *Hell* 94–95). Big Japonesa replies: "This house" (95).

It is worth mentioning that this bet implies the interruption of a performativity to move to another one, a performativity around the enjoyment of power by attempting to force a stable and fixed gender, that is male or female, on la Manuela. Power, then, is portrayed as that which relies on a stable, fixed discourse of gender, whereas Manuela's gender indeterminacy defies this possibility. Likewise, this bet involves obtaining land, property, to perpetuate a system based on trafficking in flesh, such as the brothel. Don Alejo, looking through the window while Big Japonesa and Manuela have sex, enjoys the effect of his power to alter sexual roles and determine sexual identities, eliminating the gender indeterminacy that Manuela represents.

Perhaps for this reason, *El lugar sin límites* ends by showing how Cruz betrays Manuela. They must be eliminated because their existence is not suitable for the Chilean state, represented in this novel by Don Alejo Cruz. They are not a subject that can be regenerated to become productive for the state. At the celebration party for Cruz's election victory, he promises Manuela to protect them from anyone who dares to assault them because of their *travestismo* or their gender indeterminacy, as is the case of Pancho Vega. However, later, when Vega returns to the village and pursues la Manuela in order to physically assault them, Cruz does nothing to prevent it, thus allowing their destruction:

> He had to run this way, toward the station, toward the outskirts of El Olivo because there on the other side of the town's

> limits Don Alejo was waiting for him, and he was the only one who could save him. His face ached, his frail ankles, his bare feet cut by the rocks or a piece of glass or a tin can, but he had to keep running because Don Alejo promised he would be all right, that he would take care of him, that he needn't be afraid anymore if he stayed near him, it was a promise, almost an oath, and he had stayed and now they were coming to kill him. Don Alejo, Don Alejo. He can help me . . . before he could move, the men burst through the bushes and fell upon him like hungry animals . . . nothing is left and now la Manuela scarcely sees, scarcely hears, scarcely feels, sees, no, doesn't see, and they escape through the blackberry bushes and she is left alone by the river that separates her from the vineyards where Don Alejo waits, benevolent. (Donoso, *Hell* 152–55)

Several things are at stake in this novel. First the display of a language and a narrative that affirms the subversive role of gender indeterminacy. Likewise, it shows, through the character of Cruz, that the state, with its promises of development and progress, requires the establishment of fixed female/male identities, a requirement that the novel challenges both in its narrative language and its structure. Subjects who, like Manuela, cannot be brought into the fold have to be re-formed and if this is not possible, they must be symbolically or literally eliminated.

The novel, though, also invites us to reflect on the current state of *travestis* in contemporary Chile. In a 2021 Latin American Studies Association (LASA) conference panel where Joseph Pierce, along with Diego Falconí, and Claudia Rodríguez, discussed Pierce's article "I Monster: Embodying Trans and Travesti Resistance in Latin America," Rodríguez noted that in her experience *travestis*, besides being considered monsters by the Chilean state, are also condemned by other LGBT subjects and movements. For instance, she recounted that in the 1990s, just at the end of the military dictatorship, some of her activist *compañeres de lucha gay* would ask her not to introduce herself as *travesti* but as transgender or transexual. According to

Rodríguez, *travestis* are "the most dangerous, the most criminals, the most infected. The most excluded" (Rodríguez, "Se resiste" 22). This might be related to the fact that *travestis*, such as Rodríguez, experience their subjectivity as one that does not represent either the "masculine" or the "feminine," as stated and limited by normativity, which makes *travesti* subjectivity vulnerable to rejection, denial, and violence. At the LASA panel, Rodríguez also explained that she and other *travestis* modified their bodies, copying the "female" body as an act of survival because in this way they are perceived as women and not as beings who present an indeterminacy of gender.

We thus see that the rejection of gender indeterminacy during the re-creation of the modern Chilean national identity has been extended to the Chilean LGBT community. If *El lugar sin límites* shows us how Manuela must be eliminated because their existence is not suitable for the Chilean state, represented in this novel through the character Don Alejo Cruz, we could extend this reflection to the current realities of the *travesti* in contemporary Chile, even inside the LGBT community. Thus, *El lugar sin límites* allows us to reflect on the processes of normalization happening inside dissident communities, such as the Chilean LGBT community, and the new exclusions occurring inside these spaces that are supposed to be safe.

Horacio Legrás has noted that the historical collapse of the modern Latin American nation-state failed to grant equal citizenship to all its inhabitants (86). This is reflected in the two texts discussed in this chapter, Arguedas's *The Fox from Up Above and the Fox from Down Below* and Donoso's *Hell Has No Limits*. Both texts address the fact that the modernization of the Latin American state implied the (re)establishment of a national identity that in Peru implied placing the Indigenous heterosexual man as a symbol of its national identity, thereby excluding other subjects such as women, homosexuals, *maricones*, and Afro-Peruvians. In the case of Chile, we have seen how homosexuals and effeminate men were considered a threat to a discourse of purity and superiority of the Chilean race, the symbol of Chile's national identity.

Chapter 2 explores the figure of the *travesti* as a figure that acknowledges and embraces an "in-betweeness." Because of this, the *travesti* is presented as having the potentiality to question the modernizing nationalist discourse in Peru and Chile because it denarrativizes its construction of a collective national and ethnic identity based on the exclusion, marginalization, and subordination of, specifically, homosexuals, *maricones*, and effeminate men.

CHAPTER 2

The *Travesti* as a Language of the "In-Between"

> ¿Qué soy? ¿Importa?
> "Soy arte," digo, mientras revoleo
> las caderas y me pierdo entre la gente y
> su humo cigarro y su brillo sin
> estrellas y su hambre de ser.
>
> —Susy Shock

As we have seen in chapter 1, Latin American resistance to imperial dependency in the twentieth century focused on protecting the Latin American nation and national identity from North American domination. Different Latin American states built a modernizing nationalist discourse to face and resist this threat, (re)establishing a national identity—a homogenizing project that subordinated or excluded those considered different. During this process, a dynamic of inclusions created other exclusions, as can be seen in the work of both José María Arguedas and José Donoso. My analysis of these works addressed the consequences that the production of a national identity had for the groups that were very deliberately excluded, because their mere existence challenged the hegemonic narrative. Thus, nationalism—that is, the modern process of naturalization of social and political belonging—was understood across the political spectrum almost entirely in racial and ethnic terms, and equally invariably as a relation to the state. Anything that deviated from this standard was suspect or taken as a threat. This was the case in Peru and Chile.

The novels by Arguedas and Donoso attest to the problems of nationalism in the twentieth century in both countries and the inability of nationalism to incorporate dissident genders and sexualities. Similarly, as analyzed by Héctor Domínguez-Ruvalcaba, during the Mexican Revolution in the 1920s and 1930s, nonheterosexual expressions were read as bourgeois decadence, antinational, and counterrevolutionary. In addition, as studied by Emilio Bejel and Abel Sierra Madero in the Cuban Revolution, homosexuals and effeminate men were considered subjects that were unable to fit into the precepts of the new revolutionary citizenship established by the Revolution and were excluded from the new national project.[1]

In his research on Chile's economic exceptionalism and sexual dissidence, Carl Fischer points out that state modernization in Latin America excluded the queer/*cuir*, who was constructed as "sexually exceptional" (37). "Sexual exceptionalism" is a term coined by Jasbir Puar, who demonstrates how heterosexuality is a necessary constitutive factor of national identity (4). As we saw in chapter 1, modernizing nationalist discourses in Chile and Peru purposely excluded homosexuals as well as *maricones* and effeminate men. They were considered a threat to national identity and public morality. Homosexuals, *maricones*, and effeminate men were Others, whose exclusion defined Chilean and Peruvian modern national identity. Specifically, in Chile, the government of Carlos Ibañez del Campo, obsessed with eugenic ideas such as "depuration" and "regeneration," considered homosexuals and effeminate men as plagues that could cause racial degeneration. Meanwhile, in Peru, homosexuals and *maricones* were purposely excluded from the modernizing state's project as these subjects threatened modernity's momentum in which the Peruvian Indian was placed as the emblem of national identity and unity.[2]

This exclusion of the queer/*cuir* during the twentieth century was a continuation of similar nineteenth-century politics. For instance, as Jorge Salessi states in *Médicos, Maleantes y Maricas* (1995), *sodomitas* had to be eradicated to preserve the cleanliness of the Argentinean national body. Moreover, Joseph Pierce, in his reading and research of the life experience of the Bunge siblings during the modernization period in Argentina, explains that "the state project of normalizing culture demanded specific forms of racial identification, gender, performance, and sexuality" (*Argentine* 4), or that it was necessary to "eliminate those evils from the national body" (193) in order to defend the nation from the dangers they represented.

This politics of modern national identity from the Peruvian and Chilean states during the twentieth century, requiring self-definition as heterosexual and masculine, could be questioned and contested by practices, experiences, and subjects that conform to what in North America has been called "queer theory." Thus, as Domínguez Ruvalcaba explains, queer theory questions the essentialist constitution of sex and gender identity, proposing a view in which definition of the subject fluctuates (*Latinoamérica* 113). Or, as Diego Falconí explains, queer theory looks to collaborate in the "destabilization of the heteropatriarchal system . . . to criticize the contemporary subject and its hyper-identitarian tendencies that recycle exclusion" (179). "Queer" would be, then, a practice as much as a place to position oneself in order to unsettle and challenge identities, seeking instead identity fluidity and mobility. "Queer" would dissolve the notion of identity understood as unity, in that such a notion produces hierarchies, normalizations, and exclusions, as we have shown here in the cases of the modern state in Chile and Peru (Epps, "Retos" 223–24).

Furthermore, "queer" is a positioning that enables abject and marginalized subjects to reappropriate denigrating terms, wherein they transform these terms, resignify them, and become empowered in opposition to degradation and marginalization. Judith Butler reminds us in *Bodies That Matter: On the Discursive Limits of "Sex,"* that the term "queer" used to signal degradation, that it was used as a "paralyzing slur, as the mundane interpellation of pathologized sexuality," but that it had gone through an affirmative resignification that also led to a series of affirmative meanings (Butler, *Bodies* 169). This empowering move can also be seen in the works of the Latin American artists, performers, intellectuals, and activists I engage with in this book, who, from their dissident genders and sexualities and their exclusion/subordination, become in themselves a locus from which they question and unsettle the discourse of the modern national identity, which in turn is the reason that some of these artists and their works were also excluded.

Here, though, we need to reflect on the empowering move that "queer" represents in the case of Latin America. The term "queer" in Latin America is understood as meaning *rarx* or *marica*, and, as Falconí notes, it does not have "the same strength as in English, in which it is used to designate in a derogatory way . . . homosexuals, lesbians, trans, etc." (179). This is why, in what follows, I will also consider the knowledge and experiences around dissident genders and sexualities produced in Latin America, exploring the ways they differ from or complement those informing queer theory. This knowledge and these experiences could be grouped into what has been termed "cuir/cuyr," variant spellings of "queer" in Spanish, used to mark a distance from English and from activist and theoretical frameworks originating in the global Northern trans-Atlantic "normatively white" queer theory. Thus, as I explained in the Introduction, I recognize the limits of applying "queer theory" and its notion of "the queer" in the particular Latin American cases discussed in this book because of the multiple identities at play in the *cuir* experience of the artists, writers, performers, intellectuals, and activists I engage with.

Latin American bodies and identities have been affected and transformed by practices, meanings, and policies inherent to the historical processes of the region, such as colonization (Domínguez Ruvalcaba, *Translating* 16). In this context, the term "sodomita," as Falconí explains, played a very important role. Already present in the *crónicas* produced during the first decades of the *conquista*, *sodomita* referred to "the person, almost always a man, that practiced sodomy or the abominable sin, a prohibited act (generally speaking, anal penetration)" (Falconí 12). The act itself was considered a legal transgression, as the subject implicated (who was a man and rarely a woman) violated moral rules imposed by the conquistadores. When the term was imported to America from Europe, it became associated with racialized bodies practicing what was perceived by conquistadores and *colonizadores* as *pecados nefandos* (sodomy; literally, loathsome sins). Thus, *sodomía* also became a justification for the invasion and colonization of the "New World." As the "trans, sudaca (South American), artist" Susy Shock mentions, "The conquest not only brought Capitalism and patriarchy, but also mandatory heterosexuality. Our native people did not consider themselves heterosexuals. There is something that we need to retrace" (60).

That said, we might heed the call of the Chilean theorist Felipe Rivas, who first expressed his suspicion of North Atlantic queer theory, as he argues that although the "literal disciplinary North–South transfer " of "queerness" should not be uncritically practiced or celebrated, a flat-out rejection of the promises of what he calls *cuir* theory should not be uncritically practiced or celebrated; strict adherence to these promises carries risks of "excessive Latin American localism" (Rivas 70). If queerness, as Carl Fischer states, is generally theorized as the evasion of discursive labels that categorize sexual identities and praxis into easily surveillable categories (191), in my book I translate and intervene into this same theorization in the Latin American experience. Thus, in it, the analysis of the miseries of a modern national identity that purposely excluded homosexuals, *maricones*, and effeminate men are examined from an "in-between" position. In this, I mean to position my discussion within *queer* theory, but I also allow it to be informed, deformed, transformed, and deviated from the experiences and discourses on sexual and gender dissidence that have been produced in Latin America. This is why I work with the *travesti*, a deviant figure present in Latin American culture since before the colonizers arrived in the region. The *travesti* was condemned and punished, taken by the colonizers as a sign of weakness, cowardice, and betrayal (Domínguez Ruvalcaba, *Latinoamérica* 17).

Moreover, I use the Spanish word "travesti" and not what could be its English translation because the meaning in English does not express or contain the realities of the Latin American experience, which is a postcolonial, ethnicized, and racialized one. Besides this, and as Susan Stryker expresses, the term "transvestite" is an old word, coined in 1910 by the German sexologist Magnus Hirschfeld. The term referred to people who wear gender-atypical clothing but do not engage in other kinds of body modification (Stryker 18). Furthermore, it usually refers to men rather than women and typically carries with it the association of *travestismo* for erotic pleasure, which is not always the case in the analysis that I propose. I am also conscious that I could have used the term "cross-dresser," as a nonjudgmental replacement for "transvestite." Although this term is neutrally descriptive of the practice of wearing gender-atypical clothing rather than associating the practice with an erotic impulse, it does not contain or express the Latin American experience either. Thus, the word "travesti" in Spanish allows me to consider that, as Giuseppe Campuzano states, the *travesti* is a subjectivity that "adopts features from the opposite sex. Although this is a legitimate purpose, it turns out to be a composite of male and female features which, while common to everybody at different levels, the *travesti* makes more explicit at the same time that they unveil the inadequacy of the existing gender norms—the exclusionary male and female" (Campuzano, *Museo* 89). More important, along with Campuzano, I consider that the *travesti* implies "a full range of possibilities between the extremes of the masculine and the feminine" (*Museo* 8) and it is not "the quest or production of another identity for the long existing list," but it is, specifically for the Latin American context, a "transformative post-identity, [which moves] away from the clean racial and racist distinctions and towards ethnic overlappings" (Campuzano, "Giuseppe" 10).

To work with the figure of the *travesti* is also my way of contributing to the decolonial exercise already started by diasporic scholars such as Arnaldo Cruz-Malavé and Lawrence La Fountain-Stokes, among others, whose work translates queer theory into the Latin American and Caribbean experiences through their *queer critique of color.* Moreover, working with the *travesti* is my way of resisting what María Lugones considers a new means of colonization through sexuality (92) or, to put it in Norma Mogrovejo's words, I am not thinking in "a queer way within a Latin American context," since that is a way of "neutralizing problems of class, sex, gender or race" that are typical of the region (246).

From the diverse and complex experiences covered both by queer theory and diverse knowledge around dissident genders and sexualities from Latin America, or *cuir* theory, this chapter focuses on the study of the *travesti* to propose this figure as a vessel of features than can be translated into a language that has the potential for resisting and questioning the hegemonic discourses around the modern national identity. The term "travesti," as Lohana Berkins, one of the most well-known Argentinean *travesti* leaders explains, "has been and is still used as a synonym for thief, HIV positive, outrageous, infected, marginal." Nonetheless, just as with the term "queer," the term "travesti" has been twisted by *travestis* in order to "give new meanings to the term . . . and connect it with struggle, resistance, dignity, and happiness" ("Travestis" 5).

To propose this figure as one that is both theoretical and political has the added purpose of "disordering queer chronology" (Falconí 184), as the *travesti* has been a subjectivity present in Latin America history since before the arrival of the conquistadores, as I already mentioned. As the Chilean Claudia Rodríguez expresses in a conversation with the Argentinean social psychologist, writer, and transgender rights activist Marlene Wayar, "There were other sexualities here, other ways of living genders and sexuality, of living bodies in harmony" ("El arte" 30). So, as Wayar says, to talk with and from the *travesti* subjectivity is to "tell that part of history that was not told and that belongs to us and that is where we have to find ourselves" (30).

"No soy hombre, no soy mujer, hoy voy siendo travesti"

Sofía Devenir is a Chilean *travesti*, transfeminist, student of history, musician, performer, and activist with the *colectivo* Travesti Rabiosa. She is also a singer in public buses and a prostitute. She is "tantas cosas" (so many things), as Sofía expresses in the 2016 documentary *Sofía Devenir, una travesti rabiosa* (Barbara Díaz and Valentina Ortega). In this piece, Sofía recounts how she first dressed as a woman when she was six or seven years old. She describes her *travestismo* as a process consisting of different moments that have constituted the *sujeta* (subject) she is currently, one that is not finished or completed. Sofía considers herself a *sujeta incompleta* (incomplete subject), constantly. This is why she uses the term "devenir" (to become) as part of her name, as she feels it perfectly describes the experience of not only the *travesti* but also of *las colas* and *las tortas*, as Sofía explains. For her, this term signals that *travestis* live in a constant process, which allows for the understanding that "we were not born like this, we built ourselves throughout time."[3] In 2017, Sofía published her book *Des-ubicá: Memorias de una dinosauria travesti sudaka*, which includes literary texts, images of musical instruments, songs, newspaper clippings, and portraits, all coming from different voices and sources. Thus, besides Sofía's own texts, the book includes texts written by other *compañeras travestis* (*travesti* companions). As in the case of the Chilean *travesti* Claudia Rodríguez's work, which will be analyzed in this chapter, *Des-ubicá* is composed in a Spanish that purposely does not follow grammatical rules and uses inclusive language: a Spanish, a language, that is deformed by the *travesti* experience.

In Sofía's words, the book includes personal poems written "in spite of the deep pain and anxiety they carry with them" (Devenir 3). As the Prólogo, written by Noelia Shalá, explains, *travestis*' experience of life is a sort of "survival spectacle" (Shalá 5) given the pain and anxiety they experience due to the constant state of danger in which *travestis* live. This danger might connect to the reality that *travestis* such as Sofía destabilize notions of the masculine and the feminine and of gender identity, as well as the roles heteronormativity attributes to each of them. In one of the poems included in Sofía's book, she expresses, "I am not a woman locked in the wrong body of a man. I am a pro-abortion and cannibal *travesti* locked in a colonized body" (Devenir 14), affirming the indeterminacy of normative genders the *travesti* posits. Thus, as Judith Butler has explained, "The very notion of 'the person' is called into question by the cultural emergence of those 'incoherent' or 'discontinuous' gendered beings who appear to be persons but who fail to conform to the gendered norms of cultural intelligibility by which persons are defined" (*Gender* 23), as in the case of *travestis* such as Sofía, but also other *travestis* this book dialogues with, such as Héctor Acuña, Claudia Rodríguez, and Giuseppe Campuzano. They experience their subjectivity as not representing either the masculine or the feminine, as stated and limited by normativity. These *travestis* are, to put it in Susy Shock's words, a "fracaso binario" (unsuccessful binary) (14).

This sentiment is clearly expressed in one of Sofía's verses in which she denounces the insults *travestis* receive because of their gender indeterminacy: "HIV-positive bitch . . . fucking faggot, disgusting ass-fucker. . . . Hey, yo what the fuck is that walking down the street?" (Devenir 14). *Travestis* commit "the worst body crime" (Falconí 191), as they do not have a gender expression suitable to the masculine/feminine binary. I say this with caution, recognizing that, as I mentioned in the Introduction, the experience of each *travesti* is unique, and, like Sofía, I contend that there is no "true *travesti*" (Devenir 8).

Marlene Wayar, who considers that *travestis* are not women "locked in the body of a male" but "are automatically *travestis*" (115), explains that in her particular case, being a *travesti* does not mean renouncing her "masculinity"[4]:

> As a *travesti*, I also wear men's shoes, depending on the gathering, because if I'm going to talk about spaces of power, I want to be in men's shoes. It doesn't make me less of who I am, and I want people to understand that, so that's why they're super expensive, well-polished men's shoes, because I'm going to talk to them from this space, if we're talking in a context where you're a man and a woman, I'm not going to be in a place of powerlessness. You're going to have to deal with me in make-up, you're going to call me "Marlene," but you know I have a penis, and in my mind, you don't know if I had an operation or not, but in my mind, my penis is there. (Wayar 87)

In Wayar's case, the desire to incorporate "female" markers in her subjectivity does not make her "masculinity" invisible. This implies that sometimes privileges are lost, as the Chilean Claudia Rodríguez explains, "Trans is the person who does not resign themselves, who is willing to lose privileges in order to be in that other place" ("El arte" 43). This "other place" mentioned by Rodríguez, however, is a place of danger and vulnerability, as I will explain later.

Using these ideas and considering the particular experience of the above-mentioned *travestis*, I consider that the *travesti* is not a man dressed as a woman or a woman who looks like a man, but rather a being who eludes any fixed notion of "masculinity" or "femininity" as presented by normativity.[5] Thus, as Josefina Fernández states, the body of the *travesti* does not correspond to feminine bodies, and therefore, their corporeal and embodied experiences are different from those of biologically assigned women (19). Vek Lewis points out in this regard that "although individual *travestis* may understand and construct their subjectivities in reference to the feminine, they distinguish themselves from male-to-female transsexuals, who identify as women and often seek sex reassignment surgery (SRS) to become that vision of themselves. Being *travesti* is thus not the same as being transgender and without SRS, it is another space and another identity outside the strictures of sex and gender normativity" (7).[6]

The Chilean scholar Nelly Richard also highlights the difference between the *travesti* and the transgender but instead of considering the *travesti* a third or an other identity, she suggests that the *travesti* questions the very idea of a stable identity ("Locas" 45). Paraphrasing Richard, the *travesti* is a man representing a woman, but he keeps underneath his clothes the attribute of virility (Richard, "A treinta años" 51), as is the case with Wayar.

In her article, "Cuerpos travestis, perturbando deseos e ideologías," the Chilean feminist scholar and writer Andrea Jeftanovic adds to this discussion by pointing to the coexistence of masculine and feminine signifiers in the *travesti*: "The *travesti* does not abandon his original sex but adopts a contradictory body hosting contradictory signs; he produces an unprecedented synthesis of masculine and feminine signifiers—painted eyebrows and beard, for example. These opposing elements coexist in the tension, repulsion, antagonism that is created among them and pose time and again the question: is it a man or a woman?" (2). Because of all this, I contend that the *travesti* is a figure of ambiguity.[7] This implies that *travestis*, by means of their *travestismo*, distort the notion of subjectivity and the idea of an "original," as defined or contemplated by the binary masculine/feminine standard imposed by patriarchal social conventions. In turn, they signal that the very notion of an original is, in fact, a construction. That is, the *travesti* does not work as an individualized or defined subjectivity. Their existence would not be, to say it with Néstor Perlongher, a "conscious" existence, but a traveling existence, always adrift, in the multiplicity of flows, in the randomness and instantaneity of encounters (*La prostitución* 103). Such is the particular case of the Peruvian *travesti* Hector Acuña–Frau Diamanda—for whom the *travesti* is a "hybridized man-woman sex which offers itself as a new transhuman and monstrous possibility" (*Políticas* 6) and whose work I will review in the following section.

The Potentialities of the *Travesti* as an "In-Between"

Hector Acuña (born in 1971 in Lima) is a Peruvian performer, videographer, cultural manager, writer, and DJ. Sometime in the 1990s, they created the character of Frau Diamanda and started to develop their *travesti* performative work.[8] Through the artistic performances they have been staging since then, Acuña examines the violence inflicted on *travestis* and transgender bodies, especially during the internal armed conflict in Peru (1980–2000), and allows the spectator to recognize that a disarticulation of perceptions and affects was produced on these bodies, to take them toward a new horizon—that of the neoliberal model.[9] In Acuña's own words, "This feeling is perhaps due to the atmosphere of extreme violence that we, the pathologized-marginalized bodies, had to face continually, a permanent situation of every-man-for-himself, which forced people to design their own brazen survival and self-defense strategies—typical masculine qualities, one could say; at the end of this process we recognize ourselves as bodies in a hybrid state, for we have paid a high price for our daring move to be visible and, nonetheless, here we stand, the '*vedettes comme soldats*'" (*Políticas* 4). Besides addressing the extreme violence that the *travesti* experiences in Peru, Acuña emphasizes in this quote their experience as "in-betweens" and the strategies that they have to use in order to survive the violence against this same experience. With "in-between," I refer to the reality that Acuña does not identify themselves with one of the two normatively defined gender and sexual expressions (masculine/feminine, heterosexual/homosexual), and that they are also "in-between" nationalities and geographies, as Acuña has been living for the past five years in Barcelona, Spain.

Here, we could say that in Acuña's case, the "in-between" has to do with their state of fluctuation, fluidity, impermanence, inconsistency, and mutability (Mirassol 2), not only regarding their genders and sexualities but also their nationality and location. Thus, in the particular case of Acuña, being a *travesti* implies the production of "another Hector without giving up being Hector." This means, in Acuña's own words, that "Frau Diamanda requires the form, other or new forms of Hector to be able to claim as her own everyday spaces for interaction" ("Luchas" 6).

As Acuña mentiones in the presentation of their book *Escenas Catalanas: Errancias antropológico sexuales*, their experience as an "in-between" and *travesti* implies perceiving the world and the universe in a different way, but also thinking in a different way. Thus, Acuña considers that the *travesti* twists reality, which is related to the survival techniques and resources *travestis* have to develop in a world that rejects them and generates violence against them. This elaboration of survival strategies and strategies of selfhood that "initiate new signs of identity" (Bhabha 1) corresponds to what Homi Bhabha denominates the "in-between." Moreover, these techniques imply ways of relating, of loving, but also of experiencing sexuality in many different ways, as practices of "collaboration and contestation . . . of domains of difference" (2). In the presentation of their book, Acuña explains how *Escenas Catalanas* addresses the experience of a *travesti* in Europe through a *mirada travesti migrante, sudaca, racializada* (South American, racialized, migrant *travesti* gaze). They also mention that, in this book, the same gaze places the *travesti* not as a victim but as a *vampira* (vampire) that arrives in Spain and Europe "para commerce todo" (to eat up everything). With the brief and fragmented encounters that *Escenas Catalanas* narrates, where flirting, seduction, and other ways of expressing love and desire are happening constantly, Acuña resignifies the figure of the *travesti* as an "in-between" in that their bodies work as what Rosi Braidotti defines as "places of transit . . . in-between zones where all ties are suspended

. . . oases of nonbelonging, spaces of detachment" (18–19). This location of *travestis* as "in-betweens" implies their empowerment. For instance, Acuña expresses that in *Escenas Catalanas* the *travesti* appears as a "mestiza racialized shaman, migrant and infected . . . [who] increases the wild outburst sexualizing spaces that are or not hostile towards her" (Acuña, *Escenas* 9). In this book, the *migrant, South American, racialized travesti* is a *cazadora (*hunter*)*, an anthropologist studying white European men—a scenario that subverts colonial and historical "New World"/"Old World" positionalities. This empowerment, though, requires the development of a translation system. Thus, as Marlene Wayar signals, *travestis* have to "develop an entire system of translation that translates this world in order to find the slightest possibility for identification" (62–63), because, as Acuña states, there is no one *travesti* but rather multiple *travesti* identities. This exercise of translation is not alien to the concept of the "in-between." When approaching this notion, Santiago Silvano explains that the translator, who in this case is the *travesti*, performs a balancing act when constructing a discourse (38), as we will see in particular in the next section in my discussion of the work and life experience of Claudia Rodríguez.

I should mention that Acuña does not interpret their experience within the category of queer/*cuir*; they prefer to call it "fag art" (*arte marica*) (Acuña, "Entrevista con Erika"). For them, this art functions as a kind of subversive process in which the feminine and the masculine interact, first, to destabilize gender binarism—gender as category—and then to critique Peruvian society (Acuña, "Entrevista con Erika"). Acuña considers themself a "creature," by which they mean that they are not a man dressed up as a woman or a woman who looks like a man. "I don't identify as a masculine body who adopts a feminine form; rather, I have chosen to move freely between the masculine and the feminine," says the artist, defining, thus, their *travestido* body as a ductile matter, always in movement (Acuña, "Entrevista con Alonso" 12).

In this regard, Acuña adds that the process of *travestismo* is not in itself the quest for feminization but a mutation that implies a lot more than what is visible or can be presumed. For Acuña, what is at stake is "the fulfilment of identity dissolution, this time incarnate in tangible rebel bodies that are emptied out—of their masculinity—and filled up—with overdone femininity" (Acuña, *Políticas* 7). Here Acuña is addressing their constant crossing between genders, which results in an "in-between" experience that is not a producer of a subjectivity defined, expressed, or experienced from the normative binary masculine/feminine standard. Acuña's *travesti* performance allows them to act, constantly, as other, erasing all notions of normative subjectivity as unity. As they themselves point out, "There can be no better paradigm than the *travesti* body in permanent transformation to contest the fixity of identity, all that is taken for granted, that is, almighty heteronormativity" (Acuña, *Políticas* 6). Moreover, for Acuña, it is from this "in-between" position that their work and experience as a *travesti* breaks with the idealization of a normative community and a homogeneous collective national identity, since their position as an effeminate homosexual, *maricón*, Indigenous, and poor is inspired by the exclusion, discrimination, and rejection they have suffered to complicate such idealization (Acuña, "Entrevista con Erika").

It is interesting to observe the relationship that Acuña establishes between what they consider subaltern bodies, as would be the experience of the *travesti* embodied in Acuña themself (effeminate homosexual, *maricón*, Indigenous, poor), and the way they constantly turn around or twist the supposed essence of gender and the notion of subjectivity. Acuña believes that "subaltern bodies begin to internalize the way they are questioned both individually and collectively by transforming existential *ennui* into pure corrosive artifice that may offend, challenge, or sexualize the gaze of others" (Acuña, "Luchas" 5). The *travesti*, as expressed in the figure and work of Acuña as a subaltern and "in-between" who can "offend, challenge, or sexualize the gaze of others," could point to the possibility of considering the *travesti* as a post-hegemonic figure who holds the potential of destabilizing and resisting hegemonic discourses, as I will explain in the following section.

This subaltern experience, though, does not position the *travesti* as a victim. For instance, when I interviewed Crystal del Castillo Felices, she expressed that she rejects being included in what is termed a "vulnerable population"; she said "I wish you could be in my shoes for 24 hours and tell me if you think I am really vulnerable," experiencing the violence, insults, and rejection she has to deal with as a trans woman. The *travesti* is, to put it in Pierce's terms, "pure resistance," because, as Butler explains, that which has the status of the unthinkable is "the most critical, the most radical, the most valuable" (quoted in Pierce, *Argentine* 17).

The *Travesti* as Post-hegemonic

In his discussion of Althusser's conception of materialist thinking as a practical operation at the outside of philosophy, Alberto Moreiras addresses in *The Exhaustion of Difference: The Politics of Latin American Cultural Studies* (2001) the possibility of thinking outside of the hegemonic circle, which would be, as Moreiras calls it, "post-hegemonic thinking" (107). Pierre Macherey, a French literary critic, also worked on the proposal of a new notion of the philosophical practice, one that would also be post-hegemonic, "determined as a process which is no longer that of the exposition of the subject," that is, "a process without a subject" (33). What Moreiras is addressing in his book dialoging with the works of Althusser and Macherey, constitutes a proposal for a new framework for collectively thinking about the articulation between politics and knowledge. This new framework, as I will now explain, can help us understand the *travesti* as post-hegemonic in the sense that the *travesti* distorts the notion of subjectivity by structuring and shaping their notion of self from referents that are not hegemonically accepted or recognized. By considering the *travesti* a post-hegemonic figure, my aim is to bring to the field of Latin Americanism a discussion that entwines dissident gender and sexuality topics, realities and experiences with concepts, and notions such as post-hegemony and subalternity, among others, that have mainly been focused on issues related to class and race. After all, the notion of the post-hegemonic is related to a short essay published in 1917 by Vladimir Lenin, titled "The Dual Power," in which he presents the proletariat and the peasants—whom he calls "the people from below" (1–2)—as a weak force that is "often overlooked, often not given enough thought" (1–2). In his reading of this text, Gareth Williams explains how, in this essay, Lenin presents the notion of dual power, which is, in Williams's words, "essentially another name for anomie, or for counterhegemony," and that it "shares the same ontological ground as hegemony" (*Infrapolitical* 77). Williams continues, explaining that "hegemony represents both the experimentalism of transformational force and its opposite" (77) that is "the process by means of which social forces are integrated into the political power of an existing state—and the path along which the subaltern classes must learn to travel in a very different way in order to found their own non-state state" (Peter Thomas quoted in Williams, *Infrapolitical* 77). These first approximations to what later became the post-hegemonic would be modified and amplified by Antonio Gramsci in his *Prison Notebooks*, where we see a shift in the Leninist understanding of hegemony. Through these shifts emerges the realization that "the more authentically hegemonic hegemony is, the more open to counterhegemonic theoretical and practical challenges it becomes . . . as a result those same coercive frameworks become more open over time to the emergence of 'arbitrary' aims, energies, and forms of questioning. Hegemony's success is in fact its Achilles' heel" (Thomas quoted in Williams, *Infrapolitical* 80). The *travesti* as well as other subjects and experiences related to the dissidence of genders and sexualities are part of those "'arbitrary' aims, energies, and forms of questioning." In saying this, I mean that gender and sexuality dissidents have something to offer the field of post-hegemony studies from their own experiences and struggles as constituted outside of the hegemonic. In addition, I try to open the notion of the post-hegemonic to other realities and experiences that differ from those related to class and race. Thus, as Diego Falconí points out, certain theorizations produced in the field of Latin Americanism, are "valuable but often short-sighted and insufficient when it comes to gender" (24), as these topics tend to be taken solely from the vantage point of identity politics.

Lohana Berkins expresses in "Travestis: una identidad política," "It's generally considered that a body with a penis would align to a masculine subjectivity and a body with a vagina would align to a feminine subjectivity. *Travestismo* breaks into this binary, hegemonic logic that oppresses those who resist being subsumed into the categories of 'man' and 'woman' in Western societies" (6). The figure of the *travesti* and the practice of *travestismo*, therefore, could contribute to discussions and theorizations around the production and destabilization of subjectivity, just as the notion of the post-hegemonic does. Thus, as mentioned in the previous section and according to my understanding of *travestis* such as Acuña, the *travesti* destabilizes the notion of subjectivity, the idea of an "original" because, as Berkins explains, the subjectivity they and other *travestis* produce does not correspond to the expectations of the hegemonic and the normative regimes of genders. Acuña and others not only do not express a masculine subjectivity because of their penis, they also do not produce a "female" or feminine subjectivity because of their *travestismo*. As Josefina Fernández explains, the *travesti* is a nomad subject, a subject without a passport (or with many) that allows them to enter the sex/gender system. The *travesti*, according to Fernández, resists the dominant representations of the self because their bodies do not comply with the norms of the modern corporal order as they transgress the limits of normative gender (16), as is the case with Acuña and other *travestis* with whom my book dialogues.

Joseph Pierce states, "Queerness attaches itself and transforms the normative, pointing out its instability, its transigent reshaping" (*Argentine* 27). Thus, the *travesti*, from their indeterminacy of normative genders, points out that the entire hegemonic sex-role behavior is a role—an act. The *travesti* is therefore able to show that what is hegemonically visible—the social—is a costume, a performance, and merely an appearance, and that it can be altered and reversed, as Esther Newton points out in *Mother Camp* (109). Gareth Williams argues that hegemony is "carried out as both a potentializing force and as an active cover-up and silencing of those heterogeneous realms that expose (from within) the empirical impossibility or the violence of its language" (*The Other Side* 148). Williams's comment explains why *travestis* are not acceptable for hegemony. Because of their heterogeneity, they can interrupt hegemony's force, as they are related to and constitutive of it. Thus, if the *travesti* builds their subjectivity and their bodies using norms and symbols related to hegemonic "femininity," through this same process, the *travesti* resignifies and destabilizes these same rules and characteristics (Berkins, "Travestis" 8). This potentiality of the *travesti* interrupting hegemony's discourses around gender, is what Williams refers to as post-hegemonic, "a place within the social field in which hegemonic articulations and signifying processes no longer work, in which hegemonic discourses cease to make sense" (*The Other Side* 149).

This potentiality of the post-hegemonic in the *travesti* can be located in Acuña's *travesti* performance *El estigma y la mártir* (The Stigma and the Martyr). This performance examines the violence and oppression inflicted on certain bodies, and more precisely subaltern bodies, during Peru's internal armed conflict, recognizing that, as Vidal-Ortiz and Martinez state, "The physical and symbolic violence [*travestis*] have experienced historically is not an exception—an error—of the system, but rather an aspect that constitutes and is inherent to it" (30). This performance was presented at the Faculty of Social Sciences of the Universidad Mayor de San Marcos, during a cycle of lectures on the war between the Peruvian state and Shining Path, and it pays tribute to the victims of hate crimes and homophobia, especially those committed during that war.

El estigma y la mártir involves two individuals wearing long dresses, one white and the other black, their faces covered by blood-stained tulle. They carry flowers in their hands and walk together, slowly, as if they were heading toward an altar. The atmosphere of the performance would seem to correspond to that of a rite, specifically, a wedding. Suddenly, both characters stop and the one dressed in black scatters the petals of the flower they were holding in their hands on the floor in the form of a cross. They spread the leftover petals over their bodies and those of the people around them in a gesture that can be interpreted as purposefully involving and making complicit those who passively observe the actions presented before them. Subsequently, the character in black approaches the figure dressed in white and they dance together, in what looks like the celebration of an alliance. They stop, and then the character in white is stripped naked by the one in black and their biologically imposed "masculinity" is uncovered, canceling the *travestismo* of that character. They begin to touch themself, as their face turns pale, displaying what would seem to be fear and nervousness. Then, they lie on the cross that the black character has drawn on the ground as the latter begins to spread red paint over their face, their Adam's apple, their nipples, and their genitals—precisely the areas that would physically mark the biologically imposed "masculinity" of the individual. The black-clad character colors these areas of the character dressed in white with a fury that only stops when it appears to be over, and then they cross themself.

As I mentioned earlier, this *travesti* performance is intended to denounce the violence inflicted by the law against *travestis* and transgender bodies under the gaze of society. The law here is represented through the ambience of a wedding rite, which includes legality as granted by power and the law, but also by religion, as evidenced by the act of crossing themself by the character in black and the similarity of the figure of the character in white with a crucified Christ. The gaze of society is represented by the people who are observing the actions that are being performed, who are indifferent to the violence and have become complicit in their passivity as it unfolds.

While crossing oneself signals the end of any ceremony in Catholic rites, this is not the end of the performance. After the character in black has crossed themself and the character in white has been crucified, the latter gets up and begins to hand out leaflets with a list of names, alluding to the many others like them who were murdered or tortured because of their dissident sexuality and gender, for transgressing the hegemonic mandates on gender and the concomitant roles, represented by the red-painted Adam's apple, nipples, and genitalia. Before handing out the leaflets to the attendees, however, the character dressed in white rubs them against those areas of his body covered in the red paint, which resembles blood and is still fresh, so that when the leaflets reach the people they are stained with "blood."

For Diana Taylor, in her work on performance in Latin America, performance is an expression whose function is not to inform or describe but to do. Performance has to do more with a process than a product and referred, originally, to a process through which something is made to happen ("Opening" 14). Performance functions, then, as a practice, an episteme, a form of communication, an achievement, a way of intervening in the world (Taylor, *The Archive* 15).[10] Carrying out this performance from a *travesti* position implies an affirmation by Acuña of their position as an "in-between," an affirmation of the transgression of hegemonic gender definition and the roles allocated to these genders. As a performance that is staged from a *travesti* position, from a positioning "in-between," from a position of fluctuation, fluidity, impermanence, inconsistency, and mutability (Mirassol) that "initiate[s] new signs of identity" (Bhabha 1), Acuña's *travesti* performance mixes up, confuses, alters, and disturbs genders, sexualities, and identities and the characters it represents, as well as their actions. These are the reasons that the bodies represented in this performance were subjected to violent acts during the internal armed conflict in Peru. In addition, the *travesti* element of this performance gives it a special character because, as it is done from a *travesti* "in-betweenness," it disfigures the notion of subjectivity and opens itself up to the multiple, to whatever does not contain an individual of a concrete and fixed gender within it, making the performative act more far-reaching and thus representing not simply a single victim of violence, but many. As Ben Sifuentes-Jáuregui suggests in his research on *travestismo* and "masculinity" in Latin America, "Travestism functions as a discursive enterprise that transforms everything it touches" (67). It is in this transformation of everything the *travesti* touches that I see, in the case of Acuña, its post-hegemonic potential.

If we examine the different historical and literary texts that have been written about the internal armed conflict in Peru, it is notorious that the violence suffered by the LGBT population during that conflict has hardly been denounced. The Lima Homosexual Movement (MHOL) has identified ten cases of hate crimes and five hundred people affected during that conflict, for which both subversive groups and military forces are responsible. However, these crimes have not been represented or written about as extensively as other violent acts.[11] On August 11, 1984, in Huanta, Ayacucho, a group of sailors kidnapped a young homosexual *travesti*. This young man was disappeared along with fifty-six other people.[12] Another example of this violence is the murder of a homosexual by the Tupac Amaru Revolutionary Movement (MRTA) whose corpse was found with a sign that read: "That's how the faggots die" (Montalvo 65). Likewise, the capture and murder of eight homosexuals and *travestis* by the members of this same subversive group on May 31, 1989, in the city of Tarapoto, Saint Martin, is another example of what the MRTA called "social cleansing" actions or "crusades against vice."[13] On August 6, 1986, in Aucayacu, Shining Path began another "social cleansing" action in which ten people were captured and executed, including homosexuals and women engaged in prostitution (*Hatun Willakuy* 337). In addition, on September 12, 1988, in La Hoyada, Pucallpa, Shining Path executed eight people who were considered "cabros" (homosexuals), "prostis" (sex workers), and "fumones" (drug users) by this armed group (*Hatun Willakuy* 126).[14]

Within the LGBT population, the "social cleansing" actions of Shining Path and MRTA were especially aimed, for moral reasons, at homosexuals, *travestis*, and transgender people (Montalvo 61). As pointed out in the MHOL annual report (2005), these subversive groups, homosexuals, *travestis*, and transgender people in addition to posing a danger—triggered by prejudices and the stigma associated with these transgressive sexualities—were the very denial of the authoritarian order based on a model of exacerbated "masculinity" that was practiced and reproduced within these subversive groups (68). Thus, these hate crimes were aimed at restoring the hegemonic normality broken by the existence of these sex dissidents, since they represented a rejection of both sexual and gender identities as defined and imposed by hegemonic norms, the very same that these subversive groups, interestingly, reproduced while calling themselves revolutionary. Moreover, these acts of violence against sexual and gender dissents were contemplated with indifference by the civilian population, which often approved such acts, as they were regarded as acts of "moral prophylaxis."

As I mentioned before, these crimes have not been properly addressed or represented in the construction of the official narratives of the Peruvian internal armed conflict. While four landmark cases were included in the Final Report of the Truth and Reconciliation Commission (TRC), setting aside cases of torture, cruel treatment, and forced displacement against LGBT members of the population, its main objective was not to investigate and document these crimes in a particular and systematic way (Anaya and Valle 13), since the subject was addressed in only two pages of a twelve-volume report.[15] It is evident, then, that there has been some marginalization in the way memories of the internal armed conflict and the victimization of LGBT people have been constructed. Some representations, therefore, have displaced others, in the attempt to gain visibility and constitute themselves as hegemonic. Hence the importance of Hector Acuña's *travesti* performance, *El estigma y la mártir*, as an act of commemoration and denunciation that implies, to echo Félix Reátegui, a renewal and negotiation of the acts themselves (the practice) and the accounts about the events (the hegemonic narrative) of the internal armed conflict (Reátegui 371). This is carried out from the position of a figure, the *travesti*, who transgresses genders and their roles as hegemonically stipulated. Acuña's *travesti* performance thus commemorates and denounces the violence inflicted on homosexuals, *travestis*, and transsexuals during the internal armed conflict from their own position of dissent and simultaneously recognizes and affirms their sexual and gender dissent, resisting the way the hegemonic discourse articulates them.

I point this out because the few pages devoted to the denunciation of these hate crimes in official narratives included the names of those affected as understood from the perspective of hegemonic legality. For example, with regard to *travesti* and transgender people documented in the pages of the TRC report, it is notable that their names were printed according to their identity documents. Recognition then avoids remembering these people with their chosen names, their *travesti* and transgender names.[16] Acuña's performance, by affirming the memory of *travesti* and transgender people from the "in-between" position of the *travesti* recognizes their dissident existence. It affirms the transgression of hegemonic sexual and gender orders that these *travesti* and transgender people performed. If, according to Mauricio Albarracín and Juan Carlos Rincón, violence against *travesti* and transgender people during a period of armed conflict or dictatorship "is a performative act that seeks to recast a social, moral and political order" (7), I propose that Acuña's *travesti* performance resists and responds to such recasting, further affirming the existence of a different order.

Let us now consider my proposal to recognize the *travesti* as a post-hegemonic figure. If we recall that, according to Williams, post-hegemony would point out "a place within the social field in which hegemonic articulations and signifying processes no longer work, in which hegemonic discourses cease to make sense" (*The Other Side* 149), Acuña's *travesti* performance functions as this place described by Williams with regard to hegemony. Acuña's practice of denunciation and memory construction regarding hate crimes against homosexual, *travesti*, and transgender people rescues the part of armed conflict's history that has been suppressed by the official hegemonic narrative, since this latter narrative consists of an official heterosexual memory in which the experience of subjects who practice dissident genders and sexualities—those outside of hegemony—is discarded. All this is staged through a figure, which is also rejected by hegemony, the *travesti*, achieving with this performance an alternative history of the internal armed conflict, one that includes sexual dissent that, to signal Williams's words, "haunt[s] the inherent incompletion of hegemony's social articulations" (*The Other Side* 151). Acuña's *travesti* performance functions as the maker of another narrative that resists and destabilizes the one presented by hegemony, "a narrative constructed as result of, and from within, the fissure in narrative itself" (153).

As I mentioned in chapter 1, the main reason that homosexuals, *maricones*, and effeminate men were excluded from the (re)establishment of a modern national identity in Chile and Peru was because of their indeterminacy of gender, or because they were thought to practice the incorrect gender, which thus marked the subaltern experiences of homosexuals, *maricones*, and effeminate men. As I also mentioned in the previous section, the *travesti* is a figure that experiences this same gender indeterminacy to the extreme. We could argue then that the *travesti* contends to the extreme those features that made homosexuals, *maricones*, and effeminate men dangerous and threatening to the Peruvian and Chilean modern national identities, which also means that the *travesti* is a subaltern figure. In fact, this has to do with the reality that *travestis*, like homosexuals, *maricones*, and effeminate men, did not comply with the historical hegemonic orders of the nation-state that allowed its reconsolidation and extension in the twentieth century.

In his dialogue with the ideas of Gayatri Spivak, Gareth Williams argues that post-hegemony grounds itself not so much in the incorporation of subalternity as an inferior position within a hegemonic articulation but, rather, in the opening up of the political field to a certain form of unintelligibility that marks the "absolute limit of the place where history is narrativized into logic" (Spivak quoted in Williams, "Subalternist Turn" 16). To think of the *travesti* as a post-hegemonic figure and in reviewing the work of different Peruvian and Chilean artists that critically address the modernization of the Peruvian and Chilean nation-states from this perspective could allow us to denarrativize the Peruvian and Chilean modernist discourses around the construction of a modern national identity based on the exclusion and marginalization of homosexuals, effeminate men, and *maricones*. This affirms the need, from my own perspective, to extend a bridge between the fields of Latin American *cuir* studies and post-hegemony/subaltern studies, as in this case we see how the *travesti*, with their indeterminacy of genders, signifies the post-hegemonic from a perspective that has not been productively developed. In this way, the *travesti* and *cuir* studies interrogate the work of post-hegemony studies and remind it of the interesting (and perhaps necessary) collaboration these two fields could or should engage in.

In the next section, I will push the boundaries of the *travesti* to propose a narrative that puts into action the features of this figure, especially their "in-between" positioning and their nonaffirmation of subjectivity. This narrative is thought of as post-hegemonic in that, in Williams's words, it opens up a "reflection to an outside that is capable of signaling the possibility of an entirely different telos from which to think," in this case, the discourses of a modern national identity (*The Other Side* 149). The potentiality of this narrative might be easier to understand by looking at the experience of the Chilean Claudia Rodríguez.

From the Body Complex to the Narrative Body

> So what is this divided being introduced into language through gender?
>
> It is an impossible being, it is a being that does not exist, an ontological joke.
>
> —**Monique Wittig**

Claudia Rodríguez (born in 1968 in Santiago, Chile) is a trans writer, activist, performer, and founder of the first Compañía Teatral de Activistas Travestis (Travesti Activist Theater Company).[17] Unlike Acuña, Rodríguez experiences herself as "female," and often identifies herself as a "travesti sidosa y resentida" (resentful, "poz" *travesti*).[18] Nevertheless, Rodríguez states that in her case to be a *travesti* is not necessarily to want to be a woman (Cabrera). In 2013–2014 she published her book *Cuerpos para odiar: sobre nuestras muertes, las travestis, no sabemos escribir* (Bodies to Hate: We *travestis* Don't Know How to Write about Our Deaths), a text that Rodríguez describes as a reflection based on hate crimes against homosexuals, *travestis*, and transgender people.[19]

In its form, *Cuerpos para odiar* is a hybrid text composed of different literary genres. It includes stories, poems, and chronicles but also photographic images and drawings, as well as different fonts styles, colors, and font sizes to address the violence experienced by homosexuals, *travestis*, and transgender people in Chile.[20] This text was brought to the stage in 2015, and it included activism, poetry, performance, and theater.[21]

For Rodríguez, writing *Cuerpos para odiar* was especially important and necessary because it implied making the existence and experience of *travestis* visible through writing. To put it in the terms of Matthew Edwards, this book brings to the fore marginal subjects that have historically been "outside the law and outside textuality" (6). Edwards explains in the context of Argentina that in queer lives "the unknown is misunderstood, undocumented, waiting in the wings to be included in a textual reality that is favored for its tangible, concrete, and solid nature" (6). Edwards and Rodríguez's comments coincide with Marcia Ochoa's assertion that there is a dearth of written and archival forms of cultural production by transgender individuals themselves (Ochoa 231). Thus, "We're the ones [the *travestis*] who should write about us" (Rodríguez, "Ecofeminismo" 12), as part of a claim to a different existence.[22]

In the context of the Chilean military dictatorship (1973–1990), Nelly Richard, alludes to this claim when she argues that practices outside the social contract—such as *travestismo*—emerge from the multiplicity of the social to claim their right to difference and position it against the repressive uniformity from which the standard identities arise (*Masculine/Feminine* 3). This claim to the right to difference in *Cuerpos para odiar* is also carried out from the editorial margins, since the book was self-managed by Rodríguez herself.[23] In Rodríguez's words, the book "is a precarious work, self-produced, that disobeys omnipresent cultural industries. . . . It is a work that one could dismissively call a LITTLE BOOK, a work of failure, without a publisher" (*Cuerpos* 2). That is to say, the production of *Cuerpos para odiar* arises from precariousness, not only from different bodies, these other bodies that are narrated and inscribed in the text, but also from the space from which these bodies are narrated. And I say different bodies, other bodies, because these bodies live in an indeterminacy of genders, thus becoming bodies that may be vulnerable to rejection, denial, and violence. It should also be added that these bodies are poor, Indigenous, and live with HIV and AIDS. Hence, as Jack Halberstam would say, in them "monstrosity and humanity reside at one and the same time," to the extent that they exhibit "gendered, raced and classed skins" (152).[24]

Because of these same characteristics, the bodies that appear in Rodríguez's text call into question who counts as human, as much as the rules that govern what should be considered human. Judith Butler argues that "the very notion of 'the person' is called into question by the cultural emergence of those 'incoherent' or 'discontinuous' gendered beings who appear to be persons but who fail to conform to the gendered norms of cultural intelligibility by which persons are defined" (*Gender* 23). The bodies that Rodríguez narrates in her text are indeed "improperly or inadequately gendered," and they experience double exclusion because of the race and class to which they belong. They are socially categorized as "inhuman" or "less than human," as they are "'marked by class subalternity and a bodily incongruity that leaves them exposed to economic precariousness and transphobic and sexist violence" (Butler, *Gender* 37). On the other hand, however, due to the same characteristics, these bodies resist reduction to single principles. These bodies, as post-gendered bodies, come from a nondecipherable place, even beyond the human, insofar as they are figures of absolute alterity. This is why they represent a break away from the certainties of the known and the usual because they are in constant alteration. Therefore, and following the Chilean feminist critic Alejandra Castillo, we could think of these same bodies as bodies that are a "place of dominance but also of resistance" (29), thus coinciding with what is noted in the previous section with respect to the post-hegemonic potential of the *travesti*. Here, I refer to the fact that these marginalized post-gendered bodies, because of their heterogeneity, can interrupt hegemony's unitarian force. That is perhaps why Pierce considers *Cuerpos para odiar* "an archive of precarity and of possibility, a homemade body (of work) that nonetheless reflects a collective will to survive" ("I Monster" 314). Thus, Pierce does not consider *Cuerpos para odiar* as simply a poetry collection, but rather names it a *travesti* archive, in which those other bodies constitute the archive. These bodies are related to and subjected to hegemony's force as they are opposite to normal or normative bodies. Besides this, the bodies that appeared in this book interrupt hegemonic articulations around gender and sexuality as their voices or "hablas" (speech, discourses) go "in the opposite direction," as the narrator and cultural critic Juan Pablo Sutherland would say, and they are "*hablas* without a canonical alphabet" ("Repensarlo" 208), since they are participating in a construction of their life experience outside the rules, norms, and mandates of hegemony. This "habla" (speech, discourse) is related to an *hacer travesti en la escritura* or *travestir la escritura*, just as other Latin American *cuir* writers have done before, such as Perlonger, Lemebel, Puig, and Sarduy.

The heterogeneous *travesti* experience of Rodríguez is inscribed outside of hegemony, and as a work based on that experience, *Cuerpos para odiar* inscribes a memory and an other historical archive for the ignored or negated *travesti*, thus, in Gareth Williams's words, "interrupting or suspending, hegemony's signifying processes and its necessary destitution of heterogeneity" (*The Other Side* 149). As Rodríguez herself puts it, "Since people think that what's different is grotesque I've been so hated, I have reasons for writing" (*Cuerpos* 5).[25] *Cuerpos para odiar* thus translates into a claim for visibility of the experiences of the most desolate and forgotten group in Chile, especially in terms of education, culture, and memory. Excluded on account of their gender and sexual diversity and dissent, they seek recognition of these experiences. Focusing on the experience of the *travesti* for the purposes of this chapter, *travestismo*, as Sutherland suggests, disallows the regime of truth that negates the *travesti* in a constant aggression that expels them, insofar as it considers the *travesti* a nonnarratable body within the normative sex order ("Recepción" 84). Thus, and following Williams, *Cuerpos para odiar* would function as "site of a dislocation within the hegemonic . . . field that keeps the supply lines of reflection open to the notion of the Other(s)," in this case of poor, Indigenous, and HIV+ homosexual *travestis*.

As stated in *Cuerpos para odiar*, "If girls like me don't exist, it's because our lives haven't been told in children's stories; 'once upon a time, there was a boy who transitioned and was happy for forever after'" (Rodríguez, *Cuerpos* 15). Rodríguez challenges traditional dogmatic writing of literature and canonical and academic education, which has been responsible for editing and erasing everything that does not fit into heterosexist, binary, patriarchal, and heteronormative regulations, as much in form as in content. Rodríguez's text becomes a place to denounce and challenge the same hegemonic educational discursive devices that maintain those bodies and practices situated on the edges of desire/sex/gender invisible. By using a narrative of a "marica sucia, perversa, callejera" (dirty, perverse, street-walking fag) and by writing, using a (purposefully) bad Spanish, a narrative that is fragmented translates how the *travesti* experiences reality, how the *travesti* writes and expresses a particular style of being.

Thus, some of the above-mentioned characteristics with regard to the bodies that are inscribed in Rodríguez's text can be extended, likewise, to the narrative of the book. That is, the narrative presents (1) a language that is different from the hegemonic language, because it does not follow orthographic or grammatical rules, (2) an "in-between" language that confuses the masculine-feminine genders, and (3) a narrative voice that is constantly being interrupted by other voices and that questions the authority of the omniscient narrator at the same time that it prevents the construction of subjectivity. *Cuerpos para odiar* thus proposes a particular way of narrating, one that emerges from the post-hegemonic position, in this case, of *travestis*.

In the first pages of the book a photograph appears in which we see Rodríguez with other *travestis*. The photograph is titled *Cuerpos para odiar* and next to it, in the margins of the page on which Rodríguez herself appears, the precarious context of the life experience of, perhaps, Rodríguez is mentioned: "Reading the images surrounding me: hunger, cold, childhood, alcohol, drugs, men, always tied to a risk of dying" (Rodríguez, *Cuerpos* 7). In this way, *Cuerpos para odiar* opens a space to narrate, in addition to the individual experience of, perhaps Rodríguez, that of other *travesti* subjects. I use the term "perhaps" here because although the reader could assume that the content of the book is based on Claudia Rodríguez's (the author's) life experience, *Cuerpos para odiar* constantly puts this into question.

For instance, the narrative makes the reader doubt whether the Claudia mentioned in the following quote is in fact Rodríguez, our author, as the voice states "éramos vecinos" (we were neighbors) in the masculine form, while Rodríguez refers to herself throughout the book as feminine: "Intuitively I knew you liked to wear your hair light and down to your waist, and that now they call you Claudia. I remember we were neighbors when I saw you on the news. Right away, I remembered the punishments I got for looking for you, for dreaming of you" (*Cuerpos* 26).

In any case, if we assume that the content of the book does include biographical information about Claudia Rodríguez (the author), this information is not the core of the narration. As the book's first pages suggest, *Cuerpos para odiar* is not addressing the experience of Rodríguez as an individual self but, on the contrary, proposes that her existence as a *travesti* is cocreated through multiple existences such as Zuly's, "who was a boy just like me" (*Cuerpos* 27), la Marce, "the most beautiful mom" (29), or la Lola. These lives have taught, perhaps Rodríguez, how to be a *travesti* and survive: "I'm *travesti*! And at my age she was just like me, I said . . . and I realized that I had always been *travesti*, not a coward or ugly, just *travesti*, just like Lola" (33). This resonates with Perlongher's affirmation that *travesti* subjects are not to be conceived of as individualized or defined subjectivities, since they are always "adrift, in the multiplicity of flows, in the randomness and instantaneity of encounters" (*La prostitución* 103). *Cuerpos para odiar*, then, proposes that the construction and survival of the *travesti* is a cocreation that depends on the dialogue and relations it maintains with other marginalized or subaltern lives. The *travesti* would not be, then, an individual existence but rather a subject who constructs and inscribes themself and survives in a multiple form. Or as Rodríguez would say, "You learn to be *travesti* by watching other *travestis*" (58). For Pierce, these experiences of the *travestis* generate knowledge but also develop a pedagogy and a solidarity ("I Monster" 316). In this sense, I agree with Pierce when he states that the *travesti* body is affected by its reverberation with other bodies, those other bodies that must exist in order for hers to make sense, to be" (316).

This relation, though, is not exclusive to *travestis*. As stated in the initial pages of the narrative, "Travestis are just like the Mapuches in the countryside, just like women of the olden days . . . by talking with the older ladies we learn to think about what the body has to do with it, about desire, which is the same as learning to see" (Rodríguez, *Cuerpos* 6). Susy Shock also sees the importance of the relation and solidarity between *travestis* and other subaltern groups. Thus, Shock expresses, "We see ourselves as *travestis*. And that's where there's some crossover between our struggles and those of the first nations or the Indians" (61). However, Rodríguez and Shock are not the only *travestis* who recognize this relation. Wayar points out that "subjects like *travestis* and first nations communities have been, and we continue to be, victims" (109). There is a mutual understanding and sharing of experiences *desde el despoder*, but also a call for unity among these bodies who empathize in their subalternity and precarity. Here, also, we find a kind of pedagogy, in Pierce's terms, in which one can learn to be *travesti* and to survive in dialogue with other lives, such as those of Mapuche women out in the countryside, old and ancient women. This is complemented throughout with the images the book incorporates. *Cuerpos para odiar* includes many pictures of *travestis*, but also of Mapuches and other indigenous women (Rodríguez, *Cuerpos* 43). The bodies of all these lives are monstrous bodies, bodies to hate. Here, the book points out that the *travesti* belongs to a community of "lo diferente y grotesco" (the different and grotesque) (5). Moreover, from this, *Cuerpos para odiar* affirms that the writing of the book itself stems from this multiple existence of the *travesti* and the community of "lo feo y grotesco" (the ugly and grotesque). The narrative voice, perhaps Rodríguez, notes: "I write because I haven't been the only one. My *travesti* friends and I, we've been rejected . . . that's why I write" (5). The narrative of *Cuerpos para odiar* seems to be a narrative that is for, with, and because of the other and not the self.

While *Cuerpos para odiar* is narrating the life experience of, perhaps, Rodríguez, this same narration is interrupted by other voices that bring other stories. This gesture affirms the multiplicity of the *travesti* but can also be connected to what has been discussed in the previous paragraph regarding the pedagogy of the other, as these interruptions continue expressing that the *travesti* learns to be and to survive from and through other lives that are also considered "grotescas y monstruosas" (grotesque and monstrous) and from "an origin that must be erased" (Rodríguez, *Cuerpos* 59). This can be seen in the following words, uttered by an unidentified voice, "And who you are? Have they thrown you in jail ever? . . . to be *travesti* you have to be brave, you have to show you can do it" (50). Or in these words, where different voices get confused, "We didn't have borders, or skin, or faces, or surfaces up to meeting Lola. She said; I'm *travesti* and I'd never heard this word before and it complemented me, and it became real because she was" (62). Sometimes, these different voices in *Cuerpos para odiar* differ by the type and color of the fonts in which they are typeset. For example, on page 13, when, perhaps, Rodríguez approaches her own experience with the maternal figure, "Mother (maere), came from the most southern place in the south, she had three daughters there. When my father's father died, they moved north to this ranch where they were the first inhabitants," at the same time that she goes back to her own origins, she opens up the text, its space, to accommodate the voices of others in solidarity. In the page margins and using another color and typeface, someone says, "Mom, it's a horrific feeling knowing that one will disappear from a world that will continue on just as content, without *us*" (130). We can tell this is a different narrative voice from that of, perhaps, Rodríguez by the way the word "mamá" (mom) is used, since, when Rodríguez is speaking, she uses the term "maere" for "mother."

Rodríguez's book is performing an act of multiplicity, holding the voices of many within a space she could have withheld for herself. In this sense, Rodríguez's narrative can be understood as destroying or undoing the notion of the self because these voices, speaking alongside her own, demonstrate that Rodríguez's story is both hers and not hers, in text as in life, as I have explained in the previous paragraphs. Besides this constant interruption by other voices and stories, a narrative that is jumping from one experience to another without settling anywhere, never staying in any of them permanently, indicates that *Cuerpos para odiar* is not putting forward or affirming a clear subjectivity, neither for Rodríguez nor for the different voices and experiences that are included in the book. This lack of subjectivity and the impossibility of constructing a clear self through the book's narrative is supported by the use of an "in-between" language. Thus, the narrative is fluid, impermanent, and inconsistent when expressing the genders that potentially refer to Rodríguez herself. For instance, the narrative uses sentences such as "Niñas como yo" (Girls like me) (*Cuerpos* 15), which may refer to Rodríguez, and others such as "but more than anything, I jumble the path of words. My mom tells me I'm a silly boy (tonto)" (24), that may also apply to Rodríguez. If we suppose that *Cuerpos para odiar* is narrated from the voice of a normatively defined "male" narrator—Rodríguez—in the book this same narrator is a normatively defined "female" being, thereby disordering the hegemonic "masculine-female" mandate as it confuses the genres. The same happens in the following passage: "My aunt asked my mom about *the boy* because she liked the causing trouble, and she knew I was a *loca*. . . . I woke up at the last minute, my lashes stuck together with mascara, smelling like clubbing and at least 50 *lucas* in a pisco flask. How's the boy doing? She asked, like always, and my mom responded: she woke up early to go to the clinic because she felt sick" (36). The narrative voice of what could be Rodríguez refers to herself in an "in-between" way, sometimes as a normatively defined "male," sometimes as a normatively defined "female." This confusion of the genders goes hand in hand with the voices of other subjects who try to impose a fixed gender to, perhaps, Rodríguez and explain to her that she is a boy not a girl: "And I stopped feeling my body when they'd yell at me: You aren't a girl! You're a boy!" (42). Or when the narrative voice informs that the mother uses masculine nouns and adjectives when referring to her: "My mother doesn't want me to keep playing, she hits me and says I'm a silly boy (tonto)" (52). This is extended to other subjects who are included in the narrative, such as la Barby: "With her, we were all little trainees, *bardudas* and vulnerable asses" (74).

Besides this, and as I mentioned before, the language of *Cuerpos para odiar* distances itself from hegemonic discourse in its form, as it does not follow orthographic or grammatical rules. This has to do with the need to break language in order to break the old and traditional patriarchal ways of existing. The language is fluid and does not use commas or full stops to organize the discourse. It has orthographic mistakes and does not use accents where needed, as part of the stylistic torsions that Rodríguez employs:

> Tenderly kissing chumiga is a sin. Seems like in the world of adults, everything is a sin. It's a sin to not want to play with my siblings, to go toe to toe with the trees with my girlfriends; to be as funny as that girl who climbed the tallest fig tree and with a dirty face said: "no-come-here-any-yankee" as if we could go in and out of stories, put ourselves inside the tv and occupy the spaces of artists without any risk of running into some angry old person who pulls my hair or kicks me out of the movie, or skins my knees as I go by the edges of the tv, or who gives me an electrical shock and we die laughing because nobody can talk to us about the end of the world. (*Cuerpos* 24)

The long sentences contribute to the fluidity of the language, a language that does not pause and that also supports the confusion of genders. Thus, although the narrative voice that may pertain to Rodríguez (normatively defined as biologically "male") narrates herself as a feminine being, she reverts to the masculine form when, as is the case of the previous quote, the voice expresses itself in a masculine form: "Ocupar el lugar de *los artistas*" and not of *actrices* or actresses. In this we see how the fluid language and the narration from an "in-between" position are intertwined.[26]

As the Spanish sociologist and trans activist Miquel Missé points out, "Language plays a very important role in our identity because we define ourselves, think, act and, in fact, exist through it" (106). The language of *Cuerpos para odiar* that I have been describing, like the *travesti*, distances itself from and at the same time destabilizes the reality constructed by hegemonic normativity, which excludes and impedes the existence of the *travesti*. This is why, through this same language, the narrative reinscribes the *travesti* experience, which is violated by hegemonic language, as the following quotes suggest: "Faggot, they yelled at me. The language became quite and destroyed everything in its path" (*Cuerpos* 45); "The words twisted me, they turned into pulling forces that erased me" (47); "The vowels had nothing compassionate to say. When the teachers taught me to combine letters, I mixed them up and interpreted them incorrectly because they didn't have anything to do with me. I was always incomplete" (21).[27] These phrases go against orthographic and grammatical norms in Spanish as they include misspellings and follow oral- rather than written practice.

As Nelly Richard points out, sexual otherness requires other languages that break with the transparency of expressive conventions ("Locas" 34). This other language, in the case of the *travesti*, is a language of dissent that disrupts the notion of belonging to a specific gender and expresses, in turn, a dissent with regard to gender identity.[28] When it becomes writing, it also mishandles the regulations of hegemonic discursivity as it deterritorializes the power regimes of a normativized and officially centered identity.

Here we have explored the other language of the *travesti* in *Cuerpos para odiar*, a language that emerges from the very same *travesti* experience, and how it works as a site of encounter and common learning and construction. In other words, the book poses a language that is an experience of commonality, an experience in common outside of hegemony. The language of the text, as we have seen, goes from the individual to the collective; it is written from a position that breaks away from the concept of normative subjectivity, which belongs to the field of hegemony, and opens itself, instead, to the experience of the multiple, away from normative homogeneity and toward radical heterogeneity.

This experience of the *travesti* and their language as expressed in *Cuerpos para odiar* embraces a productive category, the category of community, which teaches us, as Jean-Luc Nancy would put it, "how to be in common, to allow our existence to exist . . . how we allow our otherness to exist, to inscribe itself as community and history (Nancy 166). This would be the case regarding not only Rodríguez's work but also Acuña's because as we could see in my reading of the performance *El estigma y la mártir*, Acuña constructs an alternative history of the internal armed conflict that acknowledges and affirms the sexual and gender alterity of the *travesti* and transgender people, as well as the violence inflicted against them during the conflict by inscribing and affirming the experience and existence of this community from a place outside of hegemony.

The experience of the *travesti*—and its language—in its alternate communitarian dimension, thus holds the potential for transforming the community to a political reason.[29] Therefore, as we have seen in the cases of Acuña and Rodríguez, the *travesti*'s experience and its language can not only transform the real circumstances of their social group so that they can access more egalitarian conditions with respect to other groups with which they coexist but can also change the historical discourses that only foster the construction and articulation of stable and firm subjectivities, since these historical discourses produce, from an ideology of homogeneity, inequality and discrimination based on identity. Such was the case of the modern national identity in Chile and Peru, which was articulated around discourses based on a conception of homogeneity to structure a new social, political, and cultural order excluding homosexuals, *maricones*, and effeminate men for not complying with the precepts of such an identitarian construction. In chapters 3 and 4 I will study the case of three writers, performers, intellectuals, and activists whose narrative of the "in-between" contests and challenges this historical construction.

Before ending this chapter, however, I would like to recognize that the realities and potentialities I have expressed in the work and life experiences of Acuña and Rodríguez point to the fact that they are also producers of theoretical frames that currently are neither considered nor applied in the fields of Latinoamericanismo or Latin American cultural studies. The Argentinean journalist Sergio Ciancaglini, in a conversation with Shock and Wayar, reflects on the figure of the intellectual in the context of a theorization by both *travestis* around their practices and experiences: "If we think that an intellectual is somebody who thinks about their times, who tries to identify questions, problems, the answers to them and more, none of the people who normally pose as or use that label are actually intellectuals. And Suzy and Marlene play a central role in that they open your mind because their intellectuality is right there, they choose their words carefully, wanting to give them a positive value, they create these numerous ruptures that are at the same time easy to understand because they go along showing you different horizons, even different rainbows" (Ciancaglini 81). As the Argentinean journalist explains, *travesti* lives imply a rupture, and that rupture "nos hacen pensar" (makes us think) in their intellectual practice; *travestis* "provide new answers to the crucial questions of our times" (81), something that should be taken into account in the fields of Latinoamericanismo or Latin American cultural studies. Moreover, the materials by Acuña and Rodríguez that have been discussed here are based in lived experience and are activist in nature, therefore, they produce theory from spaces that are different from academic spaces. Thus, as Marlene Wayar expresses, "Not [from] their beautiful academic words or their gorgeous art that doesn't change anybody's life. We speak from experience" (112). In this, Wayar addresses the need to break, deviate, or *cuirizar* academic language, invading it with the experience of knowledge that is being produced from other spaces, in a way of breaking with "the canonization of white, cisgendered . . . theorists whose work dominates the academic landscape globally" (Pierce, *Argentine* 274).

CHAPTER 3

Pedro Lemebel

The *Loca Travesti* as a Site of Resistance

As we described in chapter 1, during the mid-twentieth century, Chile experienced a great national crisis that led to a denationalization of the Chilean economy, an exploitation of social misery, and the administrative corruption of the oligarchic sectors. The Chilean economy had already experienced serious devastation in the 1930s as a consequence of the Great Depression and the collapse of the nitrate industry. In the face of the renewed midcentury crisis, the Chilean state practiced ongoing mobilizations of nonelite sectors, forcing a dramatic expansion of the entire political system. Furthermore, the Chilean state resumed the discourse of Chilean racial purity and superiority established during the War of the Pacific (1879–1883) to create (or re-create) a modern national identity in its path to rescuing the country from this crisis. Chile, along with many other Latin American nations, was going through a period of strong nationalism in which national identity, tradition, and values were intensely debated in the context of modernization, and it turned, once again, to racial purity and superiority as the authentic values of Chilean national identity. This identity, as we saw, relied on the exclusion of those populations and groups perceived as "different," as subclasses or subaltern formations, in order to keep and protect the homogeneity of Chilean identity. The governments of Carlos Ibañez del Campo—along with others—obsessed with eugenic ideas such as "depuration" and "regeneration," considered homosexuals and effeminate men as plagues that could cause racial degeneration, by which they meant that they were threats against Chile's modern national identity. This is what causes Carl Fischer to state that Chile's supposedly exceptional economic and political status, particularly since 1965, exists in tandem with models of masculine and heteronormative behavior (5).

In the same sense, Ericka Beckman reminds us that throughout the course of the twentieth century, the myth of Chilean racial purity and superiority did not disappear, as the true claims regarding "the Chilean race" found their way into official state discourse (86). Chile, against all appearances, continued to be a racist state, but also a state that defended certain models of masculine, feminine, and heterosexual behavior where homosexuals and effeminate men were considered threats to national identity.[1] For instance, during the military dictatorship (1973–1990), these same subjects—homosexuals and effeminate men—were considered threats to Chilean national identity as they questioned and resisted the dictatorship's heterosexual narrative that placed the family as a core institution to secure the reproduction of the Chilean pure and superior race, as I will explain in the following section.[2]

The Militaristic-Patriarchal Discourse of the Military Dictatorship

On September 11, 1973, a military junta led by Augusto Pinochet carried out a coup against the democratically elected government of Salvador Allende. The ensuing military dictatorship deployed savage repression mechanisms, such as torture, extrajudicial killings, enforced disappearances, arbitrary imprisonment, and a wide range of human rights violations, especially against those thought to oppose the regime, whether politically or morally—that is, any and all who in one way or another questioned or resisted the ideological tenets of the military junta. As José Joaquín Brunner described it, the military dictatorship aspired to reduce Chilean society to passive conformism and expected people to adapt their behavior to an environment defined by repression and the market (172).

Among those who transgressed such passive conformism and resisted the dictatorship's commands and orders were homosexuals, *travestis*, and effeminate men. The military dictatorship sought to reinforce conservative societal conventions, particularly the preservation of the heterosexual family, with a heterosexual head of household as its ideal figure, and the Chilean woman, identified with La Patria (or the motherland), as the national symbol of "garantía y comunidad del orden" (assuring community and order) (Richard, "Perversiones semánticas" 124).[3]

In March 1974, the military junta published its *Declaración de principios del gobierno de Chile* (Declaration of Principles of the Chilean Government), which delineated the roles of Chilean men and women based on the premise that "a morally and legally constituted family . . . must match the natural-biological destiny of each body with the maternal and paternal vocation of the roles assigned to men and women by human nature" (quoted in Richard, "Perversiones semánticas" 129). The military regime established a culture of fear and violence that permeated the entire social fabric, in which bodies and the polis itself were ruled by force, prohibition, exclusion, persecution, and punishment against practices and subjectivities considered to be a threat to the defined mission and destiny of Chilean men and women (Richard, "Bordar de pájaros" 75). In this context, homosexuality, *travestismo*, and male effeminacy were deemed a danger to society, as the dictatorship had put forward a precise idea of nation, family, and national identity with gender-specific roles for men and women (Brito et al. 56).[4]

The dictatorship imposed a militaristic-patriarchal discourse that exacerbated the virile identifications of the ruling rhetoric, where homosexuals, *travestis*, and effeminate men were deemed to be, at the level of discourse, clear transgressors. During the Chilean dictatorship, as in other Latin American dictatorships, they were blamed for corrupting and distorting the fundamental social values of family, gender, and sexuality.[5] They were also considered a threat to the physical body of the nation. After the diagnosis of the first HIV case in Chile in 1984, during the dictatorship, the state established a relationship between HIV and "risk groups," identifying homosexuals as the main carriers of the disease (Contardo 350).

In addition, during this period, two articles of the Chilean Criminal Code that criminalized homosexuality and other conducts that were considered a threat to Chilean society not only remained in force but were enforced more rigorously (Robles, *Bandera* 20). Article no. 365, for instance, criminalized sodomy and, more specifically, homosexual relations between men, stating that "crimes of sodomy shall be punishable by a minor prison sentence of up to three years, of which a minimum of 541 days must be served" (Ministerio de Justicia, Código Penal, 1874.).[6] Article no. 373, in turn, condemned "any acts of transcendence or causing serious scandal not expressly stated in other articles of this code that may offend modesty or good customs [which] shall be punishable by a minor prison sentence of up to three years, of which a minimum of 61 to 541 days must be served," and which was enforced to prosecute and imprison homosexuals, *travestis*, and effeminate men.

Using this legal framework as justification, especially in the 1980s, discotheques were subject to frequent police raids in which gay men were arrested most frequently for "wearing unusual clothes, engaging in suspicious amorous behavior, or dancing with a person of the same sex" (Contardo 334). This was a time when the military and the carabineros (the Chilean police force) had full legal authority to exert violence. However, discotheques were not the only spaces intervened into by the violence of the military dictatorship against homosexuals, effeminate men, and *travestis*. As can be seen in Paz Errazuriz's *La manzana de Adán* (2014), a collection of testimonies and photographs of male homosexual and *travesti* prostitutes taken between 1982 and 1987, they were also victims of violence and persecution during the military dictatorship. In her book, Errazuriz shows one of the darkest and most horrific moments of Chilean sexual and political history, in which homosexuals, *travestis*, and effeminate men underwent horrific experiences, like that of Pilar, one of the witnesses included in this work. Pilar explains how, during the coup to overthrow the democratic government of Salvador Allende, soldiers in Valparaiso took a group of thirty *travestis* to a ship moored in the port. They were kept blindfolded on that ship for six days, during which they were subjected to numerous humiliations and torture. The soldiers cut their hair and then urinated on them and beat them repeatedly (Donoso, "A Brothel" 35).

Despite this persecution of sexual and gender dissidence during the dictatorship, homosexuality, *transvestismo*, and effeminate men started to become more visible in the 1980s thanks to organizations demanding civil rights for LGTB communities.[7] In the cultural and artistic field, the homosexual art collective Yeguas del Apocalipsis (Mares of the Apocalypse) formed by Pedro Lemebel (1952–2015) and Francisco Casas (1976) appeared in a Chile that was still under the control of the military regime.[8] With the performances of Yeguas del Apocalipsis, the practice of a nonnormative masculinity became a politicized space that not only affirmed the participation of sexual and gender minorities in the struggle against the dictatorship but also criticized the violence that the regime exerted against indigenous peoples and women.[9] Through their performative work, Lemebel and Casas homosexualized political, social, and cultural discourses. They also introduced the figure of the poor and brown *travesti* in the Chilean imaginary collective, positioning, moreover, the figure of the *Loca* as a political subject in the context of a repressive society.[10] The work of Yeguas del Apocalipsis—as with that of other transgender groups and collectives—not only provided visibility and recognition for racialized and poor *travesti* and transgender communities but also criticized the hegemonic, heteronormative political system. As Héctor Domínguez Ruvalcaba observes, transgender collectives produce one of the most dynamic spaces to queer/*cuir* hegemonic culture (173).

In the words of the poet, writer, and performer Francisco Casas, Yeguas del Apocalipsis denounced "the systemic extermination of dissident bodies by the Chilean military dictatorship and the segregation and concealment of homosexual signs in the culture at large" (6). In an interview with the journalist Luis Alberto Mancilla, published in the magazine *Punto Final* in October 1996, Lemebel pointed out that "before the advent of democracy, it was us queers/*cuirs* who were saying what others could not or did not want to say" (Mancilla 7), highlighting that it was not possible to isolate sexual liberation from the repressive conditions of a militarized state (Franco, Llanos, and Domínguez Ruvalcaba 14).[11] The exclusion of gays, lesbians, *travestis*, and transgender people was, for Lemebel and Casas, another version of the detained-disappeared. Lemebel, especially, tied the two together in his work, as we will see in the following sections.

The critic Nelly Richard argues that the work carried out in the *travesti* scene in the years of the military dictatorship emphasized "the gaps in representation through which the multivocity of meaning could dangerously seep in, the paradoxes and ambivalences of double sense that the monologism of absolute meaning seeks to suppress" (*Residuos* 20). She also argues that the *estética travesti* (transvestite aesthetic) she finds in the works of Chilean artists such as Carlos Leppe, Juan Domingo Dávila, and Yeguas del Apocalipsis "offered a possibility of rebellion, a model of opposition to the hetero-male hegemony of military control of the dictatorship" (Richard, "A treinta años" 29).[12] She stresses the potentiality of what is produced by *travestismo*, inasmuch as it enables the emergence of a nonunified, fragmentary identity, one that is not definitive but fluctuating and reversible. The *travesti* identity of these artists, in Richard's words, disassembles the homogeneous unity of the whole as a humanist—but also dictatorial—dream of the autonomy of the self ("Los extravíos" 206). In this regard, and as Domínguez Ruvalcaba states, by denouncing concrete violations to human rights and its political interventions and by creating visual and documentary archives, the transgender and *travesti* community has made its presence on the Latin American scene known through its radical questioning of the system of gender as a whole (*Translating* 175–76).

These reflections of Richard and Domínguez Ruvalcaba take us back to the *travesti* as a post-hegemonic figure, understanding post-hegemony as "a place within the social field in which hegemonic articulations and signifying processes no longer work, in which hegemonic discourses cease to make sense" (Williams, *The Other Side* 149).[13]

The *travesti* destabilizes the monologic nature of absolute meaning, which, in the case of the Chilean dictatorship, was deployed to define hegemonic roles for men and women and construct a family-oriented narrative that placed the heterosexual family as an institution that would ensure the reproduction of the Chilean pure and superior race. As Richard argues, the *travesti* and what emanates from this figure—such as the language of the "in-between"—challenges conventional conceptions of identity through a fragmentary and fluctuating notion of identity. The basis of this identity is the subject's gender indeterminacy, which accounts for both the totality and specificity from which subjectivity is produced. The *travesti*, according to this, presents a broken identity, in pieces, which questions the essentialism of the "feminine" and the "masculine" as originary elements of a natural and national body, and thus the *travesti* can guide us into deconstructing the identitarian and nationalist postulates on account of which the Chilean military dictatorship unleashed a violent persecution against dissident subjects, among which homosexuals, *travestis*, and effeminate men were included. Besides this, as Domínguez Ruvalcaba explains, the *travesti* disrupts the patriarchal order of the nation and thus questions the very notion of the nation-state as it shakes its foundations (*Translating* 189). This is especially true in the case of the Chilean dictatorship, where the nation was framed as an extension of the heterosexual family. Thus, gender dissidents, especially *travestis* and trans people, break with maternity and paternity, which are sacred, nodal pacts for any society since they imply processes of identitarian normalization in terms of male and female constructions.

With this in mind, I contend in the following sections that the exclusionary discourse practiced during Chile's modernization and reproduced during the military dictatorship has been questioned and contested by the Chilean author Pedro Lemebel. As I will show, through an "in-between" narrative, Lemebel questions and destabilizes the fixed and single meanings that the military dictatorship imposed on sexuality and gender to construct and elevate a heterosexual family-oriented narrative as a symbol of national identity. Although some of this has already been articulated by many scholars such as Nelly Richard, Fernando Blanco, Héctor Domínguez-Ruvalcaba, and Juan Pablo Sutherland, among others, turning to Lemebel's work allows me to discuss the way in which Latin American cultural critics and proponents of *cuir* critiques underlined Lemebel's work as the prime example of sexual and gender dissidence in Chile in the 1990s and 2000s. I contend that Lemebel's work has served as a mediator of the direct and material experiences of other sexual and gender dissidents, such as *travestis* who might be "too *cuir*" for the academic field.[14] Thus, *cuir* critique and Latin American cultural critics had failed in addressing their experiences, work, and theorizations, repeating, in a way, the exclusion perpetuated by many of the regimes and societies criticized by these same fields. In this section I ask how and why certain lives, experiences, voices, and writings have become canonical within Latin American *cuir* and Latin American cultural studies, as is the case with Pedro Lemebel. It is not my purpose to undermine Lemebel's work. On the contrary, his work may give us insights useful in addressing these same questions. For instance, reviewing the work of the author will allow me to show how Lemebel's "in-between" narrative situates poor and racialized homosexuals, *travestis*, and effeminate men, as well as other marginalized and excluded subjects within both Chilean modernizing discourse and the discourse of the military dictatorship. I contend that they are positioned as protagonists who destabilize the historical pattern of exclusionary Chilean national identity, which invites us to reflect on the exclusion of these subjects and their direct experiences and *saberes* in the fields of Latin American *cuir* and Latin American cultural studies.

The "In-Between" Narrative of a *Loca Travesti*

> Podría escribir clarito, clarito, sin tanto recoveco,
> sin tanto remolino inútil. Podría escribir casi telegráfico,
> para la globa o para la homologación simétrica
> de las lenguas arrodilladas al inglés.
>
> **—Pedro Lemebel**

When Pedro Lemebel, an effeminate Indigenous homosexual, published his second book, *Loco afán: Crónicas de sidario* (1996), the dictatorship had ended and Chile was going through the so-called transition to democracy.[15] Starting with this publication and until 2015, when Lemebel lost his voice and his life to laryngeal cancer, he turned his work into a space for critiquing the repressive, racist, and homophobic conditions of the Pinochet military dictatorship with its exclusion and marginalization of homosexuals, *travestis*, and effeminate men, as well as other dissident subjects. However, Lemebel goes further in his critique by criticizing certain Latin American leftist states that have historically reproduced this same exclusion in their effort to re-create a modern national identity.[16] For this reason, the scholar Fernando Blanco proposes that Lemebel's work was a way of doing politics that was crucial for Chile in the 1980s and 1990s ("Memorias" 95), but that, as I have mentioned, was not the only body of work functioning in this way.

Lemebel was a member of the Chilean national popular left and of the leftist underground movement that opposed Pinochet's regime. However, he distanced himself from militancy as soon as he experienced the left's homophobia and trivialization of the struggle of sexual minorities (Lewis 183). The performative work that Lemebel began to generate along with Francisco Casas as part of Yeguas del Apocalipsis and, later, the work he undertook with his journalistic and historical writings were thus generated from the perspective of a leftist ideology. However, it is a form of leftism that is shot through and steered off course by dissident masculinity. Lemebel's work is therefore the result of the combination of what the author himself calls "his biography as a fagoot and his leftist effort" (Lemebel, "Entrevista" 1). In his writings, Lemebel addresses himself to the left, which he accuses of being just as *machista*, moralizing, and conservative as the right with its production of what Richard calls "dogmatized identities" ("Los extravíos" 206). The critique that Lemebel undertakes in his texts is directed as equally to left-wing militants as it is to the military government, inasmuch as both remained within the limits of traditional masculinity (Franco, Llanos, and Domínguez Ruvalcaba 22). In the same vein, Blanco notes that Lemebel questions patriarchal bourgeois morality just as much as revolutionary morality, insofar as both rejected sexual minorities and their struggles as they were considered threats to their models of national identity in different historical periods ("El desliz" 36).

Lemebel, a passionate defender of the feminist legacy in the struggle for a more just world, published seven collections of *crónicas*, two novels, and one book of short stories. In all these texts I find the unfolding of what I have termed in chapter 2 an "in-between" narrative or a "low queer art" as described by Lawrenz and Zapata Galindo. To begin with, it should be noted that Lemebel's name implies an act of "in-betweenness." Lemebel always despised gender norms like binary sexual identities governed by the "masculine/feminine" divide, which his extraordinary character, through the eccentric contortions of the *Loca*, subverted at every turn (Richard, "Bordar de pájaros" 75) and this is expressed in the way the author changed his name. Lemebel went from being Pedro Mardones to Pedro Lemebel in a gesture of complicity and encounter with the "feminine," adopting his mother's last name, "from the side of homosexual and *travesti* illegality" (Blanco and Gelpi 97). The author's name is thus formed through communion with the "feminine"—the mother's last name—and in the same process destabilizes notions of identity and gender by affirming an "in-between" existence. The name itself, as a first matrix of identity, is thus destabilized and transformed into an "in-between."

In addition, this change coincided with Lemebel's decision to stop writing short stories in favor of *crónicas*, which, according to him, "is a testimony of the context in which the writer lives . . . uses different literary genres, shelters narrative, poetics and gives the possibility of being very critical and reflexive about the cultural politics of a specific time" (Risco 31). Furthermore, as the author himself states in an interview, the *crónica* allows him to speak from within (Lemebel, "La metáfora" 12). I believe we should understand this statement as a recognition of the possibility not only of speaking from within but also of operating from within, of looking at that which is within us (Noemi 141). However, our point of reference here is not simply the interior life of the subject—that is to say, Lemebel as author—but the inner workings of the discourses that the author examines from his "in-between" position in his *crónicas*, a genre combining fiction and nonfiction that became popular toward the turn of the twentieth century in writing about the modern city. By this I mean that in his *crónicas*, Lemebel traverses the inner space of different discourses—their structures—and points out how they are constructed and designed, how they are disguised, so to speak. As he traverses them, Lemebel also reconfigures them, inasmuch as he puts them on display, undresses them, and removes their makeup. In the process, the author opens new possibilities of political, social, and literary constitution, demonstrating that these discourses are neither fixed nor definitive entities.

We need to consider, as Aníbal González explains, that the *crónica* is a borderline genre located "in-between" journalism and fiction. José Quiroga supports this idea in the prologue to *Mapa Callejero: Crónicas sobre lo gay desde América Latina* (2010), where he states that the *crónica* is a nonfiction literary form somewhere between journalistic reportage and the short story, adding that the *crónica* has also been a device to inscribe sexual dissidence in the public sphere. Julio Ramos would add to this discussion that the *cronista* is an "urban onlooker" who traverses the city to narrate the process of modernizing transformation that it experienced at the turn of the twentieth century (131). The *crónica*, then, is a genre that transgresses borders and limits, and its main function is to narrate a process of transformation, the passage from one state to another. Lemebel, through his *crónicas*, as I will explain, transforms language in a space of transgression, of extraterritoriality and deconstruction of language, as Tamara Figueroa Díaz has noted (11). Also, according to Agustín Pastén, the attention of the *cronistas* of the end of the twentieth century was focused "on the vulnerable and marginalized groups in society, to give them a voice" (106). This is exactly what Lemebel's "in-between" narrative does in his *crónicas* written after the end of the dictatorship but documenting what life was like in that period of Chile's history.

Besides his "in-between" existential position and the *crónica* as an "in-between" genre, Lemebel produces an "in-between" narrative that confuses genders when narrating, where the language does not distinguish, or rather, it erases, the normatively imposed "feminine" and "masculine" genders. Lemebel's writing is in constant transit as it never remains within gender boundaries. This is related to the way he addresses the figure of the *travesti*, also an "in-between," as I have explained in chapter 2, and as can be seen in the following excerpt of "La muerte de Madonna," one of Lemebel's *crónicas* from *Loco afán: Crónicas de Sidario*. Here the point of reference is the character named la Madonna: "Una y otra vez la Madonna mostrando el truco, la verga travesti que campaneaba como un péndulo llamando a todo el mundo, haciendo que corrieran las secretarias y auxiliares hasta la sala, provocando tanto despelote, tanto grito de los profesores y del jefe scout tocando el pito, vociferando que cortaran esa suciedad, que eso no era arte, eso era pornografía" (52).[17] The fact that this character intentionally exposes his penis during the performance at the same time that he displays his *travestido* body, which exacerbates the "feminine," symbolizes an act that seeks to erase the boundaries that differentiate the "feminine" from the "masculine" and shows fluctuation in gender. This *travesti* perspective affirms that this figure deconstructs being, as it can no longer be confined to a fixed space. Lemebel's "in-between" narrative, because of this same gender confusion or erasure, cancels the notion of a narrative self as it is constantly interrupted by other voices.

What I am calling here Lemebel's "in-between" narrative is also characterized by metaphorical and literal, hyperbolic, and social registers, with which Lemebel wraps and dresses his narrative (Ortega 75). In Jorge Ruffinelli's words, "Lemebel writes from transvestism . . . from transformation" (70). The author's "in-between" narrative deploys metaphors and images that are disguised and made-up so as not to produce a linear or unified meaning, but rather one that is charged with ambiguity and possibility. In Lemebel's "in-between" narrative, the only certainty is constant change, which excludes strict definitions.

Lemebel's "in-between" narrative could also be described as "Latin American neo-barroso," a parodic branding used by the Argentinean author Néstor Perlongher to refer to the Latin American neo-baroque trend.[18] This style would be the result of the neo-baroque crossing over from Cuba to the other side of the Rio de la Plata, where it becomes an "irregular pearl, a lump of mud" (Perlongher, "La barroquización" 101). Neo-baroque language transgresses official language as it breaks completely with the "denotative, direct, and natural level of language, as a transgression of somatic-communicative, economic, austere language, reduced to its functionality" (Sarduy, "Conversación" 315–43).[19] On the other hand, Severo Sarduy understands neo-baroque language as a process of carnivalization insofar as he considers it to be a symbolic and syncretic spectacle where "abnormal rules, in which confusions and profanations, eccentricity and ambivalence multiply" ("Escritura" 1385–404), a notion we can relate to the excess and ambiguity of signification and meaning characteristic of Lemebel's "in-between" narrative. As Figueroa Díaz explains, this style lends Lemebel's "in-between" narrative a theatrical quality, with masks and extravagant costumes, in which excess challenges the established order of Chilean society as it was in the 1980s (30). This echoes Sarduy's description of the neo-baroque as a style that "reflects structurally the disharmony, the rupture of homogeneity, of the logos as an absolute, the lack that constitutes our epistemic foundation" ("The Baroque" 33. These features are also part of Lemebel's "in-between" narrative, in its refusal to remain within fixed and single meanings and truths, and its intention, alternatively, to destabilize them, especially those related to the dictatorship's desire to homogenize Chilean society and the way gender and sexuality were to be played out. The neo-baroque style in Lemebel's "in-between" narrative performs ruptures, breaks patterns, and provokes imbalances (Figueroa Díaz 31).

Finally, Lemebel's "in-between" narrative is "pure orality" because of the enunciative voice of his texts, that of the *loca travesti*, as Blanco suggests ("La Frida" 43). Lemebel's *loca travesti*, as Víctor Hugo Robles (the Che Guevara of gay people) explains, is always in transit, it is not a man or a woman, "I would not say that it is heterosexual or homosexual, either, it's another possible place . . . but it is not a fixed place" (Donoso and Robles 81).[20] The voice of the *loca travesti*, because of its position "in-between" genders and its being enunciated from this space, marks a break, re-questions, reformulates, doubts when narrating. The voice of the *loca travesti* is neither clear nor easy to understand; it distorts words and meanings, giving them the opportunity to signify one and many things, because with Lemebel's "in-between" narrative everything is transvested, transformed. Moreover, as Katerín Barrera states, the transgressive place of Lemebel's *loca travesti* is a counterdiscourse that confronts the dominant order and national identity (41), especially in the case of the military dictatorships in Latin America between 1960 and 1990. In stark contrast with the masculinized and rigid image of the military authorities, Lemebel "creates travestis who play with tulle and sequins of many colors, creating a new esthetic order that disrupts the canon of the masculine and the feminine" (Figueroa Díaz 18).

I contend that Lemebel's "in-between" narrative has the potential for questioning and destabilizing the fixed and single meanings imposed on sexuality and gender during the military dictatorship as part of his always provocative challenge to monumentalization of hegemonic history (Epps, "Los 'fráxitos'" 146). The dictatorial praxis repressed and punished any dissident manifestation opposing its will to domination, including its will to control gender and sexuality. As we have mentioned before, the military dictatorship imposed uniformity and demanded full compliance with the exclusionary and nonexchangeable roles it had allocated in its zeal to control the nation. Lemebel's "in-between" narrative would be a way of reinventing the texture of language, something that was necessary, according to Richard. She contends that the military dictatorship disarticulated history and disrupted the subject's social organicity, and for this reason everything had to be reinvented, especially language, which "having survived the catastrophe does not know how to name the remainders" (Richard, *Margins* 16). Lemebel's "in-between" narrative renames these residues but also goes back to the past to bring about a new social historicity that resisted being subsumed to history. As we will see, Lemebel's "in-between" narrative also revises and criticizes the discourses of Chilean modernization where domination, oppression, and discrimination were exercised against certain groups, which he made the protagonists of his texts. I turn now to the analysis of *La esquina es mi corazón* (*The Corner of My Heart*) (1995) where the potential for Lemebel's "in-between" narrative to give other meanings to oppressed, invisible, and persecuted subjectivities, practices, and spaces is especially clear through what Lemebel denominates as his *lengua marucha*. Through it, the author borrows the voices of different marginalized characters, particularly *travestis*, to give them a space that society denies them (Lemebel, "Es necesario" 44). Moreover, in this work, as in others, Lemebel defends a kind of counter-hegemonic abnormality in which matters of race, ethnicity, and class, but also of age, appearance, and health—or illness—are entangled with gender and sexuality (Epps, "Los 'fráxitos'" 147).

This section, though, also discusses the importance of going beyond the work of Lemebel and his borrowing and representation of different marginalized characters, especially *travestis*. In addition, I contend that a bridge must be generated between this space offered by the Chilean author and the material and direct experiences of *travestis* themselves.

La esquina es mi corazón or the Art of the Disqualified

> The voice that testosterone propels into my throat is not that of a man, it is the voice of the crossing. The voice that trembles in me is the voice of the border.
>
> **—Paul B. Preciado**

La esquina es mi corazón was published in 1995, the same year that Yeguas del Apocalipsis, the artist collective formed by Lemebel and Francisco Casas, was dissolved.[21] As already mentioned, the group completed various works in the intersection between performance, *travestismo*, photography, video, and installation. *La esquina es mi corazón*, in particular, inherits the particularities of performance and "in-betweenness" that Lemebel and Casas deployed in their work.[22]

Following the traces of heteromasculine hegemony during the military dictatorship and in an attempt to deconstruct the discourse, values, and culture shaped by the military regime and its control of peripheral and marginal subjects, practices, and spaces, Lemebel's "in-between" narrative traverses the city of Santiago, Chile, throughout the book.[23] He presents it as a space that gives free rein to pleasures and practices considered illegal by the dictatorship because they were outside of its codifications and regulations. In this way, *La esquina es mi corazón* situates *travestis*, homosexuals, hairdressers, voyeurs, street urchins, maids, drug addicts, and prostitutes at the center of Santiago, historicizing the wayward biographies that the dictatorship made invisible (Llanos 75).

The dictatorial context is present in almost all the *crónicas* included in the book, although sometimes it is only referred to indirectly by using specific features such as "el zapateo milico" (Lemebel, *La esquina* 95) and "salvándose de las botas" (35), among others. In the *crónica* "Lagartos en el cuartel (*yo no era así, fue en el Servicio Militar*)," which recounts the experience of a young man and his military life, the narrator includes memories and actions that occurred during the dictatorship, as the following excerpt shows:

> Aún después del holocausto los compases de la Rendeski abren las "grandes alamedas." El revival fatídico de esa marcha resuena en el escalofrío de los crematorios y cárceles de tortura. Pareciera que a estas alturas del siglo, la memoria del dolor fuera un video clip bailable con un paquete de papas fritas. Pareciera que en este mismo film, rodaran juntos desaparecidos, judíos, mujeres, negros y maricas pisoteados por las suelas orugas de bototos, zapatillas Adidas y tanques. Pareciera que en cada giro de cascos se reiterara el desprecio por la democracia. Pareciera que en el ángulo recto del paso de parada, los testículos en hilera, fueran granadas de reserva a punto de detonar nuevamente sobre La Moneda. (Lemebel, *La esquina* 82)[24]

This *crónica* addresses the coup against the democratic government of Salvador Allende when it mentions the explosion of grenades in La Moneda, but also when it quotes words said by Allende in his last speech, before his death, such as "las grandes alamedas" (the great avenues). Not only this, but the segment mentions what followed the coup, as it names spaces of torture and the crematoriums used during the dictatorship. It also alludes to the mandatory virility of military life with the "testículos en hilera" relating to grenades exploiting in La Moneda. All this occurs in the context of the indifference of a society that seems to have forgotten its past, as the narrator expresses "pareciera que . . . la memoria del dolor fuera un video clip bailable" (Lemebel, *La esquina* 82).

The language used in *La esquina es mi corazón* to narrate the *crónicas* is, as already mentioned, an "in-between" language through which a process takes place, in Paul B. Preciado's words, "to translate our difference into the language of the norm; while we continue, in secret, to practice a strange lingo that the law does not understand" (254). Preciado uses the term "language of the crossing" to refer to the type of language that I call an "in-between" language that questions the legal and political architecture of gender and sexual difference and of the nation-state (330). According to Preciado, this language has the potential to radically transform that which it narrates as well as the society that rejects individuals such as those *travestis*, homosexuals, hairdressers, voyeurs, street urchins, maids, drug addicts, and prostitutes that Lemebel's "in-between" narrative inscribes in the context of the Chilean military dictatorship. Through the narrative voice of the *loca*, *La esquina es mi corazón* offers us a different version of the city, in that it demonstrates alternative ways to traverse and configure it from the place of these other individuals, excluded by the heteronormative discourse of the dictatorship.

As Jorge Ruffinelli states, *La esquina es mi corazón* makes visible the experiences of "anonymous citizens (those who are not celebrities), common citizens, the man/woman in the street, in the neighborhood, to whom Lemebel confers presence and existence, using their full names or '*travestidos*'" (42). However, by giving presence and existence to these citizens, "maids, single mothers, abused girls or women, prostitutes, workers, students, seminarists, enlisted soldiers, homosexuals, proletarians and persons living with HIV, lumpen youths" (Blanco, "El desliz" 157) and establishing a dialogue with them, Lemebel does not represent them as the voices of victims. Rather, he portrays them as languages and worlds that can be sites of new discourses and stories that cast a light on social, political, and economic conflicts. It is worth noting that these voices also represent liminal languages and worlds to hegemonic narratives, since instead of remaining silent they rise and make themselves heard above the hegemonic design attempting to render them inexistent, as is the case with the many Indigenous characters who appear in Lemebel's text. He refers on different occasions to the multiethnic origin of Chilean and Latin American people.

To begin with, the city of Santiago, as narrated through the *loca* and their "in-between" language is presented as an eroticized, *travestido*, and queer/*cuir* space. This narration, in dialogue with other voices, produces throughout the book a narrative that cancels the notion of a narrative self. The constant passage of the narrative voice of the *loca* from its external heterodiegetic position in third-person indirect discourse to a homodiegetic position (first-person direct speech) fuses with those other voices and adopts different points of view, as can be seen in the following quote: "La loca sabe el final de esas aventuras, presiente que el después deviene fatal, sobre todo esta noche cargada al reviente . . . la excita ese olor a ultraje. . . . Esas ganas de no sé qué. Ay . . . esa histeria anal . . . Ay ese fragor" (Lemebel, *La esquina* 162). The narrative voice is interrupted by that of the *loca* as we read the expressions of this character: "Ay esas ganas de no sé qué," "Ay esa histeria anal," "Ay ese fragor." The same happens in the following passage: "Aún así, a pesar de los festivales de rock en la playa y los descamisados nostálgicos de Woodstock. *Los sí pos loco y los longis pungas*, que se agarraban a botellazos de puro contentos. A pesar que la macoña llegó por fardos y las anfetas las movían por kilos" (41). Here phrases such as "sí pos loco y los longis pungas" belong to a different voice as this is not the narrator's voice. In this way, readers have direct access to the voice of "los descamisados" (the shirtless, the destitute, the underprivileged), whose history becomes visible in the narratives of *La esquina es mi corazón*. We also have access to the voices that abuse and marginalize these characters as is the case with the *teniente* repressing a *loca* in one of the *crónicas*: "Y arriba la risa del teniente le ordena que se pare, que siga corriendo, que sóbate callado, total ya queda poco" (77). The words "sóbate callado, total ya queda poco" are uttered by the *teniente* interrupting the voice of the narrator. Besides this, we see in the above passage the use of very fluid oral language. This involves the use of long sentences that transgress orthographic and grammatical rules in the Spanish language, as can be seen in the following passage: "MÁS ADENTRO, CRUZANDO el umbral de cortinaje raído la manda algodonosa que rodea a tientas, a ciegas, a flashazos de pantalla el pasillo relumbra como baba de caracol en terciopelo negro" (45). In Lemebel's "in-between" narrative, orality constitutes a register that is both metaphorical and literal, as it does not produce a linear or unified meaning, but rather one that is charged with ambiguity and possibility as can be seen here: "Volvieron platinadas bajo una llovizna de dólares comprando a diestra y siniestra noches de calentura, madrugadas de copete a destajo y toneladas de almejas para reponer la pérdida" (40). This contributes to the confusion of voices to a point that readers do not know who is speaking, as in this passage: "Se lo salsearon todo, se vacilaron el meneo riesgoso hasta quedar tiradas en la caleta balbuceando un 'Te quiero'" (40). We do not know who utters "te quiero" or "I love you."

Lemebel's "in-between" narrative adds a confusion of genders to the confusion of voices. For instance, in the *crónica* "Escualos en la bruma," which tells the story of an exiled *loca*, the language fluctuates from feminine to masculine to narrate ambiguity with regard to gender. This character is referred to in the language as ella/she in several moments, as in "ella rogaba que estuviera allí; que la modernidad tardía en Chile no le hubiese derrumbado por lo menos ese recuerdo" (61). Nevertheless, later in the *crónica,* the language narrates this character in a "masculine" form: "Así, frente a la puerta, tuvo que hacerse cargo de veinte años de ausencia lejos de este lupanar a vapor. 'Hacía tanto tiempo que no *lo* veíamos por aquí.' *Lo* sorprendió el viejo del mesón, igual de viejo, con el mismo tonito perverso, como si hubiera sido ayer ese día once de setiembre cuando los bazucazos a la Moneda *lo* pillaron ensartado en el palomo blanco que era su compañero de liceo. Aquel chico de la brigada roja que *lo* miraba . . . el mismo que *lo* llevó la primera vez a los Baños Placer" (62). We could think that the *crónica* is trying to signal that those others who see the exiled *loca* consider her a man and refer to her as *him*. Nevertheless, we notice that the narrative voice narrates this character as an "in-between," sometimes as female and sometimes as male, thereby destabilizing the binary "masculine"/ "feminine." The same happens in another *crónica* that states, "Y no mira a nadie sintiéndose como *un travesti* en el Vaticano, pensando que la ciudad entera se ríe de *ella*, sobre todo el cola que le aferró feroz palo de cuenta, sumando el nombre francés de los productos usados y que *ella* está segura los compra en el mercado persa . . . porque *la loca* la escucha o hace que la escucha, da lo mismo, total ella no tiene a nadie a quien contarle sus secretos . . . *el peluquero* es su confidente y a veces también le cuenta que *él* se pega sus relinchos" (105–6). In this paragraph a *travesti* who works as hairdresser is narrated as an "in-between" gender. Several times the narrative referred to them as a she and others as a he, such as when it mentions "el peluquero." Later in the book, the *crónicas* are even more direct in their "in-between" narratives, as is the case in the following passage where the character called Fabiola de Luján is narrated as an él/ella, him/her: "Desde entonces *la Fabiola de Luján*, el cetáceo dorado de la noche, adormece con su bolero la difícil existencia de los espectadores. Desde entonces *el/ella*, desbordante en su paquidermia, va rifando la botella de pisco equilibrada en las agujas de los tacos. Va ofreciendo los números mientras trepa la escaleta de tablones entre la gente, contestándole al que le grita guatona, que ella con su guata se fabrica unas exuberantes tetas" (132). Through this "in-between" narrative, many transgressive characters become visible in the book, enacting nonnormative practices and behaviors. Such is the case of the "New Kids" who appear in the title story, who, after a night of music and smoking weed, allow their desire to burst forth with "mina, fleto, maricón, lo que sea, reventarse de gusto, ¿cachai?" (Lemebel, *La esquina* 33) and whose, "tragic future" (35) or "obscure future" (36) as young criminals is exchanged in the narrative for a less bitter one, where they are represented as lively, happy, and free. Similarly, the "Babilonia de Horcón" walks naked through a spa full of rich people, and no one is able to stop her, not even the police (43).

Through the narrative voice of the *loca*, Lemebel's "in-between" narrative activates those marginalized and ignored places and subjects so they are able to oppose hegemonic discourses via a practice of simulation, turning the marginalization inside out and reimagining its rules and structures (Richard, *Arte en Chile* 10). We can also observe this in the story "Como no te voy a querer (o la micropolítica de las barras)," in which "la loca de cintillo indio . . . haciéndose el macho," takes refuge in the *barras*, the organized groups of soccer supporters, placing himself/herself "en medio de tanto refregón, a la deriva de los cuerpos ensopados que descargan su potencia futbolera en el arrebato de un 'te quiero adicto'" (Lemebel, *La esquina* 53). In this story, a *loca* transgresses the *machista* structure of soccer and inserts themselves into one of its most intimate and privileged spaces in order to eroticize it, so that the end of the story finds him/her fellating one of the boys from the *barra*.

With all this in mind, we can point out that Lemebel's "in-between" narrative traverses the semantic and conceptual rupture that Walter Benjamin refers to when he approaches the idea of "refractory art," "an art of denial and deviation" (18). This is because Lemebel produces his work from a language that narrates the actions and experiences of peripheral and marginal subjects and practices, silenced and prohibited by the discourse of the dictatorship. In the process, Lemebel's narrative destabilizes and reconfigures the order and the discipline imposed by this discourse. According to Nelly Richard, in dictatorial Chile this type of art was created to break with official culture and with hegemonic tradition and disciplinary hierarchies. Richard references this type of art as a part of "the new scene" (*La insubordinación* 17–18). While it is true that in *La Insubordinación de los signos (Cambio político, transformaciones culturales y poéticas de la crisis)*, Richard focuses on analyzing specific cultural artifacts produced in response to the military dictatorship, her descriptions of these works also apply to Lemebel's narrative. For example, Richard characterizes these works as forming part of the art of the disqualified, the minoritarian, the subaltern, and the heterogeneous, which is to say, everything that is not identical and uniform (23). This characterization applies to Lemebel's work insofar as, given the aforementioned examples, the author chooses marginal subjects and minoritarian and "different" practices, in order to develop an art form in which these are positioned as protagonists and creators of the art itself.

One of the spaces constructed by the hegemonic discourses that Lemebel's narrative attempts to subvert and rearticulate is the public park. Through a style of writing that, as we will see, is not passive but rather absolutely dynamic and fluid, the "in-between" narrative of the *loca* transforms the public space of the park into an intimate and private space by traversing it. In this way, Lemebel opens a space for marginal pleasure—inasmuch as those meetings in the park are among poor homosexuals and "Queens"—and creates a flow of visualization, reaffirmation, and practice, bringing about, in Richard's analysis, a rupture with the disciplinary hierarchies and hegemonic traditions as mentioned above. Here we see Lemebel's *lengua marucha*, addressed above, in action. Thus, as Berta López explains, it is part of Lemebel's unique language, which brings to the surface a marginality of a sexual nature, where the subject that enunciates is located at the margins of society. This *lengua marucha*, according to López, deterritorializes heterosexual love, which is, at the same time, a political project (127).

In the story "Anacondas en el parque," the park goes from being the place where "niños de trenzas rubias al viento de los columpios y ancianos de mirada azulosa con perros poodles asisten" (Lemebel, *La esquina* 21) to being a place where you can hear whispers of the type "no tan fuerte, duele, despacito" (22), as the lovers hidden among the trees express their marginalized pleasure and sexuality. I use the terms "marginalized pleasure" and "sexuality" in the sense that they originate—as Daniel Noemi reminds us—in the bodies of the poor, where hegemonic discourses attempt to erase any idea of sexual activity, "of the city and also of a notion of national identity" (139).

We could also argue that in this case, Lemebel's "in-between" narrative is performative in the sense pointed out by Diana Taylor: The performative is the form of expression that has as its object neither informing nor describing, but doing (14). Therefore, in the passage mentioned above, Lemebel's narrative constitutes, by means of words and actions that narrate themselves, a new notion of what a park might be. The author's own writing process is carrying out a reconfiguration of that space. This narrative is not simply describing or informing the reader about what happens in the park, but rather giving an entirely new meaning to that space, insofar as the whole story narrates prohibited sexual encounters that take place there. The park in this story is no longer the place of bourgeois leisure, but rather of marginal play and enjoyment.[25]

These marginalized characters who are having sex in the hidden spaces of the world are also engaged in a performance of their sexuality and pleasure for us, the readers. This is so in the sense that, while reading the text, we are present at the sexual encounter of these subjects. That is to say, the marginal sex of these characters, who themselves are marginalized, becomes central in the world of the text, and therefore in the world of the reader, because the act of narration itself draws them into the world of the characters. Highlighting their intersectional identities, these marginalized people are not blond, nor do they have poodles to take on walks; for us, the readers, they are the protagonists and principal actors in the sense that they have the ability to affect a performance of their sexuality and pleasure. In this way, they take back their sexual activity, even though, as Noemi reminds us, hegemonic discourses attempt to erase it from the city. Lemebel's narrative opens the space of the park to those who normally cannot traverse it because they are unwelcome, and furthermore it makes them its protagonists, in the process reconfiguring the space that hegemonic discourses give them. From the "in-between'" narrative produced by the *loca*'s movements, another architecture is constituted for the space of the park, reorganizing the very hierarchies and prohibitions that define its architecture based on hegemonic discourses. This allows Lemebel to highlight the violence and persecution suffered by poor subjects who live an alternative sexuality, while pointing out the obstacles that the official city, always under the gaze of the society of control, presents to their experience of pleasure (Noemi 140). However, Lemebel reverses this controlling gaze, replacing and overcoming it via the gaze of the reader who observes the performance of alternative pleasure and sexuality, just like those viewers mentioned in the text whom the lovers allow to watch because they are aware of "cuán caro es ver porno" (Lemebel, *La esquina* 23). We should note, however, that Lemebel is proposing something more when he reverses the controlling gaze via the gaze of the reader and those who cannot watch porn because it is too expensive. As we see, those who cannot watch porn do not consume porn, but they can see it live and directly—and even masturbate—through the performance that the lovers offer to them. The lovers choose to allow these other observers to watch, acting with the knowledge that someone is watching them and deriving enjoyment from it. Lemebel reverses the marginalization, not simply of the poor but also of those subjects who are marginalized, given their poverty, from certain forms, proposing, via an "in-between" language, another type of pleasure and enjoyment that does not necessarily stem from consumption. The pleasure that he proposes, then, is produced outside of normative economic markets, where the body, sexuality, and gender are goods traded and exchanged.

Lemebel's writing, as we have shown and as Blanco suggests, produces a way of acting in public that is not mediated by the dominant institutionality; that is, it produces a movement of resistance to or a deviation from hegemony (Blanco, "Memorias" 95).

Furthermore, in "Anacondas en el parque," Lemebel's narrative reminds readers of the oppressive dictatorial regime that characteristically threw the bodies of those who disagreed with its precepts into the Mapocho River (Noemi 142). This is apparent at the end of the work, when the *loca* explains, "Alguien en un intento desesperado zigzaguea los autos de la costanera y alcanza el puente perseguido por los disparos. En un salto suicida vuela sobre las barandas y cae al río siendo tragado por las aguas" (Lemebel, *La esquina* 27). In this way, Lemebel closes his first writing by pointing out and denouncing the persecution and punishment of those who dared to live out their sexuality within the confines of the militarized city.

At the same time, it should be noted that through Lemebel's "in-between" narrative, readers are offered a parallel between the park and queer/*cuir* culture. The culture of homosexuality, like the park itself, lives and thrives through the language that records it, in spite of the dictatorship and its discourses, which negated, persecuted, and prohibited it. In "Anacondas en el parque," the language deconstitutes the vision of homosexuality as pathology, crime, and motive for persecution and rather presents it, reconfigured, as a form of nature. At the same time, it emphasizes that it is an unproductive and excessive naturalness, which becomes an affirmation of life and an exercise of solidarity and community in the context of persecution. This is true insofar as the pleasure produced in the park is shared with its observers: "Así pene a mano, mano a mano y pene ajeno, forman una rueda que colectiviza el gesto negado en un carrusel de manoseos" (Lemebel, *La esquina* 26). This way of being in solidarity is also carried out in anonymity, as we do not know the characters having sex or those who take pleasure in watching. The anonymity of this sharing of eroticism and pleasure is a way of presenting subjects that are totally equal, erasing any race or class difference. Lemebel's "in-between" narrative, then, suggests an atmosphere of equality, a reciprocal support generated via the practice of a minoritarian pleasure in which "masturbaciones colectivas reciclan en maniobras desesperadas los juegos de la infancia" (26). Lemebel's writing thus undoes the normalizing control of masculinist/hegemonic discursivity of the military dictatorship.

La esquina es mi corazón allows us to observe how Lemebel's "in-between" narrative, uttered by the voice of the *loca*, permeates and modifies spaces, existences, and practices that have been persecuted, rendered invisible, or deemed dangerous by the discourse of the dictatorship. Moreover, Lemebel's "in-between" narrative also makes *La esquina es mi corazón* a communitarian space in the sense that Jean-Luc Nancy and Roberto Espósito understand it. I addressed Nancy's approach to this concept in chapter 2 and I would like to go deeper into it by reviewing Espósito's ideas so as to better understand the relevance of Lemebel's "in-between" narrative and *La esquina es mi corazón*.

The Italian philosopher Roberto Espósito develops his theoretical thought around the term "community," arguing that "the common" is not equivalent to a property or an essence. He points out the mistaken assumption that community is a "property" that belongs to "subjects . . . join[ed] . . . together through an attribute, a definition, a predicate" (2). Espósito's conception of the common and communal space, not as an essence shared by many to unite them but as a place where alterity is the fundamental principle, is present in *La esquina es mi corazón*. In my discussion of Lemebel's work, I have shown that the author brings together a series of characters excluded from the hegemonic discourse of the military dictatorship, such as *travestis*, homosexuals, hairdressers, voyeurs, street urchins, maids, drug addicts, and prostitutes to place them, in their alterity with regard to the hegemonic, at the center of Santiago. In this way, Lemebel's "in-between" narrative portrays the experience of the common as something characterized by the multiple and produced from the radical heterogeneity of its characters and their practices.

Not only this, but we also see in the book a sense of reciprocity or "mutuality," two elements that Espósito describes as part of that which is communitarian (5). For example, this occurs when one of the *crónicas* narrates "masturbaciones colectivas reciclan en maniobras desesperadas los juegos de la infancia" (Lemebel, *La esquina* 26), where we find a reciprocal or mutual pleasure generated via the practice of marginal and minoritarian subjects. The same happens in the *crónica* "Anacondas en el parque," where the lovers having sex in the park allow people to watch because they are aware of "cuán caro es ver porno" (23). Therefore, they also perform an act of reciprocity and mutuality from their alternative pleasure and sexuality.

Espósito adds that "the common is not characterized by what is proper but by what is improper, or even more drastically, by the other . . . the common removes what is properly one's own . . . that invests and decenters the proprietary subject, forcing him to take leave . . . of himself, to alter himself (7). Lemebel's "in-between" narrative, as that which is used to build the common space that is the *crónica* and the book, by confusing or erasing genders when narrating, but also by canceling the notion of a narrative self, expropriates his characters from their own subjectivity, and, for this very same reason, the subject who belongs to that community as described by Lemebel cannot be an "individual." This is, as we have mentioned before, what grants Lemebel's writing—as well as that of Rodríguez and Acuña—a post-hegemonic potential, as it functions as "a place within the social field in which hegemonic articulations and signifying processes no longer work, in which hegemonic discourses cease to make sense" (Williams, *The Other Side* 149). If we want to consider Lemebel's acts of reciprocity and mutuality narrated in and conducted by *La esquina es mi corazón*, and his writing more broadly as a true production of a communitarian space, with its historicization of those marginalized experiences made invisible within the context of the military dictatorship's narrative because of their alterity, it is urgent to consider the direct and material experiences of these same subjects, especially *travestis*, in the fields of Latin American *cuir* and Latin American cultural studies. I do not mean that we should stop reading and working with Lemebel's literary production in these same fields, but rather that we can also put his approach to *travestis* and *locas* in dialogue with their direct experiences and cultural production. The motivation here is to avoid reproducing these same exclusionary narratives in such fields, and falling into a situation described by the Chilean Claudia Rodríguez: "We are always victims of our research, of the dissertations that do not empower us to be ourselves, to narrate and reveal our own successes, or own inclusion in history, our direct and specific participation in history or in society. In the Academy, it is the interpreter, the translator, who has been recognized, not the primary source" (Rodríguez, "Se resiste" 23). Here Rodríguez is pointing to the fact that the academy, and particularly the fields of Latin American *cuir* and Latin American cultural studies, with some exceptions, must complement certain authors' approaches to the life experience of *travestis* by listening to their direct and material stories, by going to the primary sources, which, in Rodríguez's case, is her production of poetry, her *librillas*, and her performances.

Moreover, attending to the ideas, visions, and experiences that are being shared by other sexual and gender dissidents, such as *travestis*, through their performances, poetry, and narrative, is a way in which Lemebel's work can be actualized or continued. Lemebel brought to the surface a marginality of a sexual, gender, and racial nature, where the subjects that enunciate were located at the margins of society; therefore, it is imperative to go from Lemebel's narrative voice of the *loca*, which is already embraced by the academy, to the voice of the *loca* or the *travesti* themselves. This is especially important in the Chilean context, where as Claudia Rodríguez explains, *travestis* are "the most dangerous, the most criminals, the most infectious. The most excluded" (Rodríguez, "Se resiste" 22). In an interview, Lemebel stated: "I am interested in the homosexual as a cultural construction, as another way of thinking the self, as a different way of imagining the world, not only through theories on the homosexual but also from every locus that has been excluded from and insulted by the neoliberal and globalizing machine. I continue betting for the small spaces, for the lost ones" (Lemebel, "El cronista de los márgenes" 76). As Latin American *cuir* critics, we do not want our field to become part of the "maquinaria neoliberal y globalizante" that Lemebel is referring to, but rather to continue opening spaces for the most vulnerable and marginalized sexual and gender dissidents such as *travestis*, so they occupy a space, in their alterity with regard to the hegemonic, at the center of our fields. This is why the analysis of a text such as "Hablo por mi diferencia" (I Speak for my Difference) (1986) is so important, as in it Lemebel's "in-between" narrative, from its post-hegemonic potential, denounces and critiques the Chilean modern national identity, which, through the deployment of an exclusionary discourse, has marginalized and exerted violence against homosexuals and effeminate men. Moreover, in the next section I will explain that *Hablo por mi diferencia* also denounces and critiques other Latin American modern discourses, such as those produced in Cuba, thereby establishing a relationship between them and the exclusionary discourses of the Chilean right, especially that of the military dictatorship. These discourses have grounded their main principles in an idea of the common where gender and sexual alterity were and are still not welcomed. In this text, Lemebel states, according to my reading, that the common and the collective are characterized by the multiple. The fact that Lemebel enacted this text *travestido*, expressing and sharing his direct and material experiences as a *loca travesti*, a very vulnerable position, evidences the relevance and potential of speaking from this direct experience.

Reinscribing the "Collective Unity, Freedom, and Happiness" Equation in the Latin American Nation-State

In a Congress of the Chilean Communist Party held in Santiago, Chile, in 1986, Pedro Lemebel, wearing high heels and with a hammer and sickle drawn on his face, read his "Manifiesto: Hablo por mi diferencia."[26] Lemebel's act was transgressive, first, because it was formulated from the voice of a *loca travesti* when the country was still under the military dictatorship, thereby trespassing on the authoritarian command and military regimentation of uniform identities (Richard, "Bordar de pájaros" 85); and second, because *Hablo por mi diferencia* draws attention to the way in which several Latin American nation-states produced a modern national identity through an exclusionary discourse—pointing especially at those led by a revolutionary ideologism—that marginalized and excluded homosexuals and effeminate men. The text mentions the persecution of homosexuals and effeminate men by the Cuban government during the first years of the revolution because they did not comply with the features of the New Man, the model that the Cuban Revolution established as the ideal of national identity.[27] In this text, Lemebel also mentions the persecution that Chilean effeminate men, *maricones*, and homosexuals suffered under the governments of Carlos Ibañez del Campo (1927–1931 and 1952–1958), who ordered his police and military to harass them and "sweep them away" along with the communists.[28]

In this same vein, the text criticizes the Chilean left for its ideological censorship of homosexuals in its resistance to the military dictatorship.[29] As Nelly Richard explains, "In the name of classical Marxism as a conceptual apparatus to analyze social class conflicts, [the Chilean left] systematically distrusted the revolts of the imaginary and the symbolic overflows of fantasy, subjectivity, the unconscious, and desire" ("Los extravíos" 206).[30] During the years of the dictatorship, homosexuals within the left who resisted and fought the dictatorship were encouraged not to speak out about their sexuality (Robles, *Bandera* 39).

In *Hablo por mi diferencia*, Lemebel questions the way the modernizing nationalist discourse of the Cuban Revolution equates collective unity, freedom, and happiness—an equivalence also espoused by Ibañez del Campo—while simultaneously denouncing the persecution of homosexuals, *travestis*, and effeminate men during the military dictatorship.[31] The author thus shows that the heteronormative discourse permeates the notion of Chilean identity and it functions as a segregating strategy between those who are included and those who are excluded, and that the left does not necessarily deconstruct that particular discourse given how deeply it is ingrained in the culture.

Moreover, I contend that in the same text Lemebel challenges these discourses by affirming his difference, stating that it is from the site of exclusion and sexual and gender dissidence that he struggles against these same discourses. All this makes of *Hablo por mi diferencia* a space from which Lemebel resists and contests the exhaustion of standard and standardized genders and sexualities proposed by such discourses. Here I want to emphasize that Lemebel is challenging these discourses in his *travestido* body. This body amplifies the effect of his "in-between" language since his discourse is also coming from an "in-between" body that, on this particular occasion, exhibited and reconciliated dissident gender (wearing high heels) and revolutionary ideologism (the hammer and sickle drawn on his face). Here I mean that with his *travestido* body, which disrupts the canon of the "masculine" and the "feminine," Lemebel was able to create, with his body, a common space where gender and sexual alterity is welcomed.

The text starts by establishing the gender and sexual difference of Lemebel himself, who self-refers as *maricón*. As Emilio Bejel points out, in the Cuban *Diccionario razonado de legislación de policía de 1889*, the *maricón* was defined as an effeminate and cowardly individual who carried out tasks deemed to be of a feminine nature, behaved like a woman, and adopted her mannerisms (7). Bejel explains how *maricones* were considered as squandering the natural privilege of being born male, an expression of the importance given to the male in the years of struggle for Cuban national independence. I take this definition as a starting point to understand the context of Lemebel's text and its emphasis on how Cuban revolutionary ideology influenced the way sexual and gender roles were conceived in the Latin American left. The exclusion of subjects who transgressed normative masculinity has been, as already discussed, part of the construction of a modern national identity in Latin America, a process that began with nineteenth-century nationalism and resumed in the twentieth century, especially in the context of the Cuban Revolution.

Lemebel presents himself not only as a *maricón* but as a poor one. "But don't speak to me of the proletariat because to be poor and queer/*cuir* is worse" ("Manifiesto" 35), he says, signaling the intersectional nature of the hatred and rejection he has endured throughout his life. Lemebel does not renounce or reject his difference in order to speak, but, on the contrary, as the Chilean scholar Juan Pablo Sutherland notes, Lemebel "assumes homosexual dignity as a reaction to the political repression of the dictatorship in Chile" ("Repensarlo todo" 19) that was taking place while Lemebel was reading his text:

> I don't need a disguise
> Here is my face
> I speak for my difference
> I defend what I am
> And I'm not so strange (Lemebel, "Manifiesto" 35)

It is important to consider the affirmation of the author's sexual and gender difference while *travestido*, as it was an extremely vulnerable position to take when Chile was still under military control, but also because Lemebel's reading took place at a Congress of the Chilean Communist Party, which, as we have mentioned, rejected LGBT people. As stated in the testimony of Silvia Parada, the first president of TravesChile (a *travesti* and transgender organization), the violence of the dictatorship against LGBT people was more intense than has been documented. For instance, Parada points out that several testimonies of this violence were not included in the report by Chile's National Commission for Truth and Reconciliation:

> I was subjected to fierce repression by the *carabineros* of the Fourth Precinct. I remember they would throw us (all those who seemed physically to belong to the world of sexual diversity) into the Zanjón de la Aguada. Transsexuals had their women's clothes taken away; their rights were not respected and it was assumed they were men in disguise, so we were never supported. We were being held under article 373, that is, for serious offense to morals and good customs. . . . What I expect is just the most obvious thing: that our gender identity be recognized, that our *compañeras* be recognized in the reports for reparation. Let an investigation be done that includes the entire homosexual community that they killed during the military dictatorship. (Testimony on CNN Chile, November 25, 2018)

The precepts of the right (the military dictatorship) as much as those of the left (the Communist Party) exposed the LGBT community to special danger and vulnerability. Thus, in the verses of his "Manifiesto," Lemebel emphasizes the lack of solidarity with gender and sexual minorities on either side, as both persecuted and excluded homosexuals, *travestis*, and effeminate men.

After affirming his sexual and gender difference, Lemebel addresses the left militancy directly by pointing out that the hate and rejection he had endured "because of bad habits, because of bad luck" ("Manifiesto" 36) is just as bad as the experience of the dictatorship. As in both experiences, certain bodies, because of their difference, suffered oppression and persecution. Moreover, Lemebel accuses the left of not being a space where gender and sexual minorities could be safe, because, on the contrary, it was also a place of persecution and oppression. Thus, Lemebel states that his experience within the left as a brown, poor, effeminate homosexual was worse than the dictatorship because "the dictatorship ends, and democracy comes, and right behind it socialism, and then what? What will you do to us, *compañero*?" (36). Lemebel here highlights that the oppression and persecution of sexual and gender difference is constant and that it is exercised from the right as well as from the left.

After these comments, Lemebel directly addresses the exclusion that the Latin American modernizing nationalist discourse practiced against homosexuals and effeminate men with its creation of an exclusionary modern national identity. The text mentions two examples, the Cuban Revolution and the dictatorship of Carlos Ibañez del Campo in Chile. Lemebel expresses:

> What will you do with us, *compañero*?
> Will you tie us into bails by our braids, destined to arrive in
> some AIDS-ridden quarter of Cuba?
> Put us on some train to nowhere
> Like general Ibáñez's ship
> Where we learned to swim
> Although no one reached the shore.
> ("Manifiesto" 36)

The text relates and connects the sweeping up of homosexuals ordered by Ibañez del Campo in Chile with the persecutions of homosexuals during the first years of the Cuban Revolution. I read this as a gesture to denounce and compare how both governments, the Chilean government in the 1930s and the Cuban government, the former historically described as a dictatorship and the latter as a revolutionary regime, mistreated homosexuals and effeminate men, as both shared a discriminatory modernizing nationalist discourse. All this, after Lemebel expresses that there are worse experiences than the dictatorship. The persecution and marginalization of homosexuals and effeminate men during these two historical periods would be an example.[32]

The stories of persecution and of gender and sexual difference from the past are linked to the present of the *compañero* from the left, but also to the ideal of the Cuban New Man, thereby questioning the equation of collective freedom and happiness used by the modern national identity of the Cuban Revolution, where there was only space for New Men.[33] Here we need to consider how much research into the homophobic politics of the Cuban Revolution has been advanced in the field of Latin American cultural studies. In my own experience in left-leaning cultural studies circles, I find a lack of criticism of the Cuban Revolution and other leftist movements with homophobic policies that have influenced our field as well as the lives of many people. Lemebel asks in his "Manifiesto,"

> That's why, *compañero*, I ask you
> Does the Siberian train of reactionary propaganda still exist?
> That train that passes in front of your eyes
> When my voice becomes too sweet
> And you?
> What will you do with those memories of us as children wanking each other off,
> amongst other things, on holiday in Cartagena?
> Will the future be black and white?
> Day and night, without ambiguity?
> Won't there be a fag on some street-corner, destabilising the future of your new man?
> ("Manifiesto" 36)

There are several allusions to the Cuban Revolution throughout the text, especially when it directly approaches the rejection and persecution that the Cuban Revolution practiced in the name of morality:

> Don't you think that, all alone, up in the ranges, we might have gotten up to something?
> Although you would hate me later
> For corrupting your revolutionary morality
> Are you afraid of life becoming homosexualized?
> ("Manifiesto" 37)

In this passage we see how the narrator questions the Cuban Revolution's fear regarding the impact that masculine homosexuality and effeminacy could have on revolutionary society, understanding both as corruptors of morals and as threats to the strong national identity they thought they had established through the New Man. This identity discourse framed homosexuals and effeminate men as incapable of being revolutionaries or *guerrilleros* and, therefore, incapable of protecting and fighting for the revolution.

Several times throughout the text, Lemebel refers to himself as a *marica* and its superlative, *maricón*. According to Lawrence La Fountain-Stokes, both terms come from *María*, that is, the proper name Mary ("Queer Ducks" 200). Also, in the *Diccionario de la Lengua Castellana* by Dr. Rodolfo Oroz, the first edition of which was published in 1989 under the military dictatorship—and is still in print—the homosexual is defined as "sodomita, maricón y pederasta," (sodomite, maricon, and pedophile) signaling that the definitions of certain subjects and practices established during the military dictatorship continue circulating in Chile, but also that the homosexual was and is equal to a criminal. Also, and as we have already indicated, Lemebel points out several times that he experienced exclusion in a leftist party when trying to protest against the dictatorship. *Hablo por mi diferencia*, besides denouncing the exclusionary discourse of the left and the right and the modernizing discourse, demystifies the idea that a *maricón* or *marica* does not have *hombría* or manhood to fight against and resist oppressive regimes. In the following passage Lemebel emphasizes that the *hombría* or manhood of the *maricón* or *marica* is proved everyday as he must face jokes, discrimination, and violence from society:

> My manhood wasn't given to me by the party
> Because they rejected me with laughter
> Many times
> I learned my manhood by participating
> In the toughness of those times
> And they laughed at my fag voice
> Yelling: "And it will fall, and it will fall"
> ("Manifiesto" 38)

As I have argued, the intervention of Lemebel's "in-between" narrative enunciated by his *travestido* body in the discriminatory discourses of the Chilean and Cuban modernizing process is potentiated because of the affirmation of Lemebel's position as a *travesti*—a subject that is destabilizing the binary "masculine"/"feminine." With this affirmation, Lemebel critiques but also contests the expulsion, exclusion, and marginalization of effeminate men, *maricones*, and homosexuals during the foundation of the modern Chilean and Cuban nation-states, as they were kept out of the historical and identitarian discourses these formations produced. Lemebel's narrative and performance also reclaims the manhood or *hombría* of the *marica*, the *maricón* but also the *travesti* in what I read as an attempt to resist the ideas associated with them in the Chilean and Cuban modernist discourse, as well as in the discourse of the dictatorship, with special emphasis on the Chilean left and its rejection of *maricas* or *maricones* in the resistance against the dictatorship. In *Hablo por mi diferencia*, then, there is a rewriting of such terms and their relationship to notions such as manhood or *hombría*, because Lemebel's narrative along with the *travestido*'s body challenge the "masculine"/"feminine" paradigm and bring about a space in which dissident gender and revolutionary ideologism are reconciled. This destabilizes the hegemonic definitions that the discourses of the Chilean and Cuban modernizing period, and also of the military dictatorship, had of *maricas* and *maricones*. In the next section, I review Lemebel's novel *My Tender Matador* (2001). I contend that it offers suggestions of how an alliance between those who were included under the umbrella of a national identity during the modernization of Chile—which had further repercussions in the way Chile's left conceived sexual and gender minorities—and its excluded Other might have functioned under the military dictatorship.

Resisting Together

> La revolución por venir será a partir de alianzas transversales con otros colectivos ninguneados o no será.
>
> —**Paul B. Preciado**

My Tender Matador, a novel that critics have called a post-dictatorship narrative, relates the story of a platonic love between the Loca del

Frente and Carlos, a militant from el Frente Patriótico Manuel Rodríguez who participates in the organization of a failed attack against the Dictator in the novel.[34] The Loca del Frente is a romantic *travesti* who is sensitive and flexible and enjoys pleasure, while Carlos considers emotions and pleasure distractions from his revolutionary duty.[35] For Fernando Moreno, the novel is located in a "border area in which the basic features are, without a doubt, *travestismo*, spectacle, transformation and representation. And where eroticism, sensuality and the bewilderment of a marginal, peripheric and repressed voice are the protagonists" (121).

The relationship that develops between Carlos and the Loca del Frente, and the acceptance of their differences, suggests that the inclusion and acceptance of those subjects excluded and persecuted by the Chilean and Latin American modern national discourse—an exclusion and persecution perpetuated by the Latin American left—would have made the resistance against the military dictatorship stronger. Brad Epps goes further, explaining that the novel allows the creation of "a plan of double liberation against the dictatorship of Pinochet and against the dictatorship of heteronormativity" (Epps, "Nostalgia" 118). In *Tengo miedo torero*, Lemebel's "in-between" narrative is contrasted against not only the hegemonic masculine/virile narrative of Augusto Pinochet but also the narrative of the left-wing militant who believed there was only one way of resisting and struggling against the oppression of the dictatorship.

Lemebel's "in-between" narrative comes from the Loca del Frente who is described in the novel as "a flaming faggot" and "a Queen" (Lemebel, *My Tender Matador* 2). As we mentioned in chapter 2, according to La Fountain-Stokes a *loca* "suggests or proposes a form of hysterical identity (pathologized at the clinical level, scandalous at the popular one) constitutive of an individual lacking sanity, composure or ascription to the dominant norms: effeminate homosexuals, mad women, rebels for any cause" ("Queer Ducks" 198). On the other hand, according to Lemebel himself, a *loca* should be understood as "a glittering way of perceiving and being perceived, of constantly reassembling her imaginary as part of her survival strategy. The *Loca*, then, is constantly zigzagging throughout her process of political becoming, always thinking how to survive, how to pass either as invisible or highly visiblized" (Lemebel, *La esquina* 17). The Loca del Frente presents, after all, the same characteristics as Lemebel himself. As Blanco points out, Lemebel *se traviste* and becomes the *loca*, narrating from their perspective ("Políticas" 73). This position of enunciation allows the production of an "in-between" narrative that confuses or rather erases genders when narrating, as the novel's narrative does not distinguish between "masculine" and "feminine."

The novel starts by describing the context in which the story takes place, as well as the specific moment in time in which the story is set, emphasizing that it is 1986, "a year scarred by smoking tires in the cordoned-off streets of Santiago. A city waking up to the sounds of banging pots and pans and lightning blackouts, electric wires dangling overhead, sputtering and sparking" (*My Tender Matador* 1). The story of Carlos and the Loca del Frente takes place in a context in which two forces are in conflict: one is the force of oppression, the other is the force of resistance. These forces express themselves in the novel in comments like "Stop, you piece of shit!" and the tireless "Now he will fall! Now he will fall!" (1) without a concrete referent or narrator. The reader does not know where these voices are coming from.

When the voice of the Loca del Frente is introduced, the language of the novel starts changing its syntax and the narrative begins to use many adjectives. Sentences are longer, more overloaded, and confusing, like the following: "As if by repeating his name she were embroidering those letters in the air that vibrated languidly in his presence. As if the motor of that sissy tongue were stuck enunciating his name, calling him, licking him, savoring those syllables, chewing on the word, filling her up with that Carlos so deep, that name so grand, until she was a sight held gently on the long *o* of Carl-*o*-s that illuminated her h-*o*-m-e" (*My Tender Matador* 4–5). This is characteristic of the neo-baroque style of Lemebel's "in-between" narrative, a saturated narrative that pays attention to details. In the following example, we can see how the narrative is affected by a neo-baroque style. Instead of simply expressing that the Loca del Frente was remembering, the language is decorated to say: "So, separated by curtains of smoke that they sucked in and blew out through the long vigils, she wove together, in her sissy singsong voice, thin threads of memory. Scraps from the days of street hustling, meandering along nameless dirty alley-ways she managed to transform into tropical sidewalk paradises with her swishing footsteps that clicked to the rhythm of the night" (7). As I mentioned before, Lemebel's "in-between" narrative destabilizes the "masculine"/"feminine" binary. Because of this, the identity of the narrator is unknown to the reader, as it is unstable and its gender and sexual attributes are ambiguous. The Loca del Frente is presented in the novel as a *travesti* who has an indeterminacy of genders. However, when the voice of the Loca del Frente interacts with the voice of Carlos, there is a double confusion of genders that prevents the reader from obtaining stable knowledge of the voice of both characters. For example, in the following passage the narrative of the novel destabilizes the genders of the voices: "She didn't sleep almost the whole night, tossing and turning, so excited with so many emotions, so many explosions that sent her idyllic postcard into such disarray. She was already up when Carlos arrived, dressed in a black pullover, his hair wet and glistening from the shower. Are you ready? We don't have much time because I have to return the car by six. You made food! A chicken. Fresh country air makes you hungry, don't you think? I'll carry it down, don't you bother; I'll wait for you in the car" (15). The reader cannot be sure who is speaking here. We do not know if it is Carlos or the Loca del Frente speaking, so the reader cannot recognize any stable gender in the narrative's voice. Also, the novel makes the voice of the *Loca del Frente* and the militant interact and have an impact on each other. As I mentioned before, Carlos is a member of El Frente Patriótico Manuel Rodríguez and because of his militancy in the left he practices a normative masculinity. This masculinity impregnates the narrative from the start, characterizing Carlos "with such a virile voice" (*My Tender Matador* 4) and a hard, dry language of short sentences pronounced in staccato: "What's going on? What happened? . . . They still aren't done? Don't let me fall asleep, tell me about yourself, your life. Can I have another cup of coffee?" (7). In contrast to this masculine language, the Loca del Frente uses a language that, as noted above, deviates from grammatical sentences and employs an abundance of adjectives. Both languages clash throughout the novel until the language of the Loca del Frente seduces the language that is used to narrate Carlos, transforming the discourse that Carlos embodies. Not only this, but the language of the Loca del Frente also helps deconstruct the essentialist discourse that matches the natural-biological destiny of each body with the maternal and paternal vocation of the roles assigned to men and women by human nature, represented in the novel by the character of La Primera Dama, the dictator's wife. As Epps points out, the Loca del Frente alters those common places of a domesticated femininity that this character represents by "undermining and unnaturalizing them" ("Nostalgia" 122).

The language of the Loca del Frente resists the homophobia expressed by the character of the Dictator who considers homosexuality an anomaly that should be corrected or disappeared to be in keeping with society's morality and good habits. *Maricones*, for the Dictator, are "degenerates" (*My Tender Matador* 35), like communists who exhibit their "filth in the open air" (36). In the novel, the Dictator embraces a type of hegemonic masculinity that is based on values and ideals such as order, strength, and discipline. This is why in the novel this character repudiates sexual and gender difference and everyone who does not follow the above-mentioned masculinity.

Carlos's language starts to change as it is influenced by the language of the Loca del Frente. Now the actions of Carlos are described in a different tone: "And Carlos so amused, laughing at all her jokes, swerving around the curves, saying, Hold on, one more curve, one more mile" (16). We also see that the way Carlos perceives the world has changed, as the following passage reveals: "And he stood there in amazement, staring at her perched on top of a rock with the table-cloth tied around her neck as if it were a cape on which perched birds and little angels. Her magnificence was magnified by her cat's-eye sunglasses as she bit seductively into a flower, her hands sheathed in yellow polka dots, her fingers raised above her head like a flamenco dancer" (23). We see how the language of the Loca del Frente has transformed the way the militant of the left perceives the world, transforming even his notions of beauty. The changes in the language inscribing Carlos coincide with his actions. One example is the narration of Carlos's birthday in which he is surprised by a party organized by the Loca del Frente: "And Carlos' eyes clouded over, he choked on such a sweet pain seeing those kids' dirty faces singing *Happy Birthday, Carlos* out of tune, feeling his macho chest torn to shreds by that slightly blurred image of the Queen of the Corner lit up by the candles, like Snow White among so many dwarfs" (*My Tender Matador* 74–75). This is one of the few moments in the novel where Carlos expressed affectivity, especially in regard to the feelings roused by the Loca del *Frente*, because this character avoids any kind of emotion that distances him from his revolutionary duty. In this passage, Carlos, but also the language that inscribes him as a character, is invaded by an "irrepressible wave and relaxed joy" (68) that makes him forget his military duty; and such neglect is presented as a consequence of the *actuar marica* of the Loca del Frente. This movement of Carlos toward pleasure also causes him to cross and transgress his sexual reality, as he allows himself, although he is sleeping, to feel pleasure through a sexual encounter with the Loca del Frente. This encounter is only possible because the Loca del Frente makes Carlos tell her a secret:

> One day, I don't know why, my friend and I were lying alone on our bellies in the sun on a little stretch of sand at the edge of the water. The sand was warm and, I don't know why, my friend started moving as if he were fucking and he said. It feels really good, try it. So I started to imitate him, watching his white ass next to me, the way he tightened and relaxed his buns as he pumped up and down. I watched him as I rubbed myself against the warm sand, and suddenly I couldn't stand it and I jumped on top of him. (*My Tender Matador* 78–79)

From this moment on, the language that expresses the voice of Carlos is the same as the one of the Loca del Frente, as both now share the same language. When a flirty Loca del Frente asks Carlos, "Could you take me there, Mr. Chauffeur? At your command, your highness, the carriage is waiting, and they both laughed freely as they walked with regal bearing down the stairs and got into the car parked in front" (110), both voices are *cómplices* now. The same Carlos, who at the beginning of the novel used a dry, direct, and disciplinary language; who wanted to be a Che Guevara, sharing his ideal of the New Man; who at the beginning of the novel kept a distance from the Loca del Frente, who he considered to be inappropriate and a distraction from his revolutionary duty, finally tells them, "Nobody compares to you, my princess, you are one of a kind" (112).

The novel also demonstrates that from that same difference now recognized and valued by Carlos, the Loca del *Frente* can support and collaborate with the revolutionary project in which he participates. The Loca del Frente for instance, offers to deliver a confidential and delicate package to another member of *El Frente*. As we read on, we realize that the package contains a bomb that will be used to try to kill the Dictator. On her way to deliver the package, the Loca del Frente is delayed by a confrontation between a group of protesters and the police. Nevertheless, the character uses its *loca* resources to "reassemble . . . her imaginary according to her survival strategies . . . to pass either as invisible or highly visiblized" (Lemebel, *La esquina* 17) and escape the police:

> There she was, facing the police formation, but the Queen, paralyzed with terror, didn't move a muscle, and, lifting her nose in an imperious gesture, she walked directly into an encounter with the brutality of the police. Are you going to let me through? she said to the first uniformed man she encountered. The cop was so surprised by the impertinence of this prissy faggot that he hesitated before grabbing his club, before raising his club to bring it down upon that arrogant porcelain head. What, with all these disturbances, I can't even go shopping peacefully in the supermarket? . . . In the blink of an eye, the Queen had broken through the armored wall and,

> carrying the heavy bag as if it were as light as a feather, she disappeared into the pedestrian traffic of the public walkway. (*My Tender Matador* 100)

The resources of the Loca del Frente are also shown in another scene where the character is coming back from the movies with a picture of a *desaparecido* in her pocket. The Loca del Frente encounters a group of military men, and:

> As she got off the bus, she remembered she still had the picture of the disappeared person in her pocket and felt a pit open up in her stomach, and when she heard the soldier's order for the men to go here and the women to go over there, she didn't know what to do, and just as she was getting totally flustered and all in a tizzy, she sensed the emergence of her emergency drag queen. What are you waiting for, don't you know where to go? The uniformed man shouted. I'd have to split myself right down the middle so I could be in both places at once, she answered, with a smile . . . on your way then, the soldier said, lowering his machine gun. (*My Tender Matador* 140)

In this way, the novel shows that dignity and courage are not related to notions such as masculinity and manliness, and that from difference, resistance can be produced against oppression and domination. As Jean Franco states, "In a society that celebrates military and militants, *La loca* questions the discipline carried out by the State and corrects the slogans of the party with her own slogans 'pan, justicia, sexo y libertad' and 'el pueblo caliente jamás baja la frente'" ("Pedro Lemebel" 63).

Tengo miedo torero shows what the Chilean, as well as the Latin American left, is missing out on by excluding the participation of sexual minorities from its struggle. Moreover, by proposing a bond between Carlos and the Loca del Frente, the novel, as Bernardita Llanos expresses, "cancels the masculine socialist realist model that privileges the ideology of the revolutionary heterosexual militant worker traditional gender roles" (198). Besides this, the novel is another example of how Lemebel's "in-between" narrative produces a communitarian space defined by alterity, exchange, and mutuality. In *Tengo miedo torero*, Carlos and the Loca del Frente exchange places, because the individual who was conceived as a coward and without *hombría* or manhood—the Loca del Frente—by the left, represented by Carlos, is the one who ends up helping the resistance. Carlos, the individual who at the beginning of the novel avoided any kind of emotion that could distract him from his revolutionary duty, the militant of the left who believed there was only one way of resisting and struggling against the oppression of the dictatorship, ends up asking the Loca del frente to move with him to Cuba. They enrich each other's lives as they move through new experiences and feelings together that transform them and allow them to better contest and resist the dictatorship and its mechanisms.

In ending this section, I want to return to an idea put forward by Héctor Domínguez Ruvalcaba, who states that the principle of *cuirizar*, or to queer, consists in opening an anti-hegemonic space for excluded, oppressed, and marginalized individuals (*Translating* 76). Lemebel's "in-between" narrative does this by making visible and protagonizing marginalized and excluded practices, and opening a post-hegemonic space from which to question and contest exclusionary discourses like those practiced during the modernization of Chile and reproduced during the military dictatorship. As we have seen in the analysis of these three works by Pedro Lemebel, by deconstructing the gender system his "in-between" narrative also questions the foundations of the modern national identity and of national identity under the dictatorship, especially regarding their notions of the natural biological destination of each body, gender, and sexuality.

Today, as in the past, queer/*cuir* modernity rejects national identity as it has been wrought through exclusionary and oppressive discourses, proposing, moreover, a reconfiguration of concepts such as citizenship and national subject. As Dominguez-Ruvalcaba suggests, a queer/*cuir* critique addresses not only homosexuality but also much broader epistemological formulations, as well as the representation and knowledge of sexuality and its broad implications for the social structure (*Translating* 107). This is exactly why I have proposed in this chapter the need to *cuirizar*, or to queer (more), the fields of *cuir* Latin American and Latin American cultural studies by bringing the direct and material experiences of those excluded, oppressed, and marginalized individuals, especially poor and racialized *travestis*, opening, as Domínguez-Ruvalcaba notes, "an anti-hegemonic space" (76) for them in the academy—not to theorize about them, but to include their own lived experiences, work, and theorization. This will allow us as *cuir* and Latin American critics to address the potential of these lives, their vulnerability and resistance. As the Chilean *travesti* Sofía Devenir states, "For *travestis'* bodies, daily survival is a strategic performance, an activism, a political action" (40). Devenir brings her songs and protests—which include the biographies of and tributes to other *travestis* that had been murdered—to public buses in Santiago, a public, marginal space where she surely reaches a diverse audience. As with others, Sofía makes her body vulnerable on behalf of her art, her political action, and her community, and these direct experiences should be addressed in the above-mentioned fields.

As I stated at the beginning of this chapter, Lemebel, through his *crónicas*, transforms language in a space of transgression, of extraterritoriality and deconstruction of language (Figueroa Díaz 11). I suggest that this same transformation should be undertaken in the fields of Latin American *cuir* and Latin American cultural studies, to transform their academic language, *cuirizar*, or queer it, just as the Loca del Frente's did with Carlos's language, allowing this character to perceive the world in a different way.

In the particular case of *travestis*, "our way of expressing ourselves is different," as Claudia Rodríguez states, and explains in an interview that she had to find her own language "to say what I, as a *travesti*, want to say" (Rodríguez, "Se resiste" 21). Hence, the need for reflecting and respecting these voices in the fields of Latin American *cuir* and Latin American cultural studies by including and exploring their ways of expressing themselves. *Cuir* Latin American academics such as Joseph Pierce had already started doing this with his work on the trans and *travesti* experiences of Claudia Rodríguez and Susy Shock. His article "I Monster: Embodying Trans and *Travesti* Resistance in Latin America" was published in the journal *Latin American Research Review* and is probably the first article published in the journal that addresses the direct life experience and cultural production of these two artists as theorization. On a LASA panel where Pierce, along with Diego Falconí and Claudia Rodríguez discussed Pierce's article, Pierce mentioned the need to practice "an ethics and a collaborative politics together with the people who are creating these art works and these activisms in different parts of Latin America" in the fields of Latin American *cuir* and cultural studies. This is in the sense that, as Rodríguez expressed, it is important to enact "a collaboration that produces knowledge, rescues histories, creates a record, integrates this rudimentary writing into other scenarios" "building a different Academy," where theorization is not applied to the bodies and experiences of *travestis* and other gender and sexual dissidents but, on the contrary, is constructed by or with them.

CHAPTER 4

The "In-Between" in the Works of Giuseppe Campuzano and Claudia Salazar

En el Perú hay ciertas cosas que no se deben hablar,
y nuestra debilidad por los hombres es una de esas cosas.
En el Perú puedes ser coquero, ladrón o mujeriego,
pero no te puedes darte el lujo de ser maricón.

—Jaime Bayly

As pointed out in chapter 1, the political, economic, and social crisis of Peru during the mid-twentieth century involved peasant mobilizations, the Indigenous question, and the increasing participation of different urban sectors in Peruvian national life. In the political and cultural fields, under the influence of the Mexican and Russian Revolutions, this resulted in a reconceptualization of Peruvian Indigenous culture, traditionally regarded as an "obstacle for progress" (Rama, *Writing* 22). Indigenous culture became the matrix from which to rethink Peruvian national identity. The reconceptualization of Indigenous culture proposed the Indian as the emblem of modern Peruvian national identity; however, it used him (rarely her) for the promotion of an ideology of national progress, popular incorporation, and transculturation. In this way, the incorporation and affirmation of the Indian was always and exclusively limited and conditioned to their remaining a dominated and subjugated subject. This could be considered a modern modality of domination and subjugation under which Indigenous peoples are incorporated symbolically into the national imaginary while being excluded in practical terms from enjoying citizen rights.

This modality continued to be applied by successive governments in the second half of the twentieth century, including the governments of presidents Juan Velasco Alvarado (1968–1975), Francisco Morales-Bermúdez (1975–1980), Fernando Belaúnde-Terry (1963–1968 and 1980–July 28, 1985), and Alan García (1985–1990 and 2006–2011). These governments followed an authoritarian tradition that, far from being a ghost of the past, is a constant presence in contemporary national policies that to this day continue to build identities and legal subject positions by condemning those from marginalized groups, as Giancarlo Cornejo, Eloy Neira, Patricia Ruiz Bravo, and Rocío Silva Santisteban have pointed out.

During the Peruvian internal armed conflict (1980–2000) and especially during the ten-year-long authoritarian presidency of Alberto Fujimori (1993–1995, 1995–2000, and 2000), it became evident that when Indigenous peoples resisted—in ultraradical ways—this modern identity that subjugated and dominated them, the Peruvian state responded with devastating violence. Thus, along with other scholars (Talía Dajes, Nelson Manríque, Cecilia Méndez, and Rocío Silva Santisteban), I consider this conflict to be an explosion of what lies beneath the surface of a modernizing project, and its further reproduction, founded on exclusion, domination, subjugation, and racism toward Indigenous populations. Moreover, the brutal violence practiced against these populations, in particular during the internal armed conflict, together with the forced sterilizations of Indigenous women during Fujimori's presidency, indicate that the subjugation and domination of the Indigenous populations during the modernization of the Peruvian nation-state had evolved into a desire of the Peruvian state to reduce and, in some ways, exterminate these populations.

The aim of this chapter is, first, to review the work of the Peruvian researcher, artist, and philosopher Giuseppe Campuzano, who, by means of an "in-between" narrative structure, questions and resists the project of a modern national identity by positing a mobile national identity, in which alterity plays a major role. As I have already pointed out, the construction of modern Peruvian national identity integrated into the nation some of the populations considered nonnational. Yet, at the same time, they appeared as exceptions or as emblems of forms of belonging that were incorporated into the nation without actually being part of it, thereby continuing to subordinate them. Although the Indigenous populations were the most visibly affected by these politics of exclusion, it was also the case for homosexuals, *travestis*, *maricones*, and effeminate men, as I have discussed in previous chapters. Campuzano's work, specifically his interactive museum-book *Museo travesti del Perú* (2008), addresses this failed integration by reorganizing and redesigning the history of Peru and the history of its modern national identity through a narrative structure informed by the figure of the *travesti* and *travestismo*.

This chapter also discusses the novel *Blood of the Dawn* (2016) (*La sangre de la aurora*, 2013) by the Peruvian writer Claudia Salazar to argue that through an "in-between" narrative the novel shows how the place of Indigenous populations as dominated and subjugated in the construction of Peruvian modern national identity has evolved into a desire of the state to reduce and, in some ways, exterminate these populations. Salazar's novel focuses particularly on addressing the multifaceted and brutal violence that the Peruvian state exercised against Indigenous women, but it does so by presenting them not as passive victims, which is how they have been portrayed in hegemonic discourses, but as individuals capable of agency and self-empowerment. In this way, *La sangre de la aurora* affirms the post-hegemonic potential of the "in-between" narrative, as I will contend in the following sections.

An "In-Between" Redesigning of Modern Peruvian National Identity

In *Muerte en el Pentagonito: Los cementerios secretos del Ejército peruano* (2004) (Death in Little Pentagon: The Secret Cemeteries of the Peruvian Army), which reports on crimes committed by the Peruvian Armed Forces during the internal conflict, the journalist and researcher Ricardo Uceda points out that agents of the Peruvian state regarded sexual rapes of Indigenous Quechua-speaking women as a minor ill, for it prevented other rapes or aberrations, such as the outbreak of homosexuality (122). As we discussed in chapter 2, these attitudes clearly show that during the armed conflict, violence was also exerted on the basis of gender and sexual dissidence. This violence has been practiced throughout Peruvian republican history.[1] However, there have been moments of greater intensification, such as during the internal conflict. In that period, there were at least ten cases of hate crimes and five hundred people were affected, with both rebel groups and military forces responsible for the attacks. An underlying reason for this violence in the midst of the conflict is the place—or the no-place—dissident genders and sexualities were allocated during the rearticulation of the Peruvian national identity. As I have discussed throughout the book, this was understood across the Peruvian political spectrum almost entirely in racial and ethnic terms. Gender and sexuality were not included, since heteronormative ideals were taken as the default standard.

Giuseppe Campuzano (1969–2013) contests and challenges this historical construction, reorganizing and redesigning it through experience and knowledge derived from the figure of the *travesti* and the praxis of *travestismo*. In 2003, Campuzano began working on the *Museo travesti del Perú* (Travesti Museum of Peru), a project that explores *travestismo* and its aesthetic possibilities while also contrasting *travestismo* and its forms of knowledge with those of official discourses. The project has been shown in Peru and many other countries, such as Cuba, Canada, Brazil, Colombia, and Mexico, in exhibitions, performances, lectures, protests, and publications. As Tomás Ruiza-Rivas comments, "The collection of works and documents that constitute this museum without a permanent site to house it tells a story of hegemonies and subalternities, of the construction of memory on the basis of what has been forgotten, of the exercise of power from institutional culture" (18).

In 2008, Campuzano published a book with the same title and on the same subject in which he moves the *travesti* from the margins and brings to the fore their historical tradition in order to rethink Peruvian national identity (*Museo* 77). In an interview with the Argentine critic Daniel Link, Campuzano stated that if the *travesti* has a function at all, it would be to destroy clichés about sexuality and gender. This statement indicates one of the book's possible aims: to carry out a discursive destabilization that vindicates the condition of the *travesti* at the same time that it criticizes any exclusionary reaffirmation of identity. This discursive destabilization is part of the composition of the book. It is not clear whether this work has been written or collected or retrieved or documented. Should this book be considered literature? More than literature? *Museo* is a museum because it is made up of literary texts, newspaper clippings, ordinances from the viceroy during the colonial period, portraits, chronicles, and chronologies, all coming from different voices and sources. For Campuzano, "the exhibition—the images, ordered and narrated as irrefutable truth—represent a blunt political statement that many viewers accept; and when we confront what it is showing us, we learn that we are not the protagonists of our own history" (49). *Museo* puts forward an alternate archive, with the figure of the *travesti* and the practice of *travestismo*—a nonhistorical subject and practice—at the center, disobeying official historiography and highlighting what is hidden: those practices, spaces, and cultural productions discredited by a hegemonic aesthetic order complicit in the creation of a national identity that left out those who were considered "different." In this sense, Campuzano's *Museo* integrates a sort of *travesti* archival palimpsest, similar to Claudia Rodríguez's *Cuerpos para odiar*, and also Sofía Devenir's *Desubicá: Memorias de una dinosauria travesti sudaka*, as they all activate characteristics of the *travesti* in organizing these texts.

In the "Prologue" to *Museo*, Campuzano explains that the book "was born from the need to have a history of our own—an entirely new history of Peru . . . to propose the development of a more productive metaphor than any exclusionary taxonomy" (8). In this way, Campuzano's project not only considers making the life experience of *travestis* visible but also shows how this experience is constitutive of Peru's history. He goes further to recognize that Peru's history is incomplete if it does not include the experience of *travestis* and how they have permeated and influenced it. For Gustavo Buntix and Susana Torres, this book is "a sharp rewrite of our history and its representations, its documents and its gazes" (12). Personally, I think that in addition to conforming to the definitions of Campuzano, Buntix, and Torres, *Museo* questions and resists the project of a modern national identity and proposes a mobile national identity in which dissidence is recognized as one of its main features and no totalizing categories are projected. Thus, using performance, photography, and literature, this book can be characterized as positioning itself against the discriminatory modern national identity that, as I have mentioned, relied on a process of subordination/exclusion to the margins of those who were considered "different."

As I will discuss here, *Museo*'s "in-between" narrative structure activates features of the *travesti* and *travestismo*, especially their indeterminacy of gender and their distortion of subjectivity. In doing so, Campuzano's forceful work gives voice and visibility to Indigenous populations and their oral and written manifestations, and simultaneously puts forward an open, multiple, plural, and unstable national identity that does not exclude those groups considered "different." This "in-between" narrative structure is, as I will explain, a post-hegemonic one that, in Gareth Williams's words, opens up a "reflection to an outside that is capable of signaling the possibility of an entirely different telos from which to think" (*The Other Side* 149)—in this case, the discourses of a modern national identity that situated Indigenous populations as dominated and subjugated, at the same time that it subordinated and excluded homosexuals, *travestis*, *maricones*, and effeminate men, among many others.

Before starting the analysis, however, I believe it is useful to look at the way Campuzano conceives of the *travesti* and *travestismo* because these conceptions influence the structure and organization of the book. In the "Glossary" included in *Museo*, Campuzano argues that the *travesti* is a "person who assumes the characteristics of the opposite sex. While this is in itself a legitimate action, it results in a compound of male and female characteristics which, although common to all in varying degrees, the *travesti* makes explicit at the same time that he/she questions the inadequate prevailing gender norms—the exclusively male and female distinctions" (89). Similarly, the author argues that the *travesti* position implies "a whole range of possibilities between the extremes of the masculine and the feminine" (8). *Museo* questions modern Peruvian national identity from an "in-between" conception of the *travesti*, and by doing so, it enables a rearticulation of the fractured nation that has emerged from Peruvian nationalism, thus revealing its identitarian fallacy. Presenting Peruvian national history and identity from a *travesti* position—from an "in-between" position—also implies conceiving the *travesti* "not at the level of the subject but of a discourse that has a self-referencing starting point; that conceives of identity as a relational and, therefore, unstable phenomenon; that refers to a colonized and mestizo body-territory endowed with agency" (Campuzano, "Giuseppe Campuzano y El Museo" 10). In this sense, Campuzano considers *travestis'* bodies as does Rosi Braidotti, who defines them as "places of transit . . . in-between zones where all ties are suspended . . . oases of nonbelonging, spaces of detachment" (18–19), but also in the sense that *travestis'* bodies make visible the racial and ethnic "in-betweenness" of all Peruvian bodies. Interestingly, Campuzano's understanding of the *travesti* allows us to perceive Peruvian bodies as also "in-between" because of their "colonized and mestizo body-territory" reality, thereby affirming that *travestismo* is a form of knowledge. However, Campuzano does not propose the *travesti* "as the research or production of another identity for the long existing list," but rather as "transformative post-identity, away from the clean racial and racist distinctions and towards ethnic overlappings" (Campuzano, "Giuseppe Campuzano y El Museo" 10). This is something that could be extended to all Peruvian bodies.

As I mentioned earlier, *Museo* proposes a distortion of subjectivity. The history of Peru and the Peruvian national identity that the book addresses consist of different sources and multiple voices that are changing, dissimilar, and constantly interrupting each other. There is, therefore, "no recognizable subject, only mutation and deidentification processes, where some bodies become another" (Miguel López 15). The voices and sources included in the book mutate and metamorphose; they belong to different historical periods, to different contexts and disciplines. We may well find the voice of a writer, a viceroy, a historian, or a prostitute. *Museo*, for instance, includes a quote from the *indigenista* writer José María Arguedas's novel *El sexto* (1961) with the voice of one of its characters, Rosita, a *maricón*, *travesti*, or effeminate man. Likewise, it includes the passage from Enrique Planas's *Orquídeas del Paraíso* (1996), in which we learn about Achilles's experience of having Nancy "powdering his face" (Campuzano, *Museo* 3). Among archaeological findings and ceramics produced by different pre-Hispanic cultures, documents of Andean symbolism, and maps of the Kingdoms of the Indies, Campuzano situates the narrative of the above-mentioned writers—and of others, like Mario Bellatín—who address in their fiction the experience of homosexuals, *travestis*, *maricones*, and effeminate men in a gesture that, I would like to suggest, seeks to interrupt the hegemonic Peruvian historical narrative and the construction of the country's national identity. There is also a gesture that seeks to make visible the way in which different Peruvian literary figures have approached homosexuals, *travestis*, *maricones*, and effeminate men in their work, despite Peruvian political discourses that not only excluded them but dismissed any kind of ambiguity or heterogeneity in the national narrative. We thus return to Diego Falconí's statement that Latin American literary productions "misregard . . . certain subjectivities, cultural organizations and *cosmoviciones*" (34). These authors Campuzano mentions recognize the inclusion of gender and sexual dissidences in Peruvian literature in their literary production, as do Oswaldo Reynoso, Mario Vargas Llosa, Juan Carlos Cortázar, Jaime Bayly, Karen Luy de Aliaga, María Luis del Río, Violeta Barrientos, and Morella Petrozzi, among others.

The inclusion of different and diverse voices that interrupt each other implies that *Museo* addresses not only the *travesti*, but other individuals who were also subjected, subordinated, or excluded in the name of modern Peruvian national identity. For instance, the book includes the experience of immigrant Chinese opera singers on account of their *travestismo* on stage (*Museo* vii), of Afro-Peruvians, and prostitutes. In the case of the latter, the book addresses in particular the clandestine prostitution sought by low-income women, making visible the injustices affecting this also marginalized and excluded group. Campuzano points out: "The allegation of immorality of the act carried out between the sex worker and the client is contradictory, since she is the only one to be arrested. . . . It looks like one particular sector is always being protected. Who is the immoral person here?" (101). The experiences of the "nation of minorities," as Hannah Arendt would call them in "The Decline of the Nation-State and the End of the Rights of Man" (375), had been erased from modern Peruvian national identity because they were considered the experiences and conduct of illegitimate inhabitants of the modern Peruvian nation. Campuzano makes this status visible, questions it, and reformulates it by presenting the experiences of these minorities at the center of their post-hegemonic historical narrative. In this sense, *Museo*, just as did Lemebel's *La esquina es mi corazón*, produces a communitarian space, with its historicization of those marginalized experiences made invisible by the discourses of the modern Peruvian national identity.

The language used in *Museo* sways between a narrative and a poetic language, but it also records the many different language registers of the archive, including legal, literary, photographic, performative, and journalistic language, in the collage it composes with loose quotes, newspaper clippings, old ordinances issued during the viceroyalty, photographs, portraits, chronicles, and chronologies drawn from different sources and uttered by multiple voices. This makes it possible for the book to "coexist simultaneously with all recorded eras" (Bellatín 10), displaying the past and history as something prevalent and continuous that has not reached closure.

In addition, *Museo* analyzes the criollo nationalist project, from which Peruvian national identity originated, as well as its literary manifestations. These manifestations have traditionally regarded and represented Indigenous populations "as a real obstacle for progress" (Rama, *Writing* 22), excluding and erasing their oral and written cultural manifestations. In contrast, *Museo* makes a series of manifestations and cultural traditions from these populations visible. The book includes, for example, a photograph of a Moche spout vessel in which a "berdache" is portrayed, "a person who performs an-other gender, neither feminine nor masculine" or "in whom female and male attributes are combined creating a symbolic nexus with the magical" (Campuzano, *Museo* 16). Also included are a series of texts written by Spanish chroniclers in which discussions of homosexuals and *travestis* in the pre-Hispanic Indigenous populations appear. For example, in addition to extracts from the chronicles of Felipe Guáman Poma de Ayala, *Museo* includes this fragment from Pedro Cieza de León written in 1553: "It is true that generally, among the *serranos* and Yungas, the devil has introduced this vice under the guise of sanctity. And each temple or main shrine has a man or two, or more, depending on the idol. And they were dressed like women since childhood and talked like them, and in their manner, attire, and everything else they imitated women" (quoted in Campuzano, *Museo* 17). This text quoted by Campuzano about pre-Hispanic Indigenous populations emphasizes the completely different vision of sexuality, the body, and the relationship between sexual and social roles that they practiced. It also shows that this conception of sexual and gender diversity was condemned and punished by the Spanish conquistadores. In his article "Are Two Genders Enough?" Campuzano notes that "before the arrival of the Spanish conquistadores there was an Indigenous identity of people who did not see themselves as women or men. The colonizers suppressed this identity by punishing these people with lashes and public humiliation" ("¿Son suficientes?" 63). For this reason, *Museo* also includes a document that illustrates the processes through which these practices were punished during the Spanish colony, an excerpt from an ordinance of 1566 that states:

> Additionally, if an Indian man were to dress like an Indian woman, or an Indian woman like an Indian man, said mayors are to arrest them and if it is the first time to give them one hundred slashes and shave their head publicly; and if it is the second time they are to be tied for six hours to a pole in the tiangueza to be seen by all; and if it is the third time that the Indian is arrested for this reason, he or she is to be sent to the Corregidor of this valley or to the mayors of the Villa de Santiago de Miraflores so that they be prosecuted in accordance with the law. (quoted in Campuzano, *Museo* 38)

This ordinance contains the punishment that any person who practiced what would later be called homosexuality or *travestismo* should receive. In addition to this ordinance, *Museo* lists other cases brought before the Court of Castile and the Real Audiencia of Lima, where these punishments were repeated, especially for *travestis* and effeminate men. *Museo* records how the Spanish conquistadores segmented "the *continuum* of the Indigenous knowledge of gender, in masculine and feminine while suppressing alterity" (Horswell 16–28). Furthermore, *Museo* includes texts revealing how the pre-Hispanic Andean world was divided, citing, for example, an excerpt from Oscar Ugarteche's book *Historia, sexo y cultura en el Perú* (1989), in which he points out that "the Andean world placed the male world at the top right and the female world at the top left. At the bottom right was the female masculine and at the bottom left the male feminine. The lower part corresponds to ambivalence . . . these categories apply to both the pre-Inca and the Inca world" (quoted in Campuzano, *Museo* 25). *Museo* thus "disorganizes the queer chronology" (Falconí 184) by affirming the presence of sexual and gender "dissidents" such as the *travesti* in the history of Latin America since before the arrival of the conquistadores. If, according to Marlene Wayar, "there were other sexualities here, other ways of living genders and sexuality, of living bodies in harmony" (*Travesti* 30), *Museo* returns to such *armonía* by bringing them back in a memory apparatus, such as the museum. Thus, *Museo* presents the nonaffirmation of subjectivity by means of a plural narrative voice in which diverse voices and different sources and historical temporalities come together. Using a diverse language, the historical post-hegemonic proposal of *Museo*, in addition to making visible a series of cultural manifestations from the pre-Hispanic Indigenous populations, records the notions of sexuality and gender that influenced these populations and the cultural traditions that came from these notions. The notions and traditions were erased and replaced during the colonial period and were not rescued or included during the process of modernization of the Peruvian state, which suppressed these same traditions within the crafting of modern Peruvian national identity.[2] *Museo* highlights that these traditions are still alive and present, for example, in the examples of the Tunantada, the Limpiacequias, the Festival of Compadres, and the Festival of the Cross of Freedom of Huancayo, making visible and affirming the existence and survival of these practices over time, despite historical attempts to make them disappear. In this way, the historical post-hegemonic proposal of *Museo* unveils how the modern nation has created an Indigenous past that fits into the image it wanted of the nation, and erases from the past what it seeks to erase in the present. Campuzano denounces these exclusions but also the way inclusions are made selectively.

In the same vein, in the final section of *Museo*, called "Archivo" (Archive), Campuzano puts together a series of twentieth- and twenty-first-century newspaper and magazine clippings and articles that deal with the existence of homosexuals, *travestis*, and effeminate men in modern and contemporary Peru. The choice of articles for this section and the way they are displayed suggest that "Archivo" has a specific purpose. It opens with a 1974 newspaper clipping in which Peru is accused of being "a society confronted with the evidence of its own diversity, but, unable to become aware of it, denies it" (92). This, it seems to me, is a way in which the book stages a critique of the erasure and exclusion of the traditions and legacies of Indigenous peoples, which has persisted throughout Peruvian republican history and has resulted in the intensification of violence against homosexuals, *travestis*, and effeminate men for considering their behaviors "obscene, immoral or dishonest" (103). Another article addresses the violence that Peruvian police have exerted (and still exert) against homosexuals, *travestis*, and effeminate men. The article explains that while Peru's Penal Code does not consider *travestismo*, homosexuality, or sex work a crime, those who practice these acts are regularly harassed and even arrested by the authorities. This abuse of police power goes unpunished because it can be justified under an old provision:

> Article 450—Other Misconduct
> The following shall be punished with community service that shall have a term of ten to thirty days:
> 1. Making any immoral or dishonest proposal to a third party in a public place. (quoted in Campuzano, *Museo* 101)[3]

Another article included in this section, "El tercer sexo en el primer poder" (The third sex meets the first power), has to do with the group of *travestis* who went to the Peruvian Congress to demand inclusion in what defines Peruvian citizenship during the last year of the Revolutionary Government of the Armed Forces (GRFA), led by Francisco Velasco Alvarado (118). In 1968, the armed forces seized power by means of an institutional coup, deposing President Fernando Belaúnde and establishing the GRFA. This regime sought to promote a popular "revolutionary reform" based on anti-imperialism and cultural nationalism. The GRFA defined that its main purpose was to correct the injustices inherent in the foundation of the Peruvian republic. As an opposition movement, however, the GRFA never distanced itself from the practical and conceptual limits set in the nineteenth-century model—although it sought to redefine it in different terms—in which the national community excluded homosexuals, *travestis*, and effeminate men.

Alongside this article is another that addresses hate crimes against homosexuals, *travestis*, and effeminate men during the Peruvian internal armed conflict, and highlights that these crimes,as well as the violence that the armed forces exerted against these excluded groups during the conflict were understood as actions of "National Security" (Campuzano, *Museo* 111).[4] This implies, then, that the defense of the Peruvian nation required or involved physical and psychological aggression against homosexuals, *travestis*, and effeminate men, which, in turn, places the conduct of guerrilla groups at the same level as that of the Peruvian Armed Forces. Yet another article points out that guerrilla groups reproduced the violence practiced by members of the Peruvian Armed Forces against these populations when it stated, "With the protection of the Army and the National Police, drug addiction, prostitution and homosexuality spread rapidly in Tarapoto. The Tupac Amaru Revolutionary Movement (MRTA) decided to end these social scourges, which were used to corrupt the young" (Campuzano, *Museo* 112). The members of the MRTA considered homosexuals, *travestis*, and effeminate men to be antirevolutionary or products of bourgeois decadence, "and therefore a threat to the leftist political project" (Campuzano, "Reclaiming" 133).[5] Besides this, the MRTA also "executed" drug addicts and prostitutes as it deemed them social scourges that "were used to corrupt the young" (Campuzano, *Museo* 112), reproducing the logic of the Peruvian police and armed forces.

The "Archive" section also illustrates those contributions that homosexuals, *travestis*, and effeminate men have made to Peruvian society. Such is the case of the article "The Boys of Pink Volleyball," which highlights the talents of these historically marginalized groups, since they make up the metropolitan volleyball selection. The article also underlines that this volleyball team is supported by many Peruvian citizens and concludes by arguing that "the volleyball they practice proves that marginalized beings will do whatever it takes to integrate into ordinary social life" (quoted in Campuzano, *Museo* 98). These comments tell us that today homosexuals, *travestis*, and effeminate men continue to exist outside of what is considered Peruvian national identity despite their various contributions to national society.

Museo closes this section, and the book, with information on two *travesti* candidates in the twenty-first century, one for the Andean Parliament and another one for the Peruvian Congress (121). This emphasizes the true inclusion that these citizens seek and deserve not only in Peru's social and economic life but also in politics. In short, *Museo* shows a state that has historically been incapable of, and has lacked the will to include ALL citizens—in theory, the ones who grant the state its legitimacy. We can establish, then, a continuity of the modern Peruvian state with European colonial rule (in our case, Spanish). If before independence, only heterosexual white men who owned property were granted full privileges, and all other subjects, especially Indigenous, homosexual, and *travesti* bodies, remained in the condition of "others," then after the establishment of the republic, they continued to be external to the nation. We thus see that in this archive, *Museo* denounces the exclusion, persecution, and murder of *travestis*, but also includes information that empowers and recognizes the positive presence of *travestis* in Peruvian society. Furthermore, this section shows, as Marlene Wayar explains in *Travesti: Una teoría lo su-*

ficientemente buena, that *travestis* reproduced themselves by producing "subjetividades capaces de empatizar con la otredad" (18), such as the above-mentioned Indigenous bodies.

Finally, I would like to discuss three images that *Museo* includes through which we can see how Campuzano explores a post-hegemonic vision of identity. The first image is a photographic sequence by Cecilia Noriega Bozovich titled *El ultimo Brunch* (The Last Brunch), which was part of the exhibition *Tout est fetichiste / Tout est politique* at the ICPNA Cultural Center (Lima, Peru). The panoramic photograph in the book shows a group of individuals belonging to the "lower classes" (Buntix and Torres, "Micromuseo" 22) who work in different trades, sitting in chairs decorated with bands bearing the Peruvian national colors (white and red). These individuals belong to different age groups and their traits indicate that they belong to the many different ethnic groups in Peru, without establishing any hierarchy. A *travesti* is also seen among the characters featured in the photographic sequence, precisely the author of the book, Giuseppe Campuzano. The fact that this photo includes only subjects who have been excluded from what is considered the modern Peruvian national identity can be read as a desire to transform the narrative that constitutes it and to offer a post-hegemonic version of it, through the presence of the *travesti*. Alongside this photographic sequence is an image titled *La libertad guiando al pueblo* (Freedom Guiding the People) by the Peruvian artist Jaime Higa (2003). Based on painting by Eugéne Delacroix, *La liberté guidant le peuple*, Higa uses only the female figure of freedom flying the French flag, replacing her face with that of a "male," Higa himself—emphasizing the artist's Asian features—flying the Peruvian flag. In this way, the photograph, it seems to me, destabilizes the notion of freedom in the original image, while Higa's image keeps the "female" body of freedom but replaces her face with his own, a "masculine" one. In other words, an "in-between" subject makes the Peruvian flag fly. This image explores a post-hegemonic vision of identity, recognizing the Asian population as part of Peruvian identity, stating that Peruvian people are not exclusively Indigenous, mestizos, or criollos. The fact that the "in-between" figure in the photograph is, in addition, flying the Peruvian flag indicates an intention to highlight their membership in the Peruvian nation.

One last important example of what we might call Campuzano's intention to offer a post-hegemonic vision of identity is the inclusion of a national identity document (ID) in which two overlapping photographs of the Peruvian citizen are recorded, which represents the indeterminacy of gender. This ID also shows the alterity and mobility of Peruvian identity through the presence of the "in-between," in contrast to a modernizing project that, on the basis of exclusionary and racist references to the Indigenous world and to other groups considered "different," conceived of Peruvian national identity as fixed and stable. As Campuzano points out in his article "De engendro fabuloso a performatividad creadora" (From Fabulous Engendering to Creative Performativity), the "successive transformations of the identity document itself are a comment both on the impossibility of containing identity in a fixed document, and to the very idea of unity regarding an identity that is always convoluted" (95). In this way, on account of its organization and *travesti* narrative structure, of its "in-betweenness" inasmuch as it includes different voices, languages, and sources that are changing, dissimilar, and carrying out a distortion of subjectivity, *Museo* (1) gives voice and visibility to Indigenous peoples, their popular, oral, and written manifestations, and (2) proposes an open, multiple, plural, and post-hegemonic identity that does not exclude those groups considered "different." Let us now explore how the conditions (re)established during the modernization of the Peruvian nation-state with respect to the notion of national identity and Indigenous populations, criticized and resisted by Campuzano, have evolved into a desire of the state to reduce and, in some ways, exterminate these populations.

From Emblem of the Peruvian Modern National Identity to "Terrorist"

As mentioned before, from 1980 to 2000, the Peruvian state and the Peruvian Communist Party (aka Shining Path) were involved in an internal armed conflict that left behind approximately 69,280 victims. Seventy-five percent of these victims were Indigenous Quechua-speaking people.[6] In *El tiempo del miedo: La violencia política en el Perú 1980–1996*, Nelson Manrique argues that out of these violent political circumstances a severe social crisis arose. This crisis brought to light the unresolved historical problems that faced this multiethnic society, characterized by the subjugation and domination of the Indigenous populations by the Peruvian state.

The abbreviated Report of the Truth and Reconciliation Commission states that in the conflict there was a clear relationship between social exclusion and the intensity of the violence (*Hatun Willakuy* 22) toward these "othered" populations, reinforming their lack of recognition as members of the nation. The report indicates that instead of protecting Indigenous peoples from Shining Path, the state acted as if it were protecting Peru from Indigenous populations (44). This behavior was in part due to the capital-centric military's view that these Indigenous groups were "alien to modernity" (Franco *Cruel* 7) and, thus, they were not worthy of being treated as populations to be protected.

The Peruvian Communist Party, founded in 1970 by a Huamanga University professor, Abimael Guzmán ("Presidente Gonzalo"), anticipated fifty years of armed struggle to take over power and establish a dictatorship of the proletariat, thereby inverting the logic of the national hegemonic paradigm and reformulating the terms of the republican and modernizing projects within an ultraradical framework.[7] In "Somos los iniciadores" (We Are the Initiators), a document written by Guzmán, he declares: "Centuries of hard exploitation have passed. The masses have been hit hard. They have been exploited, subjugated, implacably oppressed. But the exploited masses have always fought back through the ages. They have no desire besides class struggle. Nonetheless, the masses were always history's orphans" (quoted in Degregori, Sánchez León et al. 311). Shining Path offered the exploited masses, mainly the Indigenous peasant populations, the fulfillment of the promises of the modernizing project to achieve integration and national unity. In fact, many marginalized subjects found in their adherence to Shining Path and in their participation in the actions organized by the party a space of visibility that opened access to the political sphere, which had been historically denied to them on the basis of identity, and cultural and socioeconomic factors. Thus, what Shining Path offered for some was a viable alternative since, in a sense, it seemed able to fulfill the unmet promises of integration and unity of the nineteenth-century national project.

In light of Shining Path's first acts, President Fernando Belaúnde-Terry (1980–1985) defined his counterinsurgency policy as an "internal war" and, in essence, allowed the military to deploy at liberty all means necessary to eliminate the subversive group. Alan García Pérez (1985–1990), his successor, implemented the same counterinsurgency policy, and the human rights violations continued as paramilitary and criminal groups, such as the group that called itself Comando Rodrigo Franco, carried out a series of clandestine killings to combat and eliminate the rebels.[8] Such incursions as well as the multiple massacres of peasants carried out by agents of the Peruvian Armed Forces during Garcia's first administration, which they defined as "armed clashes with subversive criminals" (Manrique 122), contributed to the general population's weakening respect for the state.

While many actions took place in remote regions, the uprisings in the Lima prisons of Santa Barbara, Lurigancho, and El Frontón on June 18, 1986, and the government response to them made more evident how much the human rights situation in the country had deteriorated. The government murdered three hundred prisoners who had taken a group of hostages and were demanding improvements in the quality of daily life. This event was deemed a genocide organized directly by Alan García (*Hatun Willakuy* 231).

On the other hand, it should be mentioned that in the first two years of his administration, García enjoyed great popularity, and there was a sense that the country was entering a new political phase. In the next three years, however, García proved how wrong this perception had been. Peru experienced unprecedented hyperinflation, in addition to the expansion of the subversive front, the violation of human rights by state forces, urban crime, and corruption. The García administration ended in a severe crisis of the state as a system of institutions and practices, which is what Alberto Fujimori promised to "reconstruct" or transform when he came to power (Degregori, *La década* 305).

When Fujimori assumed the presidency in 1990, the country was suffering the consequences of Alan García's government. Peru was going through an acute political, economic, and social crisis, with a state of emergency declared in sixty-five provinces and one district; the Peruvian state was about to collapse (*Hatun Willakuy* 310). As Cecilia Blondet argues, "In the face of hyperinflation, terrorism, the crisis in leadership and authority at the beginning of the decade, people lost their sense of security and self-esteem and found in Fujimori a protector to whom they surrendered unconditionally" (59). The end of García's first term, therefore, had produced an economic crisis in Peru and also a crisis of political representativity, of cultural communication, and moral authority. Fujimori's rise to the presidency of Peru was possible, according to Carlos Iván Degregori, due to this widespread crisis of the country, politics, and parties (*La década* 22). Fujimori presented himself as an outsider, a nonpartisan politician, who was not contaminated by association with established Peruvian institutions and who had emerged from ordinary people to offer Peru a new alternative (Roberts 287).[9]

Fujimori's rule was authoritarian and violated the rule of law; frauds, irregularities, and abuses were rampant. He was corrupt to a degree rarely seen before in the history of the republic (*Hatun Willakuy* 309). For example, Fujimori tasked the military with counterinsurgency, and enforced a decree stating that members of the military would not be tried in civilian courts for human rights violations, thus granting them immunity and enabling them to engage in open repression without any consequences (Klarén 232).[10] Fujimori's government also adopted selective elimination procedures and other forms of human rights violations (*Hatun Willakuy* 313). Such is the case known as "La Cantuta." On July 18, 1992, there was a military incursion into the student residence of La Cantuta University that ended with the abduction and disappearance of nine students and a professor. This operation was carried out by the Grupo Colina squadron, which before Fujimori's self-coup had carried out a massacre in the Center of Lima, in Barrios Altos (*Hatun Willakuy* 319–20).

As has been widely documented regarding the management of the armed conflict during the Fujimori administrations, the state and its representatives perpetrated numerous atrocities, especially against Quechua-speaking Indigenous peoples. During those years, it was common to argue that the demographic growth of Indigenous and, in general, poor people constituted an obstacle to national progress. Indigenous peoples, especially the Quechua-speaking, were not only seen as dangerous and impossible to assimilate but were also regarded as an obstacle to the development and modernization of the country.[11] In that same vein, the Fujimori regime considered racial and linguistic heterogeneity a threat, the very same heterogeneity that was used as a starting point for the construction of the stereotype of the terrorist, the subversive, or—more popularly—the *senderista*. The image that had the greatest effect on the imaginary of the upper and middle urban social classes and even some sectors of the popular classes around the *senderista* was that of the "resentful *cholo*," that is, the peasant migrant who moves to the cities looking for better opportunities and who, in spite of having studied, cannot move up the social ladder, and therefore acts out their frustration against "decent people" (Silva Santisteban 82).[12] Thus, the final report of the Truth and Reconciliation Commission notes that members of the Peruvian Armed Forces selected potential suspects according to a "prototype of the *senderista*." The testimony of a detainee included in the report highlights this prototype: "The policemen told me that my background was ideal for becoming a member of Shining Path: I was the son of Ayacucho parents, spoke Quechua more or less fluently, studied at UNMSM [Universidad Mayor de San Marcos] and lived in Callao" (*Hatun Willakuy* 57). The Quechua-speaking Indigenous person, linked to the remote mountains, was/is the suspicious, rejected, and persecuted Other. They constituted the subjects who had to be watched for their potential adherence to Shining Path, which threatened the survival of the Peruvian nation.

Fujimori presented racial and linguistic heterogeneity as suspicious in order to manipulate and enhance fear and insecurity in Peru in the 1990s. This was part of a strategy to perpetuate his authoritarian and corrupt regime. This treatment of heterogeneity was related to Fujimori's neoliberal form of government, in which a suspect—any Quechua-speaking Indigenous person deemed a potential terrorist—was considered more dangerous than any enemy. In this regard, Jo-Marie Burt points out that fear was the main driver for manipulating Peruvian society. She mentions that while conducting interviews in various marginalized neighborhoods of Lima, an interviewee stated that she and the others in her community did not protest against Fujimori's government and his outrages because it was known that "whoever speaks out is a terrorist" ("'Quien habla'" 34). Fear was used to raise suspicions about the Other. In Peru, this activated acute social segmentation by class and race.[13]

Fujimori, who had promised to bring peace and order back to Peru and to combat Shining Path "with a heavy hand," waged a sustained campaign of state terrorism during his two presidential terms. In this period, ethnic, racial, and linguistic heterogeneity was portrayed as suspicious, and the culture of fear was intensified, as numerous violations of human rights were committed, mostly against those citizens whose social, racial, linguistic, and economic background limited their chances of being heard. A particular aspect of the atrocities committed during the internal armed conflict were the acts of sexual and physical violence that members of the Peruvian Armed Forces, in the name of state security, perpetrated against alleged terrorists and innocent women, mostly members of Indigenous communities. In the next section we will see how this specific aspect of state terror under Fujimori is addressed by Claudia Salazar in her novel, *La sangre de la aurora*.[14]

Female Resistance and State Extermination during the Peruvian Internal Armed Conflict

In the context of the Peruvian internal armed conflict, several literary texts were published that were eventually categorized as "Peruvian literature on the violent years."[15] Since 2010 new novels, testimonies, and short stories have been published. Using new narrative techniques, these texts continue inquiring as to the causes and consequences of the conflict, but, I argue, some recent publications offer additional insights, such as Claudia Salazar's *La sangre de la aurora*, which tells about the personal tragedies of three women during the conflict.[16] This is the first Peruvian novel that "breaks with certain conventions that have become too simplistic and opens up a space for a plurality of female subjects that enter the social and political scene . . . their voices show the presence of women where dominant discourses gloss them over or relegate them to the most domestic of places, to the silent kitchen in the battlefield" (Eltit 202). Eltit's quote alludes to the fact that in Salazar's book we listen to the histories, voices, and memories of Indigenous, Quechua-speaking, lesbian, guerrilla, and peasant women, which makes *La sangre de la aurora* multilayered and multitextured. This allows Salazar to show the complexity of experiences that we could group under the term "subaltern subjects" during the internal conflict, from an intersectional perspective. Following Antonio Gramsci's definition of subalterns as individuals who belong to those groups in society that are subordinated and oppressed by the ruling classes (253), subaltern subjects may include peasants, workers, and other groups denied access to "hegemonic" power. These subaltern subjects appear in novels about the Peruvian internal conflict like *The Blue Hour* (2012) by Alonso Cueto, *Death in the Andes* (1993) by Mario Vargas Llosa, or *Un lugar llamado Oreja de Perro* (2008) by Ivan Thays. However, the subjects are portrayed from a hegemonic position that reproduces the official discourses constructed around the conflict. For instance, the Indigenous Other—especially women—is represented as archaic and dangerous or, conversely, as a passive victim.[17] What distinguishes Salazar's novel is that it presents the voice of the subaltern subjects—Indigenous, Quechua-speaking, lesbian, guerrilla, and peasant women—not as needing salvation but as capable of agency and self-empowerment. The book allows us, as Ranajit Guha would put it, to "listen to the small voice of history," the voice of subaltern subjects that are never represented or included in official historical narratives as active, narrative agents (quoted in Beverley 305).

Moreover, the book offers a post-hegemonic version of the conflict. As Gareth Williams explains, the post-hegemonic "permits us to give a name to hegemony's subaltern residues, negative languages, fragmentary responses, cultural leftovers, and fissured experiences" (*The Other Side* 327). The enunciating voices in Salazar's text—of Indigenous, Quechua-speaking, lesbian, guerrilla, and peasant women—would be part of "hegemony's subaltern residues." Therefore, they produce a negative language, which, as we will see, allows me to discuss how the subjugation and domination of the Indigenous populations during the formation of the modern Peruvian nation-state evolved into a desire of the state to reduce and, in some ways, exterminate these populations.

La sangre de la aurora presents an "in-between" narrative that uses (1) a language that is different from the hegemonic one, because it does not follow spelling or grammatical rules, (2) an interior monologue that is interrupted by a narrative in the third person that questions the authority of the omniscient narrator at the same time that it prevents the construction of subjectivity, and (3) a narrative that is fragmented and nonlinear, that presents its memories piecemeal without informing the reader as to which of the three main characters is speaking. In this sense, we see a similarity to what Claudia Rodríguez, Pedro Lemebel, and Sofía Devenir do in their texts. They share with Salazar the use of an "in-between" narrative but with different purposes in terms of each book's overarching argument. All of them, though, are in my opinion interested in historizing experiences, especially those that have been made invisible by official discourses. Rodríguez and Devenir's works clearly relay *travesti* experiences, and Lemebel's work, we could say, relays the same in part. As I will try to explain in what follows, the use of an "in-between" narrative by Salazar has the purpose of structuring the armed conflict from a gendered and racialized position that is focused on a specific context, which is that of the Peruvian internal conflict. This implies forcing the reader to pay close attention to the narrative, emphasizing that the memories the narrative describes are both individual and common, distinctly personal yet somehow representative of experiences lived by many others. This is translated in an indeterminacy of subjectivity and the impossibility of constructing a clear narrative self through the book's narrative, which is supported by the use of a language that erases the "masculine/feminine" normative gender distinction.

Claudia Salazar Jiménez, a queer writer and scholar of color, is originally from Lima, Peru, although she now resides in New York City. She studied literature at the Universidad Nacional Mayor de San Marcos and holds a PhD in Latin American literature from New York University. She is the editor of two anthologies, *Voces para Lilith: Literatura Contemporánea de Temática Lésbica en Sudamérica* (2011), and *Escribir en Nueva York: Antología de narradores hispanoamericanos* (2014). Her short fiction has been published in several anthologies and journals. In 2016 she published *Coordenadas Temporales*, a book of short stories. *La sangre de la aurora*, published in 2013 and translated into English by Elizabeth Bryer as *Blood of the Dawn* (Deep Vellum 2016), was awarded the prestigious Premio de las Americas in 2014, establishing Salazar as a new voice on issues surrounding the effects of armed conflict on Indigenous populations and women. The novel follows three women whose lives intertwine and are ripped apart during the Peruvian internal armed conflict, because of its violence against women, especially those who are Indigenous peasant and Quechua-speaking. Thus, as we will see, although these three women come from different worlds, they all suffered the violence produced by a hypermasculine and racist state, "which had as its epicenter the lateral body of the peasant. Peasants become the site of experiences that operate as annihilating impulses" (Eltit 201).

In *Blood of the Dawn*, Melanie is a lesbian photographer in love with a female artist who has moved to France. She lives in a big city, but travels to different small villages located in the mountains to document the atrocities occurring there. In these travels, Melanie gets to see what the government is keeping from the public. Facing the horror, she reflects: "Sometimes I'd rather not look, I wish the camera would bear sole witness. The frame will shout what is sooner stifled. . . . May eyes smell all this and feel the smoke clearing to reveal what I want and don't want to keep seeing. May my camera see it" (Salazar 63). Despite—and maybe because of—her class and race privilege, Melanie experiences sexual and physical abuse by members of a communist group—presumably Shining Path.

Modesta, the second main character, is an Indigenous peasant who lives in a tiny village located in the mountains. She is a devoted mother and wife who is happy raising her family and breeding guinea pigs. We learn that members of Shining Path and also those from the Peruvian Armed Forces invaded Modesta's land, killing her loved ones and raping her. The final character, Marcela, is a poor teacher of Indigenous descent who is frustrated by the oppressions suffered by Peruvian peasants and other minorities. In response, she leaves her family to join a guerrilla group, seduced by the promises of the revolution. The novel narrates her experiences as a member of this group, showing us Marcela's metamorphosis as she exerts the violence required to become an active member of the insurgent group: "My hands demanded the revolver I had been assigned to liberate the wounded from their last breath. As if my fingers had lengthened and were injected into the temples of the wretched. Bullet fingers. Gun-barrel arms. Revolver body" (Salazar 34).

The stories of these three women converge in a series of violent experiences at the hands of the guerrilla group and the state, rewriting the Peruvian internal armed conflict from their own perspective. It is important to note in these stories that each woman is part of not one but two oppressed minority groups. Focusing on Modesta and Marcela for the purposes of this chapter, the fact that both women are poor and Indigenous is crucial to my analysis, because during the internal armed conflict women in general, and Quechua-speaking Indigenous women in particular, represented a special target for members of the Peruvian Armed Forces, who abused them physically and sexually (Degregori, Sánchez León et al. 346).

Although this situation was to be found throughout the country and all armed groups participating in the conflict had a shared responsibility, 83 percent of the cases of sexual violence are attributed to agents of the Peruvian state (Henríquez Ayin 84). As scholars have noted (Rocío Silva Santisteban, Iván Degregori, Jean Franco), the sexual violence exerted by members of the Peruvian Armed Forces was a racialized violence, as white women did not experience this kind of treatment. This assertion is based on the experiences of females suspected of being members of Shining Path; they were insulted with racial slurs as they were mistreated, tortured, and raped. Members of the Peruvian Armed Forces would call them "chola asquerosa, chola de mierda, india bruta" while raping them (Wiese). Although it is difficult to do justice to these insults in translation, roughly speaking, they are something like, "disgusting half-breed, shitty half-breed, stupid Indian." The use of these slurs indicates that state agents intensified the use of violence when attacking Quechua-speaking Indigenous women, that is, those who belonged to a different region, subaltern ethnic group, or economic and cultural formation. During the administration of Alberto Fujimori, these groups were considered suspicious and dangerous.

Many of these women, regardless of whether they were members of Shining Path or not, threatened the social norm that assigned a passive role to Peruvian women in general, but even more so to Indigenous Quechua-speakers. In the context of the internal armed conflict, women not only "worked as men," but "became male," both regarding physical work and in the settlement of everyday conflicts. "Being male" involved doing armed surveillance, an act that was far removed from the normative perception of what a woman was supposed to be in Peru (Henríquez Ayin 63). However, the women associated with Shining Path posed the greatest threat to this normative perception, since many women played a leading role within the movement. As a former Shining Path militant argues, joining the group allowed them to break with the exploitation they were subjected to by men, the state, and the Church, which is why, she believes, they were made to appear especially monstrous (24). This rebellion against male domination also made insurgent women a target for agents of the Peruvian Armed Forces.

With Jean Franco, Giulia Tamayo, Kimberly Theidon, and Rocío Silva Santisteban, I believe that the physical and sexual violations perpetrated against these women involved a will to exterminate the Quechua-speaking Indigenous population. This is especially evident if we consider, as explained by Bülent Diken and Carsten B. Laustsen, that, in the case of wartime sexual abuse, the soldier attacks a woman who is a civilian (not another combatant or male soldier) to generate trauma and destroy family ties and collective solidarity within the enemy camp (111). What Diken and Laustsen point out suggests that violence against Quechua-speaking Indigenous women was exerted with the intention of damaging and destroying ties, links, and solidarity networks that sustained their communities, while making women abject subjects. Silva Santisteban refers to this process as "symbolic trashing," because within the communities these women became "leftover human beings, who clog the fluidity of a symbolic system and must therefore be resignified outside it" (71). Sexually abused women become unsuitable for marriage or motherhood because the community condemns them, thus affecting their reproduction and the perpetuation of communities. It must be highlighted here that for the people of the Andes, honor is related to the integrity of the family and the community (Franco, *Cruel* 89), so sexually attacking these women also damages the honor of their families and the entire community. Furthermore, in many cases, these rapes resulted in physical damage that prevented these women from ever reproducing, thus affecting the birth rate of the Quechua-speaking Indigenous population.

The Peruvian state's willingness to exterminate the Quechua-speaking Indigenous population was also felt in other forms of sexual violence practiced by the Fujimori regime in the name of development and progress. I am referring here, more concretely, to the forced interventions of surgical contraception under the National Program for Reproductive Health and Family Planning (PNSRPF 1996–2000), which involved the permanent alteration of the bodies of 270,000 Quechua-speaking Indigenous women (Theidon 16). As shown in the research carried out by Giulia Tamayo, a lawyer and human rights researcher during the Fujimori administrations, surgical contraception interventions were organized in order to dramatically decrease the birth rate in Peru's most impoverished Quechua-speaking Indigenous areas.[18] These interventions clearly violated the right to decide and the reproductive health of the poorest members of the population. In 1996 several local women's and human rights organizations reported these abuses, and in 1997 the first complaints were filed with the Ombudsman's Office. They pointed out the pressures that were imposed on health personnel at the time to meet quotas for increasing surgical contraception in different urban and rural localities in Peru. This revealed the existence of numerical targets set by the political-administrative health authority with respect to such procedures (Tamayo 16). Staff were given monetary incentives to recruit more women. Those who recruited women who would be subjected to a surgical contraception process received between 10 and 13 soles (5 or 6 dollars) for each woman (57).

Jo-Marie Burt traces back the origin of these surgical contraception procedures to a report called "Coup Plan," written by a select group of military officers in the 1980s. The authors of this report stated that Peru's most serious problem was that its demographic trends since World War II had reached epidemic proportions. Hence, they suggested, there was a need to immediately reduce population growth. The report concluded by indicating that the most convenient method to solve this problem would be the generalized use of sterilization among the culturally and economically underdeveloped and impoverished groups, which in Peru coincided with the Quechua-speaking Indigenous peoples (Burt, "Sterilization" 2). Notably, to confront what was purportedly an overpopulation problem in Peru, the solution they put forward was the reduction of the sector of the population considered less productive, because it was considered racially, linguistically, and economically "inferior" to the rest. This same population was associated with social disorder, criminality and, as we have seen, terrorism. Thus, forced interventions of surgical contraception and sexual rape of Indigenous Quechua-speaking women during the internal armed conflict are an expression of the state's desire to exterminate these populations.

Before the publication of *La sangre de la aurora*, cultural objects dealing with the internal conflict had not directly addressed the relationship between race, ethnicity, and gendered violence.[19] This mixing of racial, ethnic, and gendered violence on the part of the government-sanctioned military shows how the Peruvian state considered its Indigenous subjects to be, as Franco notes, "alien to modernity" (*Cruel*

7) and not worthy of being protected. The novel goes even further to show how the sexual violence practiced toward Quechua-speaking Indigenous women was deliberate and went beyond the ostensible purpose of eradicating Shining Path. It had the intention of breaking apart the Indigenous populations as a whole, since they were not really incorporated into the state's modernizing goals. The rapes, as portrayed by Salazar, show a desire to damage and destroy the bonds that held Indigenous communities together, turning their women into abject subjects. This is especially addressed in the book through the character of Modesta, who was repeatedly raped by members of the army who arrived in her village to "take it back" from the guerrillas. After her experience, Modesta is excluded by her female peers, and rejected by men who considered her "damaged." Modesta is thus isolated and decides to leave her village and live with other women who have gone through the same experience of rape.

What makes *La sangre de la aurora* so important is not only its political critique of the government-sanctioned violence, a critique that parallels the work that anthropologists have already done, but also its depiction of the ways in which this violence was resisted. Unlike other narratives dealing with this period of Peruvian history, Salazar's violated subjects are never completely stripped of their agency. Rather, their agency is affirmed when the women make small decisions for themselves. Marcela decides to join the guerrillas and she successfully assumes one of the main positions in the group; Melanie leaves her bubble of privilege and comfort where Indigenous peasants are considered "the worst" (Salazar, *Blood* 42); and Modesta, who, against her will, was not allowed to go to school—because her father "didn't want [her] to. What for. She should see to the smallholding, or learn to weave. When she marries, her husband will take care of everything" (53)—leaves her village to join other women in a new community: "I grab the pot of boiling soup and pour it over his parts. He screams as if his soul is escaping him. His rifle has fallen down, and we lift it to strike him across the head. *So you're not so brave after all, little soldier. You're not going to do any of that rotten business to anyone else, you swine.* He has fainted. We leave him lying there. *Let's leave, mamachas, let's get out of here.* They follow me; we'll continue on together. I hold tight to the rifle" (87). The novel emphasizes that the subaltern, as Dipesh Chakrabarty would put it, "is the maker of his own destiny" (22), also portraying the possibility of constituting a different kind of community.

Beyond the storyline of empowered women who were once victims or passive subjects, *La sangre de la aurora* offers another strategy of resistance that is based on the nature of the literary text itself. Salazar's "in-between" narrative stands against traditional/hegemonic writing of the internal armed conflict, suggesting that thinking and writing about the violence in that period requires not only telling different stories but also telling them in different ways, in different languages. For instance, the novel uses an interior monologue that is interrupted by a narrative in the third person:

> She was more settled now so I left her with the other little ones and joined the community members to discuss the upcoming projects. They needed a network of potable water, drainage and public lighting to cover at least ten streets. They had also asked the municipality for a health post with basic services and for a school to be built. Education is fundamental to breaking free from the structural inequalities that social organization is founded on; without it, the potential of change *Mami!!!* is practically non-existent. My years of experience as an educator give me the authority to confirm *Mamiiiiiiii!!!!!* that without the appropriate level of *Señora Marcela, your daughter!* (Salazar 7)

Also, *La sangre de la aurora* uses a fragmented narrative that is interrupted and nonlinear, as we see in the following passage:

> Dah dit dah dit behind dah he snaps his fingers liquor in his blood everyone in the capital dah dit dah dit he dances with three of them now it's down to two he dances with her applause she straightens her hair dum dum dum do you remember how it went? She raises heer arms dum dum dum crosses

> her legs dah dit dit dit spins spins spins everyone else applauds smiles sings they think we're in the mountains let's dance dum dum dum spin again dum dum move your feet they look at each other smile he she three now two all the women want to dance with the leader they dance circle of comrades mao lenin marx wath us from their position on the wall dah dit dit dit it your all comrades applause now everyone hold hands dah dit dum dum holding on out in foot forward foot back to the side moving forward in a circle dum leadership dum leader and another comrade singing applause applause applause dum dum dum jump jump jump everyone in a circle look at the camera dum dum in hiding jubilant. (82)

This fragmented, interrupted, nonlinear narrative erases the "masculine-feminine" genders. For instance, the above quote does not give a specific gender to the voices speaking and those among them being interrupted. Furthermore, the narrative presents its memories piecemeal without informing the reader as to which of the three women the pieces belong. This has the effect of forcing the reader to pay close attention to the narrative, but it also emphasizes that these memories are both individual and common, distinctly individual yet somehow representative of many. Moreover, the novel presents these stories in a way that purposefully resists normative grammar. Sentences are long with no periods or commas. It is a fluid narrative that includes onomatopoeia and metaphors. As Eltit puts it, Salazar's narrative "disrupts grammar, changes the rules, and turns onomatopoeia into a patrimony to highlight the mental noises that inhabit the bodies when language fails in the communicative act" (203), as we can see in the following passage:

> how many were there it hardly matters twenty came thirty say those who got away counting is useless crack machete blade a divided chest crack no more milk another one falls machete knife dagger stone sling crack my daughter crack my brother crack my husband crack my mother crack exposed flesh broken

> neck machete eyeball crack femur tibia fibula crack faceless earless noseless swallow it crack right now eat it up pick the ear up off the floor don't spit it out don't crack five put them in a line machete crack blood soup spattering making mud their boots slipping comrade crack screaming screeching machete bones crack just ten were enough. (Salazar 10)

This way of narrating in a nonlinear fashion is transgressive because of its repetitions, and its grammatical and spelling mistakes. In this sense it parallels the act of memory itself, because it "designates an area of voluntary and involuntary associations . . . that are conceived as incomplete formations" (Richard, "La crítica" 16). This (post-hegemonic) memory of the internal armed conflict not only offers up memories through multiple perspectives via three separate protagonists but also never allows the reader to be completely sure of the source of the information they are receiving. The narrative makes it impossible to trace a specific and conclusive origin for the stories, suggesting that they could belong to any of the three, and thereby impeding the construction of a clear narrative self. This is the case in the following passage:

> blackout total darkness Where was it all? All over Where did it come from? High tension towers fell to their knees bombs explode all raze blast burst Were you with the group? Cocking at home while I waited for my husband blackout typing up the meeting's minutes blackout developing some photos blackout get candles I don't have enough six pages two towers the outskirts of the capital What did you say? you can't sign comrade darkness excluded from history submit or blow up bomb Did you find out what they did? wow you cleaned your whole plate smile no candles eat here towers they say now more time more towers. (Salazar 5)

With this repetition of the exact phrasing at various intervals along with its refusal to assign origin to one individual or another, the book presents collective experiences more than individual ones, speaking from the "we" rather than the "I." Moreover, the voices of the three main characters intertwine with others, with witnesses, the innocent, and the different victims and perpetuators of the acts of violence that are included in the book, as we note in the following quote:

> The bonds strengthen like this bloody womb everyone together we're all one inside her she who won't look at us now or talk now soaked bloody chest the women everyone brothers everyone the entire troop in her in them in the whores the Indians the terrorists the journalists the daughters the mothers all of them it grows more until what point it looks like it's not enough it grows it hardens on everyone everyone huge and hard present your identity card open her divide her slice her penetrate her cut her everyone brothers just a hole that's what they're for rip into it break it your turn you and you and him and him and them everyone brothers ranks comrade soldier combatant drive into her sergeant revolution army committee navy it grows more a bit of fun it grows more we multiply in the pampa the mountains huge like the hills we burst in river emptied joint forces we divide the mountain we fracture the dawn we penetrate the land we slash the sky we open everything up nothing is closed to us we're brothers. (Salazar 79)

Salazar, like Lemebel, constructs a narrative that does not involve a clear individual self. The novel builds a communitarian experience of the internal armed conflict where, as Espósito notes, "the common removes what is properly one's own . . . that invests and decenters the proprietary subject, forcing him to take leave . . . of himself, to alter himself" (7). Salazar's "in-between" narrative addresses the general state of violence in Peru that was both specific to individuals and pervasive throughout society through a narrative that is fragmented and nonlinear, that presents its memories piecemeal without informing the reader as to which of the three main characters the pieces belong, that does not follow spelling or grammatical rules, and that erases the "masculine-feminine" gender distinctions. This is the case in the following passage, which describes a rape scene. This same paragraph is repeated verbatim throughout the book to narrate the rape of the three main characters: "She was a lump on the floor. It didn't matter what her name was, they were only interested in the two holes she had. Sheer emptiness to be filled up. No questions or need for replies. They knew all there was to know about this lump. But really, she meant nothing to them. Her four limbs were enough: with them she could be held down, immobilized, restrained. They wore rifles and the same clothes as the campesinos. With balaclavas or kerchiefs covering their faces. It was all the same, she was just a lump" (Salazar 70). Significantly, the moment of rape is described identically for each of the three characters, with differences only in the insults and slurs addressed at them as their bodies are being violated. What could appear as an isolated, personal experience is shown to be collective and systematic. The act is always the same; and the insults, rather than a recognition of the individuality of each woman, are a way of turning them into the collective body of the enemy, of justifying the rape, of blaming her for it. For example, when violence is inflicted against Melanie, it seems that the fact that she is a white, middle-upper-class woman is the reason she is being physically and sexually abused: "Blows on the face, abdomen; legs stretched out to infinity. *White traitor.* They line up to enjoy their part in the spectacle. No orifice is spared in this bloody dance. *Anticummunist journalist, we'll make an example of you for any others who come around here.* Only pain in this lump, like a tightened knot that could never come undone. How much longer could they keep it up? If only they'd stop now. Stop, stop, stop" (Salazar 70). When violence is inflicted against Marcela, it is her adherence to the guerrilla group that causes the violence: "Blows on the face, abdomen; legs stretched out to infinity. *Fucking terrorist.* They line up to enjoy their part in the spectacle. No orifice is spared in this bloody dance. *Fucking subversive.* Only pain in this lump, like a tightened knot that could never come undone. How much longer could they keep it up? If only they'd stop now. Stop, stop, stop" (Salazar 73). And, when violence is inflicted against Modesta, it is her ethnicity and race that causes the violence: "Blows on the face, abdomen; legs stretched out to infinity. *Fucking mountain whore.* They line up to enjoy their part in the spectacle. No orifice is spared in this bloody dance. *Lousy Indian.* Only pain in this lump, like a tightened knot that could never come undone. How much longer could they keep it up? If only they'd stop now. Stop, stop, stop" (Salazar 74). In *La sangre de la aurora*, the voices of the main characters of the narrative—the voices that narrate it—are those normally excluded and marginalized in the construction of historical and literary discourses regarding the conflict. In Salazar's novel, Indigenous, Quechua-speaking, lesbian, guerrilla, and peasant women become central in the world of the text and, therefore, in the world of the reader. We are invited to experience the catastrophe of this violent period from a plurality of perspectives allowing us to see different versions and histories about the conflict, because as the novel points out, "We live many voices so many too many all of it" (Salazar 98).

Salazar's narrative gives us insight into the ways in which the subjugation and domination of the Indigenous populations during the formation of the modern Peruvian nation-state have evolved into a desire of the state to reduce and, in some ways, exterminate these populations. But it does much more: *La sangre de la aurora* produces a post-hegemonic memory of the Peruvian internal armed conflict. The use of a fragmented narrative and the intertwining of heterogenous and non-hegemonic voices—Indigenous, Quechua-speaking, lesbian, guerrilla, and peasant women along with others, those of witnesses, the innocent, and the different victims—allow the construction of a communitarian reality that destroys the construction of a hegemonic history, of a hegemonic truth about this conflict. Moreover, it reflects on the devastating reality of violence, a reality that cannot be revisited or narrated from a regular/normative language that is expressed in terms of wholeness. This is also how we remember this violence, which comes to us in trace residues, just as Salazar inscribes it in *La sangre de la aurora*.

EPILOGUE

An Invitation to Opening

> Si las humanidades tienen algún futuro como crítica cultural y si la crítica cultural tiene hoy alguna tarea, es sin duda la de devolvernos a lo humano allí donde no esperamos hallarlo.
>
> —Judith Butler

While preparing the second draft of this manuscript, incorporating suggestions from my anonymous readers and editor, I noted a repeated theme in all the reports, "This manuscript needs more of the author's own voice." For someone who learned, through years and years of sexual molestation as a child, that her voice did not matter, incorporating my voice has been a difficult task. Nevertheless, through the interviews I conducted for this book with *travestis*, nonbinary or genderqueer, and trans people from Peru, Chile, and the United States, I learned firsthand about courage, survival, risk, and creativity. In a way, we might say that my interviewees motivated and pushed me to release my voice from its enclosure. Now, as I look at the final version of this book, I understand that this liberation was what allowed me to cocreate a *Language of the In-Between.* It let me tell the story of how recent trans, *travesti*, and sexually dissident artists, writers, performers, intellectuals, and activists in Chile and Peru have been challenging the normative regime of subjectivity, in particular during the periods of military rule and internal armed conflict. I said "cocreate" because this book and these ideas are mine and are not mine. They are the result of the encounter of different languages and life experiences that, in dialogue, have given birth to what you have just read.

In traversing my own limits and those imposed by others, I came to understand the importance of voices, my own included, when telling my story. But I also realized that I needed to find my voice when telling others' stories too. Finding and embracing my own academic voice while writing this book meant maturing as a scholar and understanding that, if I am going to continue developing a career that addresses how subaltern subjects, like Indigenous women, queer/*cuir* people, and the dispossessed, empower themselves to confront hegemonic society, I must bring their voices directly to my pages, as well as to my classes. This is what I have tried to do in *Language of the In-Between*, just as other *cuir*/queer colleagues who have inspired me have done in their own work; I refer to individuals such as Lawrence La-Fountain-Stokes, Joseph Pierce, Diego Falconí, Héctor Domínguez Ruvalcaba, Fernando Blanco, and Carl Fischer, among others. Through their work, these *cuir*/queer scholars, some of whom are also Latinoamericanistas or Latin American literary and cultural critics, have been calling for a change in the Latin American literary, cultural, and *cuir*/queer academy, and the academy in general. Such a change aims to center the direct voices of the individuals so that we do not simply *study* them but *dialogue with* them in the pages we write and, of course, the classes we teach.

Cuir/queer studies and Latin American literary and cultural studies do not always include individuals or subaltern subjects as objects of study, but as Gustavo Verdesio points out, "They [we] are always, studying texts that either produce subalternity (because of their endorsement of the official narratives of nationhood) or represent it in various derogatory ways: either as background (almost like part of the landscape or decorative folklore) or as a lack that should be eliminated in order for progress to develop" (29–30). With this in mind, I would like to enter into dialogue now with Verdesio's introduction to the 2005 *Dispostio/n* issue devoted to the Latin American Subaltern Studies (LASS) group cited above. This essay touches on some concepts that are key to what I want to propose in this Epilogue; that is, the building of a much-needed bridge/dialogue between *Cuir*/queer studies and Latin American subaltern and post-hegemonic studies.

In reviewing the life and "death" of the LASS group, Verdesio mentions in his introduction the ideological and theoretical confrontations inside the group that, supposedly, led to internal conflicts, because "there was a core of people more interested in social activism (or in understanding the subaltern as a real-life, social subject) and another sector of the group that favored a more philosophical approach to subalternity" (11). In this context, Verdesio quotes Ileana Rodríguez, who stated that "the question was whether or not we could really limit ourselves to thinking the subaltern solely as a metaphor or negation and limit of hegemonic knowledge or whether we were willing to seriously entertain the agency of flesh and blood sufferers" ("A New Debate" 15). I do not want to intervene in this old debate. However, I will note that looking at the work published by the members of the so-called more philosophical approach to subalternity and how it has inspired generations of young scholars, including myself, to be deconstructionist or to be more preoccupied by theoretical and philosophical issues, does not cancel a concern for "the flesh-and-blood subaltern" (Verdesio 12). Rather, we can explore the two approaches as they manifest in myriad ways. Besides, as Verdesio comments in his introduction, he and Bruno Bosteels consider that "we do not need to choose between the two forms of subalternism, but to seek a harmonic combination of both" (34).

This harmonic combination is one that, humbly, I have tried to practice in the *Language of the In-Between*. In this work, I have centered and dialogued with the direct (new) voices of what we could call "*cuir*/queer subaltern subjects," such as Sofía Devenir, Claudia Rodríguez, and Héctor Acuña. I have considered their voices along with the work of more canonical *cuir*/queer writers and performers such as Pedro Lemebel and José Donoso, and other noncanonical ones such as Giuseppe Campuzano and Claudia Salazar, using philosophical and theoretical frames. While writing with and about them, especially Rodríguez, Devenir and Acuña, I have attempted, as Verdesio advises, "to bring subalterns, or their opinions, to academia, in order to get their input about our research agendas so that they can be a part of the process of shaping them" (30). I also hope to have practiced what Alvaro Felix Bolaño, quoted in Verdesio's introduction, proposes: "To bring the subaltern (the real person, flesh and blood) to the university . . . a milieu that has almost always been deaf to their message" (Verdesio 30–31). This was my aim in including their own plural definitions of what a *travesti* is and how their own life experiences and survival strategies, formulated and explained directly by them, could and should inform our research and teaching. By dialoguing with and studying these Peruvian and Chilean artists, writers, performers, intellectuals, and activists within a subalternist and post-hegemonic theoretical frame, I have tried to manifest "the subaltern as a real-life, social subject" but also, to consider their subalternity from a philosophical perspective. Moreover, in this book I have expressed that the life experiences and survival strategies of these artists, writers, performers, intellectuals, and activists, especially those of "c*uir*/queer subaltern" subjects and *travestis*, are in themselves producers of knowledge and theory that complement the conceptualizations and theorizations of the cultural critics and academics I have included in this book. This positioning is an invitation to rethink and listen to those voices that are often left out of discussion and denied recognition not only in our societies but also, sadly, in the academy, where the direct voice of the (subaltern) subjects we work with has been dismissed or these subjects have been used merely as discursive figures. In this sense, I align with Verdesio's thought that "without a basic respect for the oppressed and their knowledges, it will be impossible to take their contribution to humankind seriously. This respect should be the point of departure of our research, understood less as a merely academic enterprise than as de-totalizing practice of solidarity with the Other" (33).

Dialoguing with the direct voices of "c*uir*/queer subaltern subjects," such as Devenir, Rodríguez, and Acuña within philosophical and theoretical frames (subaltern, deconstructionist, and post-hegemony) has allowed me to question the fields of Latin American *cuir*/queer studies and Latin American literature and culture. This, in turn has allowed me to question the hegemony of Pedro Lemebel's work as the prime example of sexual and gender dissidence in Chile, as well as in Latin America in the 1990s and 2000s. Again, I am not underestimating the great and powerful work of Lemebel, but I think that the work we undertake in *cuir*/queer studies must advance the inclusion of the direct and material experiences of other sexual and gender dissidents, such as *travestis*. I mean that building a bridge/dialogue between Latin American subaltern, post-hegemonic studies and *cuir*/queer studies can lead us to new and innovative perspectives of thinking.

This positioning has also allowed me to question the field of Latin America literary and cultural studies, which, in the many theoretical approaches that apply when engaging with a cultural object, disregards theoretical approaches such as those offered by Latin American subaltern, post-hegemonic studies and *cuir*/queer studies. For instance, why are there no serious critiques of Arguedas's homophobia as expressed in his literary work and how is this homophobia entangled with the indigenista project? This could have been asked by and in literary and cultural analysis, but it has been disregarded. Thus, Arguedas adopts a mestizo and heterosexual gender perspective as an important part of national identity, as did many of his contemporaries, which then justifies his homophobia and his portrayal of the Andean or Quechua world as heterosexual.

Moreover, the introduction to Verdesio's volume states that "there is a lot left to do with regards to both the knowledge we produce in universities and what we do with it." To this I would add several questions regarding what he calls "the knowledge we produce in universities, which came to my mind while listening to the work and the direct voices of Devenir, Rodríguez, and Acuña. As an academic researcher, I ask: What or who produces this knowledge? What is a researcher's role in elevating this knowledge? How do we decenter the academic exclusivity of knowledge production? How do we recognize our own interpretation of the knowledge with which we dialogue as researchers? How does the lived experienced of knowledge producers impact academia? I think these questions relate to a premise that Verdesio brings to his introduction, one that I think is good but limited. Verdesio stands for an "intervention of scholars of Latin American studies that goes beyond the boundaries of the academy" (Verdesio 26), but maybe we should also consider how the knowledge that is produced beyond the boundaries of the university could inform and benefit Latin American subaltern, post-hegemonic, and *cuir*/queer studies? I am not the first person to express this concern. For instance, as Horacio Legrás, quoted in Verdesio's introduction, explains, "The incorporation of subaltern knowledges and cultural production to our research agendas should be done in the understanding that they deserve the status of critical discourse" (Verdesio 27). I think that a bridge/dialogue between Latin American subaltern, post-hegemonic studies and *cuir*/queer studies could allow academics to permeate one another's fields and go deeper into questions related to excluded dissident genders and sexualities and their forms of knowledge.

I should emphasize that I am interpreting the post-hegemonic as it was first addressed by Alberto Moreiras and Gareth Williams in their books *The Exhaustion of Difference* (2011) and *The Other Side of the Popular* (2002), respectively. According to Williams, in Moreiras's book, "Posthegemony emerged as active solidarity with subalternity as a result of the negative work, or deconstruction, it carries out in relation to hegemony" ("The Subalternist Turn" 10). As Williams continues, he mentions something that I find important to rescue nowadays that can sustain a bridge/dialogue with *cuir*/queer studies: "This was posthegemony's affirmation and insistence at that time, as well as being the ground of its double aim of knowing the world and transforming it" ("The Subalternist Turn" 10). This aim of post-hegemony studies of "knowing the world and transforming it" from a gesture of "active solidarity with subalternity" could benefit, and gain benefit from, *cuir*/queer studies.

Perhaps, here I might posit a question to Latin American subaltern and post-hegemonic studies: Why have you disregarded the power and force of gender and sexual dissidents or *cuir*/queer subaltern subjects as constituted outside of the hegemonic? Particularly the poor and racialized *travesti*, whose voice and mere existence and survival exhausts hegemony, as they themselves resist the very ordering of life into hegemonic and subaltern spheres. If post-hegemony is that space wherein hegemonic discourses reach their limits in making sense of the world, *travestis'* lives do a different kind of work as they cannot be comprehended or grasped by hegemony, and they highlight hegemony's discursive and authorial limitations, and even failure. As I have explained in chapter 2, the life experiences and work produced by *travestis* presents not only political strategies but also alternative post-hegemonic theories. It is my perception that Latin American subaltern and post-hegemonic studies have focused mainly on the case of peasants, Indigenous groups, and, to a certain degree, on women. What about other oppressed groups that not only resist hegemonic power but also create alternative futures, alternative post-hegemonies? *Dónde están las locas, los maricas, les travestis*?

I should mention another issue for the emergent field of Latin American *cuir*/queer studies in the sense that, to my knowledge, it has not yet attempted to dialogue with Latin American subaltern and post-hegemonic studies as fields that touch on the constitution of *cuir*/queer individuals outside of the hegemonic. It would be productive to push the field of Latin American *cuir*/queer studies toward new and different theoretical directions with the intervention of subaltern and post-hegemony studies, as I believe it would allow us to think about cuir/queer works and life experiences from a different perspective. Doing so would also question "the canonization of white, cisgendered queer theorists whose work dominates the academic landscape globally" (Pierce, *Argentine* 274). It would also address the fact that, as contended in chapter 3, in contemporary Chile, the indeterminacy of *travesti* gender, or not belonging to a specific gender, either "masculine" or "feminine," is questioned and rejected in the LGBT community.

So, *The Language of the In-Between* ends with more questions than answers. I hope that my colleagues from the fields of Latin American subaltern, post-hegemonic, literary, cultural and *cuir*/queer studies will help me discover answers to them. The invitation is always open to expand our boundaries, our bodies, and, especially, our fields of study.

NOTES

Introduction: There Was Something Different in the Way That Body Danced and Sang

1. The Shining Path (translated from the Spanish, Sendero Luminoso) refers to the Peruvian Communist Party.

2. When, in 1990 Alberto Fujimori was elected to the office of the presidency, he swiftly instituted authoritarian practices for dealing with the violence in the countryside, setting the stage for what became a de facto dictatorship despite, ostensibly, continuing to be a country ruled by democratic elections.

3. Salessi also studies the case of female homosexuality, especially as it related to the corruption of the Argentinean educational system during the first decades of the twentieth century. He addresses what was denominated as *tribadismo*, "sexual practices among women, behaviors considered incorrect for their biological sex" (214). These entities were considered as people without a national or patriotic spirit. All translations of texts originally in Spanish are mine, unless otherwise indicated.

4. As will be explained shortly, since "travesti" is a term that developed in Latin America and does not have the same political, cultural, or historical valence as "transvestite" or "cross-dresser" in English, I have chosen not to translate it in this book.

5. Although this book does not directly addresses the experience of Afro-Peruvians I should mention that this population faces widespread racism and discrimination, especially in the job application process, and they are relegated to low paid positions. This is why different Black civil rights groups or *colectivos* such as Ashanti Perú push the Peruvian government and society for a more inclusive participation and leadership of this group in business or the military.

6. I also recognize that as Vidal-Ortiz and Martinez explain, in some Latin American countries, the term "travesti" "is extremely offensive and expresses abjection and violence" (34).

7. The *travestis* of this book are related to the *chaupi* which in Quechua means "intermediate" or "in-between" (Horswell 39) in the sense that these *travestis* present an ambiguity of gender.

Chapter 1: *Cuiring* the Birth of the *Modern(a)* Nation-State in Chile and Peru

The term "moderna" here refers to a designation LGBT people use in certain parts of Latin America when asked about their role in bed. *¿Eres activa, pasiva o moderna?* *Moderna* means that you play both sexually active and passive roles in bed.

1. Moreover, the scholar Mabel Moraña explains that by the first decades of the twentieth century, "Already located by then as a peripheral area dependent on the North American capital, Latin America will feel with special acuity the effects

of the situation . . . by then, most Latin American countries had been inserted in the international market both as suppliers of raw materials and as consumers of manufactured goods. In many cases, national economies rested on the production of a single product, which placed them in a situation of extreme vulnerability, as the price of their products was threatened by the oscillations on the world market" (*Literatura* 12).

2. This term, "dissident genders," will be used here, from among many others that are synonymous.

3. The impact of Augusto B. Leguía's governments (1919, 1924, and 1929) in this period must be highlighted. Although it was characterized as the "heyday of indigenista policies," it favored the expansion of the business bourgeoisie at the same time that it repressed the burgeoning popular movements. Concomitantly, Leguía's administration opened the financial sector to foreign capital, thus reinforcing the submission of the country to US domination.

4. Víctor Andrés Belaúnde, for example, argued that with the Conquest "the indigenous race had been subjected and it now needed to be educated and protected" (in Degregori, Sánchez León et al. 29).

5. The five core points of the APRA program were: (1) opposition to US imperialism; (2) the political unity of Latin America; (3) nationalization of land and industry; (4) internationalization of the Panama Canal; and (5) solidarity with all the oppressed peoples and classes of the world.

6. For more information on APRA and its premises, see Ricardo Martínez de la Torre (1947), Harry Kantor (1953), and Peter Klarén (1973).

7. *Tempestad en los Andes* (1927) by the Peruvian historian and archaeologist Luis E. Valcárcel is a key text for the discussion of how this tradition is reclaimed. According to Valcárcel, the *mestizaje* of cultures in Peru had produced deformities as the mestizo has not inherited the ancestral virtues of the Andean culture, but only vices and bad habits.

8. In 1982 Ángel Rama used the term "transculturation" in his study of Latin American authors such as José María Arguedas, Gabriel García Márquez, Juan Rulfo, and Augusto Roa Bastos to emphasize the capacity of Latin American writers to rework "influences" from the dominant cultures into their own narratives, combining them in innovative ways with elements from the rural cultures of their particular Latin American regions. Rama stated that these authors' literary works opened the way for a distinctive Latin American modern literature by using elements of local cultures as guiding formal principles while at the same time incorporating literary techniques from the European and US literary avant-gardes (Rama, "José María Arguedas" 32–56).

9. It is worth noting that in the 1920s José Carlos Mariátegui had already formulated a critique of *mestizaje* that could equally apply to what we call now "transculturation." Under this same formulation, Mariátegui considered that social transformation negotiated in terms of transculturation represented a principle of neocolonial social engineering that perpetuated creole modernity and reinscription and redistribution throughout the modernizing social sphere of Hispanic colonization. Likewise, regarding *mestizaje*, he argued that it "produces not only a new human and ethnic type but a new social type. . . . Neither European nor Indian tradition is perpetuated in the *mestizo*, they sterilize each other. In an

urban, industrial, and dynamic environment, the *mestizo* rapidly caches up with the White man and assimilates Western culture together with its customs, motivations, and consequences" (282). As Mariátegui suggests in his *Seven Interpretive Essays on Peruvian Reality*, his project regarding the national question does not posit national unification as an ideal, something that the dominant sectors aspire to as a condition to achieve a favorable situation to further their interests.

10. According to Cornejo Polar, the idea of transculturation "has increasingly become the most sophisticated masking of the category of mestizaje," which he considered "the greatest emblem of the false harmony a multiple mixture process would have reached" ("El zorro de arriba y el zorro de abajo" 116). *Mestizaje* would be, in this regard, a principle of social homogenization that would not cancel the existing conflicts in the Peruvian nation. Once again, for Cornejo Polar, *mestizaje* "provides harmonic images of something that is clearly torn and conflictive, suggesting figurations that ultimately are only relevant for those who find it convenient to imagine our societies as terse and non-conflictive spaces of coexistence" (116).

11. Furthermore, Rama considers that "the indigenista movement saw and explained the Indians using resources drawn from the emerging mestizo culture, which frankly was none other than the bastard child of its father, the eternal white conqueror, and was at that moment devoted to demanding the recognition and legitimacy that its progenitor had denied it. It took from the dominant culture all of the elements it considered useful, simplifying and clarifying them through its close contact with the actual functioning of the society in which it existed—that is, through its tough determination to survive in a hostile environment" (*Writing across Cultures* 99).

12. Mariátegui, however, sees Vallejo's poetry as capturing an Indigenous world vision.

13. Julio Cortázar, one of the most prominent *boom* authors, criticized the regionalist/localist vs. cosmopolitan/universalist perspective of several Latin American writers and attacked their telluric aesthetics as well what he deemed to be their "nacionalismo de escarapela y banderita" (badge and flag nationalism) that pervaded, for example, Arguedas's literature (Vargas Llosa 35). Arguedas's strong localism, so close to the dangers posed by fundamentalism and a possible nationalist exaltation, which according to the Argentine, could even recall the fascist experience, was not devoid of a parochial self-exoticization. In "Carta," Cortázar remarks that "tellurism . . . seems to me a preamble to the worst manifestations of negative nationalism when it becomes the creed of writers who, almost always . . . obsessively exalt the values of the local . . . the country against the world, the race . . . against other races" (Cortázar 8). Arguedas refers to this conflict, that started with a letter by Cortázar to Fernández Retamar and not to Arguedas himself, in his posthumous novel *El zorro de arriba y el zorro de abajo*: "Meanwhile, and from the greatest American magazine, *Life*, Julio Cortázar, who really rides out on the flaming horse of fame as if he were on a pink centaur, has cast some gleaming darts at me . . . and I repeat it now—that I am one of the provincial people of this world, that I have learned less from books than from the differences that exist" (Arguedas, *The Fox* 183).

14. Jose María Arguedas was born in Andahuaylas, a province located in the Peruvian mountains. His mother died when he was two years old. Because of the

absence of his father, a lawyer who traveled frequently, and his bad relationship with his stepmother and stepbrother, he sought comfort in the quarters of the family's Indigenous servants, establishing a relationship that allowed him to immerse himself in the language and customs of the Andes.

15. This is clear if we recognize that since *Todas las sangres* (*Every Blood*) (1964) Arguedas expressed the potential for creating a national project of peasant affiliation that would mean the preservation of the old Indigenous traditions. Cornejo Polar would denominate this aspiration a "lucid exercise of transculturation" (Cornejo Polar, "Sobre literatura" 33).

16. *Los zorros* portrays the process that turns a small fishing village into the largest fishing harbor in the world using Chimbote as a meticulously real referent. In 1940, the population of Chimbote, a small fishing town off the Pacific coast of Peru, comprising 4,224 people. Ten years later it was thought to be close to 250,000 inhabitants. By 1968, this previously tiny fishing port was thought to be responsible for the production and exportation of ten million tons of anchovy paste per year (Vargas Llosa 315). In a very few years, Chimbote grew under the empire of the fish flour industry. Chimbote would be a symbol of the unstoppable process of modernity, commerce, and national integration.

17. This text is one of the most important works in Quechua. It is the only Quechua text discovered from the sixteenth century that offers a complete and coherent framework of the mythology, rites, and societal organization of a province of old Peru.

18. It should be mentioned that the businessmen of Chimbote elaborate strategies to have the salaries of their workers reenter their financial system. These men are also owners of bars and whorehouses where they destroy their morals and harm their economic situation. As narrated in the novel, "But the 'Mafia' made the fishermen spend in due time; it whetted their brutish macho appetites. The 'Mafia' was good at trickin' them into squanderin' everything they earned; it kept them steeped in delinquency, and that stain is not easily washed out, ya understand?" (Arguedas, *The Fox* 101). As we can see, Chimbote turns out to be a chaotic and even more destructive place, where the lives of these men are torn apart by capitalism and imperialism, as well as by transculturation.

19. According to Vargas Llosa, for Arguedas homosexuality represents "the worst extreme of degradation" (318) as he belonged to a sexist and puritan world. Indeed, this representation of homosexual men is a constant in Arguedas's writing. They are always the greatest criminals and exploiters of Indians in texts such as *El sexto*, *Todas las sangres*, and of course in this novel, *Los zorros*.

20. Furthermore, the female subject is presented in the book as a reduced subject that has no agency. For instance, the mother of the above-mentioned character, Mudo, is considered "the shrewdest prostitute in Chimbote" (Arguedas, *The Fox* 34). The novel cannot recognize her just as a woman or even a mother. No, her main attribute for recognition in *Los zorros* is that she is a prostitute. Also, she is not described in the novel as a human being, but as an animal, as she does not walk on two feet but rather on four: "El Mudo stumbled over him and fell down. He could not hold the knife. Before anyone else could, La Muda, his mother, got to the knife on all fours, and she took it away" (Arguedas, *The Fox* 34).

21. In *Raza Chilena*, Palacios traces the origin and evolution of Chile's mestizo population, constructing a complicated argument of xenophobia, nativism, racial theory, and biological determinism.

22. In 1909, Tancredo Pinochet Le-Brun published *La conquista de Chile en el siglo XX*. In this book, Pinochet critiqued oligarchs for the weak state of nationalism that, according to him, had turned Chile into a nation dominated by foreigners. Evidencing the influence of Palacios on his ideological formation, Pinochet states in his book, "Every day we go on losing more respect and love for what is national, whether they are men, customs, traditions, our language, the land or flag." And he adds "It is necessary that we soon adopt a politics of Chileanization of our riches because we do not want to convert the Chilean race into an inferior one, into a slave race, in the service of other races that have in their possession our ground and our riches" (Pinochet Le-Brun 191).

23. Foucault defines the biopolitical as the control over relations between the human race, or human beings, and he also suggests that "biopolitics deals with the population as political problem, as a problem that is at once scientific and political, as a biological problem and as power's problem." Biopolitics' last domain, states Foucault, is "control over relations between the human race, or human beings insofar as they are a species, insofar as they are living beings, and their environment, the milieu in which they live" (*Society* 244).

24. In 1964, Eduardo Frei Montalva was elected president of Chile and continued with the plans to modernize the country. The Agrarian Reform Act of 1967, for instance, was one of the measures Frei Montalva proposed for this purpose. Another law he passed allowed peasants to unionize. The historian Heidi Tinsman analyzes this unionization campaign and points out that "the men who refused to unionize were derided as *maricones (faggots) amarillos* (yellows) or *mujeres* and *niñas* (women and girls), because it was understood that unions turned peasants into "real" men. Women, girls, yellows, and faggots specified cowardice, not true manliness, the opposite of union *machos*" (Tinsman 97). Homosexuality or male effeminacy continued to be an issue in the Chilean modernization process. Frei considered them problems that would be overcome by joining a union. Unions would replace depraved practices with moral behavior, barbarity with citizenship (85). Also, Frei invoked the male-headed family as a metaphor for national progress and political peace.

25. Donoso is one of the most recognized Chilean novelists. He has been placed within the group of Chilean writers belonging to the midcentury generation, whose writing represents, questions, and criticizes the values of a decadent bourgeoisie. In addition, he is one of the authors of the so-called New Latin American Narrative, which is considered to have started with texts by Juan Carlos Onetti and Jorge Luis Borges. Other authors regarded as part of this new narrative are Juan Rulfo, Julio Cortázar, José Lezama Lima, Manuel Puig, Carlos Fuentes, Mario Vargas Llosa, and Gabriel García Márquez. Some of them will be considered later as the founding members of the Latin American *boom* (1960/1970). While Donoso did have an important place within the *boom*, it was not until the publication of his novel *El obsceno pájaro de la noche* (*The Obscene Bird of Night*) (1970) that he was elevated to the ranks of the greatest Latin American novelists (McMurray 25).

Chapter 2: The Travesti as a Language of the "In-between"

Epigraph: What am I? Does it matter? "I am art," I say, as I move my hips in circles and lose myself among the people and their cigarette smoke and their starless brilliance and their hunger to be.

1. See Sierra Madero, *Del otro lado del espejo: La sexualidad en la construcción de la nación cubana.*

2. In Latin America, the gay and lesbian liberation movement appeared in the context of the Cold War—that is to say, during the years in which homosexuality was considered a threat to national identities by different Latin American states. The discourses, organizational features, and political strategies of the LGBT movement were related to the broader political struggle—such as the leftist struggle against the dictatorships occurring in the region—that characterized the Latin American public sphere from the 1960s to the 1980s.

3. For Sofía, the term "transfeminismo" is very important for understanding her *travesti* subjectivity. She defines the term as a *punto de fuga* from the binary and biologist understanding of sex. Sofía considers herself *travesti* and not trans, based on her belief that the latter term is more related to the field of medicine and its norms. She adds that in Chile trans politics have tended to focus on "hygiene," in an attempt to clean "what we have been and what we continue to be." For Sofía, Chilean trans politics deny the reality of prostitution.

4. Although in this book I try to point to a fluctuation of gender, I use hegemonic terms such as "masculine," "feminine," "male," and "female" to address what is socially accepted and requested from different subjects. I include quotation marks to express my position toward such terms that institute biological hierarchies.

5. I nonetheless acknowledge that some *travestis* see themselves as women.

6. "Transsexuals" aspire to have sex reassignment surgery, which somehow reproduces gender binarism. This is why I am interested in that particular feature of the *travesti*, because it disfigures the normative masculine/feminine gender identity and denaturalizes it (Sifuentes-Jáuregui 4).

7. This is why I maintain, following Severo Sarduy, that the *travesti* does not imitate a woman, but rather observes and makes the artificial construction of woman and "femininity" visible. As Sarduy points out, "The *travesti* does not imitate women. For him, in the end, there is no woman; he knows—and, perhaps paradoxically, he happens to be the only one to know—that she is just appearance, that her realm and the force of her fetish cover up a defect" ("Writing/Transvestism" 13).

8. Performance in Peru has precedents in what Emilio Tarazona has described as "prior incidents," including a nocturnal dance performance in the Lima Cemetery in 1917 in which José Carlos Mariátegui participated along with the dancer Norka Rouskaya; public interventions of poets such as César Moro (1935) and Jorge Eduardo Eielson (1969); and the inauguration of the New Art (Arte Nuevo) exhibition in which the actor Felipe Buendía, dressed as the president of the nation, read an ironic opening speech. In the 1980s, performance gained interest and popularity and it became a more commonly used artistic form.

9. Acuña has presented his work at international venues such as *La Internacional*

Cuir: Transfeminism, Sexual Micropolitics and Guerrilla Video, organized by Paul B. Preciado in 2011, at the Museo Reina Sofía. For more information, see https://www.museoreinasofia.es/en/actividades/internacional-cuir-transfeminism-sexual-micropolitics-and-guerrilla-video.

10. It is also worth noting that Joseph R. Roach points out in his text on performance and critical theory that performance and performing, generally, dramatize a culture of the margins or can be used, also, to impose marginality (13).

11. The disproportionate way crimes against the LGBT community during the conflict were handled is due to the historically marginalized role the community played in Peru.

12. For more information, see the work of Gio Infante, "Las otras memorias: Persecución, tortura y muerte de homosexuales durante el conflicto armado interno," https://gioinfante.lamula.pe/2013/08/28/las-otras-memorias/gioinfante/.

13. In July 2003, the MHOL and the Movimiento Raíz (Root Movement) presented the Retablo de la Memoria TLGB (LGBT Memory Tableau), which showed what had happened in Tarapoto.

14. Shining Path also organized Open Popular Committees to control marital and sexual practices (Montalvo 64).

15. It must be acknowledged, however, that the Final Report of the TRC was the first official document to record these hate crimes against the Peruvian LGBT population during the internal armed conflict.

16. The LGBT population has not been included in the reparation programs after the internal armed conflict and the violence experienced by the members of this population.

17. Rodríguez grew up during the military dictatorship. These were times in which one had to go home early because of a curfew. In an interview published by the nongovernmental organization La vaca, Rodríguez relates that her father would leave for work and many times he would find along the way the bodies of people who had been shot. "I grew up with the rustle of fear. I'm so respectful because I'm full of fear," she says ("Trans andina" 6).

18. As Rodríguez expresses in her book *Cuerpos para odiar: sobre nuestras muertes, las travestis, no sabemos escribir*, "I'm *travesti* who took hormones for years to feminize my body, then I injected silicone in my boobs and hips, and in 2000 I had my sex change operation" (Rodríguez, *Cuerpos* 56).

19. Here I am taking into consideration that many people who practice *travestismo* or are *travestis* are comfortable with their assigned sex and do not wish to change it. As I mentioned in the introduction, a *travesti* may have been normatively assigned "male" at birth but does not necessarily consider herself a woman, though some do. Thus, *travestismo* is a form of gender expression that is not necessarily indicative of a person's gender identity or sexual orientation. That is why I make a differentiation between *travestis* and transgender people. In the particular case of Rodríguez, as she refers to herself using feminine pronouns, I will also do it throughout this chapter.

20. Along with Pierce, I do not consider *Cuerpos para odiar* just a poetry collection. For me it is much more than that. As I explain in this section, I believe that the book embraces and includes several literary genres that exceed poetry. Also, although the

cover of the book includes the words "Poesía Travesti" (*Travesti* Poetry), I do not take this statement literally, in the sense that the book contains only poetry written by or about *travestis*, but as Rodríguez's gesture, considering the experience of the *travesti* as poetry.

21. For more information, see https://www.biobiochile.cl/noticias/2015/07/05/cuerpos-para-odiar-la-obra-de-teatro-que-abre-el-debate-sobre-la-transexualidad.shtml.

22. In a later publication, *Dramas pobres* (2016), Rodríguez reflects on the erasure of *travestis* as political and sexual subjects.

23. Rodríguez has also managed a series of fanzines such as *Dramas pobres: Poesía travesti*, *Enferma del alma*, and *Contodomisida*. All these projects disobey "the omnipresent cultural industries" and would be considered "production[s] of failure with no publisher" (Krampack 5).

24. In his recent published article "I Monster: Embodying Trans and *Travesti* Resistance in Latin America," Joseph Pierce approaches Rodríguez's work as the developer of a form of epistemological resistance to neoliberal politics of inclusion and recognition that Pierce denominates "monstering" (to monster). Pierce states in his article that Rodríguez "utilizes monstrosity as a project of aesthetic and epistemological dissidence" ("I Monster" 306).

25. I choose to keep the book's quotes in Spanish so the reader can appreciate the richness and complexity of Rodríguez's "in-between" language.

26. This fluid language is intertwined with a change of temporalities. Thus, until page 24, Rodríguez was narrating, perhaps, herself as an adult. Then on page 34 we go back to, perhaps, Rodríguez's childhood. This time the book addresses, perhaps, Rodríguez's violent experience with her brother who "rammed my head into the wall so I'd learn how to fight and defend myself as a man against the insults and mockery that he heard people yelling at me in school. . . . And all he did was repeat: you're not a fag" (*Cuerpos* 34).

27. Moreover, the use of the Spanish language in the narrative goes against official usage and includes terms or phrases such as "No sabi ha cómo . . ." and "Alomejo" for "no sabia cómo" and "a lo mejor" (Rodríguez, *Cuerpos* 53).

28. On the other hand, the *travesti* also destabilizes the notion of certainty by underlining the superficial quality of everything that is considered and defined as true or real. Butler explains this by noting that *travestis* make use of acts, gestures, and representations that are performative, demonstrating further that identity based on gender and, by extension, sexuality, is a pure fabrication made up of bodily signs and other discursive methods (*Gender* 187). This discovery of the fabrication of the real focused on gender can be extended to any part of the social fabric that presents norms as realities. In this way, the *travesti* not only pushes us to question what is real and what should be taken as such but also shows us that the idea of the real can be questioned, and that new ways of conceiving the real can be established (217).

29. When I use the term "political" I am using it according to Jacques Rancière's definition: "Political activity is whatever shifts a body from the place assigned to it or changes a place's destination. It makes visible what had no business being seen, and makes heard a discourse where once there was only place for noise; it makes understood a discourse that was once only heard as noise" (30).

Chapter 3: Pedro Lemebel: The *Loca Travesti* as a Site of Resistance

1. In the twenty-first century, the same discourse of Chileans as "whiter" and more "civilized" than their neighbors has been deployed against "Peruvians [who] emigrated in large numbers to Chile as maids and service workers" (Beckman 84–87).

2. During Salvador Allende's government (1970–1973), masculinity was understood around the concept of the New Man, inherited from the Cuban revolutionary regime. This concept was especially productive in Latin America during the first three years of the 1970s (Acevedo and Elgueta 11). In the particular case of Allende and homosexuality, he used to emphasize that anything could be said about him but that nobody could accuse him of being a thief or a faggot. Moreover, in 1947, when Allende was a congressman, he called another congressman, Juan B. Rossetti, a faggot during a discussion on the Chilean Parliament (Contardo 263–74). For more information about Allende's position toward sexual and gender minorities, review the work of Víctor Hugo Robles and Óscar Contardo.

3. The military dictatorship justified the coup by pointing out how UP (Popular Unity) had "broken national unity, artificially encouraging a class struggle in Chile . . . our sole purpose is to reestablish the financial and social normality of the country as well as to recuperate the lost peace" (*Declaración de principios*).

4. As noted by Nelly Richard, Chilean "citizenship consists, as Pinochet loved to say, in either ordering or obeying, and only those who do one or the other well are useful to the State" (Richard, *Margins* 151).

5. In Brazil, for instance, the 1964–1985 dictatorship furthered cleansing campaigns against homosexuals. These campaigns gave way to the creation of organizations such as the Morality Brigade of the Federal Police to cleanse the streets of homosexuals so they would be kept from disturbing "decent people" (Figari 229). Likewise, in Argentina, during the "National Reorganization Process," a series of murders of homosexuals was carried out and, in the context of the prevailing political repression, many homosexuals were arrested and tortured.

6. This article was modified in 1994, decriminalizing homosexual relations and punishing them only when they involve minors.

7. Toward the end of 1977, a group of homosexuals created the group Integración, the first gay organization to emerge during the Pinochet regime. For more information, see "El grupo Integración: (Una reina en el ropero)" by Víctor Hugo Robles.

8. In Víctor Hugo Robles's view, Casas and Lemebel brought together leftism and homosexuality, with which they were trying to homosexualize the left or politicize sexuality (Robles, *El diario* 80).

9. According to Nelly Richard, visual arts represent the first space to introduce a homosexual aesthetics as a praxis that challenges sexual identities, social repression, patriarchal culture, and liberation utopias of revolutionary desire. Richard sees the performances of Carlos Leppe and Juan Dávila in the 1980s as important precedents (*Masculine/Femenine* 44).

10. Yeguas del Apocalipsis emerged within the context of the cultural resistance actions organized by CADA (Art Actions Collective) against the Pinochet dictatorship in 1977. Las Yeguas, as Fernando Blanco notes, were a sort of "minority

backside" of this group and a historical follow-up of the urban interventions of the homosexual artists Francisco Copello and Carlos Leppe (Blanco, "De los ideales" 14).

11. Among the performances staged by Yeguas, it is worth mentioning those carried out during the Book Fair at Parque Forestal; the homage to Raúl Zurita at the Chascona, Neruda's house; the celebration of *high life* on a July 14 Bastille Day at the Alliance Française; during President Aylwin's inauguration; and at the Chilean Human Rights Commission.

12. The visual arts were the first space to introduce the theme of a gay aesthetics as a form of questioning sexual identity, social repression, and patriarchal culture during the military dictatorship.

13. For a more extended discussion of post-hegemony and the *travesti* as a post-hegemonic figure, see chapter 2.

14. In the Chilean context, *travestis*, such as Claudia Rodríguez, Sofía Devenir, and others have started being read and listened to in the North American academy, even in spaces such as the Latin American Studies Association (LASA). Its 2021 Congress included two panels and roundtables where the voices and experiences of *travestis*, such as Claudia Rodríguez, Frau Diamanda, Marlene Wayar, and Pilar Salazar, were heard.

15. In 1986, Lemebel published an anthology of short stories, *Incontables.*

16. Although this chapter deals with his narrative work, it is worth mentioning that Lemebel also addressed issues such as the disappeared and the repression in Chilean society under the military dictatorship in several performances and installations, such as his interpretation of Marcel Duchamp's *Nude Descending a Staircase* (2014) at the Museum of Contemporary Art. Also, Lemebel's show *Arder* (Burn), presented at the Museum of Memory and Human Rights, addressed the request for truth and justice that the relatives of the detained-disappeared pursued in the face of crimes of military violence during the dictatorship.

17. I choose to keep this section's quotes in Spanish so the reader can appreciate the richness and complexity of Lemebel's "in-between" language.

18. The critic Soledad Bianchi defines this style as "neo-barrocho," believing that the baroque, when it reaches Chile, "loses all the glow it has on the [Caribbean] island and the majesty of the trans-Andean estuary as it gets soaked with the filthy waters of the Mapocho River that runs through much of Santiago." For more on this term, see Soledad Bianchi "¿La insoportable levedad . . . ? Imágenes y textos, postdictadura y modernidad en Chile" (1997). See also Néstor Perlóngher, "Introducción a la poesía neo-barroca cubana y Rioplatense" (2008).

19. The Cuban authors José Lezama Lima and Virgilio Piñera also use Latin American *neo-barroso* language.

20. Lemebel's *loca travesti*, as defined by Blanco and Robles in the paragraphs above, would be the kind of *loca* that Elizabeth Grosz considers a radical term of destabilization and decentering. Thus, as Lawrence La Fountain-Stokes explains, *loca* is a radical and profoundly Latin American term that engages with postmodernism and queer/*cuir* liberation. For more information, see La Fountain-Stokes, "Translocas."

21. The book consists of twenty *crónicas* published between 1991 and 1993 in the magazine *Página abierta*, as informed on the last page of the book.

22. The book has an introduction by Carlos Monsiváis in which he reviews and comments on Lemebel's poetic trajectory as a performer and author of *crónicas* and how they have their origin in his homosexuality. Monsiváis mentions other authors who also create their discourse from their position as a sexual and gender minority. See also Fernando Blanco and Juan Poblete's *Desdén al infortunio: Sujeto, comunicación y público en la narrativa de Pedro Lemebel* (2010), which includes an article by Monsiváis in which he delves more in depth into the *crónicas* of Lemebel.

23. Lemebel's *crónica* "Pisagua En Pointe," included in *Serenata Cafiola* (2008), tells the story of Gastón, a gay dancer who was detained in the Pisagua Prison camp during the military dictatorship.

24. English translation: "Even after the Holocaust, the melodies of Rendeski open the 'great avenues.' The revival of such a parade reverberates in the shivers of the crematories and torture jails. It seems that even in this century, the memory of pain is a dance video clip that comes along with a side of fries. It seems that in this same film, *desaparecidos*, Jews, women, Black men, and faggots roll together trashed by the soles of boots, Adidas shoes, and tanks. It seems that in every spin of the helmets there is an affirmation of their hate of democracy. It seems that in the straight angle of the steps in the parade, the testicles in line are reserve grenades ready to blow above La Moneda."

25. The term "performative" was coined by J. L. Austin when, introducing the word into the philosophical lexicon, he indicated that linguistic speech and voice not only have the capacity to emit statements and declarations but also that both can also produce actions. Austin argues with regard to performative discourse that "to say something is to do something; or in which by saying or in saying we are doing something" (12). In this respect, Lemebel's "in-between" language, by exhaustively detailing the sexual encounters of various marginalized subjects in the park, is giving this space a new meaning in which every previous notion that the reader might have had about it is canceled out.

26. The text was later included in Lemebel's book *Loco afán: Crónicas de Sidario* (1996).

27. On November 21, 2006, Lemebel read this "Manifiesto" in Casa de las Américas. See "Un escritor que se expone" by Jorge Fornet for more information about Lemebel's visit to Cuba.

28. Lemebel's approach to the government of Carlos Ibañez del Campo is not exclusive of this text. In a different *crónica* the author states: "Mientras en Valparaíso los travestis eran arreados a culatazos a los barcos de la marina, para nuestra memoria la película de Ibáñez y su crucero del horror. Pero entonces nadie creía que eso era cierto, y por último; esos cuerpos escarchados de moretones eran desechos ordinarios de la homosexualidad criolla que ojeaba en las revistas de moda las imágenes importadas del gay parade internacional . . . separando en estratificaciones de clase a locas, maricas y travestis de los acomodados gays en su pequeño arribismo traidor" (*Loco afán* 164–65).

29. The Movimiento de Izquierda Revolucionaria (MIR) is the political-military party that has attracted the most interest as the subject of academic research. In recent years, a number of cases have been reported by militants who, due to their sexual orientation, had their militancy upended and even had psychological therapies applied

to them so they would supposedly overcome their homosexuality. For instance, Tania González Lorca, in "Me pusieron homosexual: Relatos y fenómenos sociales desde la dictadura" (2015), studies the case of Roberto Gajardo whose militancy was canceled because of his sexual orientation. Cristián Cottet's book *Carlos Sánchez: La razón de estar gay* (2005) also addresses the rejection of homosexuality in the MIR.

30. As Heidi Tinsman states, Popular Unity continued to be a male-dominated organization. Thus, its models of sexual revolution were within the patriarchal and heterosexual discourse of the Cuban New Man (274). According to the Chilean journalist and performer Víctor Hugo Robles, during the UP government, people could be arrested on suspicion, especially homosexuals because, as the author tells us, they were seen as scum and their demands did not appear included in the political, social, and cultural changes proposed by the government. Thus, during the UP government there would have been greater political freedom but LGBT people did not benefit from it (Robles, *Bandera* 13). On April 22, 1973, a group of approximately twenty-five working-class homosexuals held the first public LGBT event in the Plaza de Armas in Santiago. Chilean media reacting against this demonstration expressed their homophobia. The comments made by the left-wing press were especially homophobic. The communist magazine *Paloma*, for example, wrote that "50 queer/ *cuirs* gathered in Plaza de Armas," while the newspaper *Clarín* carried the front-page headline: "Colipatos piden chicha y chancho" (Faggots demand booze and pork).

31. Lemebel has written several *crónicas* that address life in Cuba under the revolution, such as "Cubana de Aviación" and "La Habana Vieja." In these works, Lemebel acknowledges the good choices of the Cuban Revolution but also recognizes its limitations and mistakes.

32. This paragraph also invites readers to ask themselves who is the "tú" (you) to which the narrator of the poem speaks. Because of the use of the term "compañero" mentioned in the lines quoted above, a common usage among the members of leftist parties and movements, we can see that the text is speaking to a sympathizer with such movements and parties. Related to this, Diana Palverich has pointed out that "the addressee of the Manifiesto is the Chilean left, which has traditionally been *machista* and homophobic. The left, that as many others, has excluded homosexuals from its struggle because the left considers homosexuality a sign of bourgeois decadency or as an effeminate degradation of men, and because of this, incompatible with the Revolution and its hyper masculine signifiers" (259).

33. The beginning of the text mentions the expulsion of the North American poet Allen Ginsberg from Cuba when he was invited to a Conference of Writers in the 1960s by the Cuban minister of culture Haydee Santamaría. Ginsberg was expelled from Cuba because he criticized the persecution of homosexuals by the Cuban government. Lemebel reproaches Marxist ideology for not considering nonnormative masculinities as part of its struggle, and he, as Palverich expresses, "modifies the narrow definition of what a marginalized subject is for the Left and includes the poor homosexual as a subject that is doubly marginalized" (259).

34. On September 7, 1986, a failed attempt to assassinate Augusto Pinochet was carried out by the Manuel Rodríguez Patriotic Front. In other words, the story of the *Loca del Frente* and Carlos is based on a true event in Chilean political history.

35. *Tengo miedo torero* is in dialogue with Manuel Puig's *El beso de la mujer araña*, inasmuch as both novels have a similar set of characters and stories that follow the same logic. These novels thus "carry out the allegorical restitution of homosexuals at the core of the revolution and of thought in the Latin American left" (Blanco and Poblete 18).

Chapter 4: The "In-between" in the Works of Giuseppe Campuzano and Claudia Salazar

1. Also, in December 1992, over 117 Peruvian diplomats were fired by Alberto Fujimori, in part because they were accused of practicing homosexual acts.

2. It is worth mentioning that these texts also highlight the marginalization and exploitation of other populations and groups during the colonial era. Such is the case of the "Carta sobre los maricones" (Letter on faggots) published in *Mercurio Peruano* in 1791 in which there is reference not only to the presence of individuals who practice a nonnormative masculinity, but also to Black and mulatto female slaves:

> Among the rare and pleasant objects that are to be seen here at every step, I have been most greatly impressed by a kind of men who seem to find the dignity of their sex a heavy burden; because in a shameful and ridiculous way they seek to defy nature. What would our fellow citizens say if they saw a body of this kind, which tries to imitate women in everything? The bodily appearance, the flair, the gait, the actions, even minor movements, everything breathes in them a ridiculous and extravagant effeminacy . . . the less perceptive see a man adorned with the clothes of both sexes. . . . But what attracted all my attention was a long stand where many black and mulatto women were seated, wearing the richest attires. I could not help but admire this reversal of things, for I saw behaving as Ladies those who in our Homeland are slaves. (quoted in Campuzano, *Museo* 55)

3. In addition, openly homophobic laws have been adopted, such as the law on the Disciplinary Rules of the National Police of Peru, approved by the Peruvian Congress in May 2009. In the list of offenses, it stipulates, "Having sexual relations with a person of the same sex that brings shame to or harms the institutional image" (Jaime 35).

4. There are several testimonies indicating that the military also threatened the lives of gays and transgender people.

5. The gay and transgender populations were targeted following an orthodox Marxist analysis that identified nonnormative sexual and gender people as expressions of the decadence of the capitalist system based on a rigid model of masculinity.

6. Fernando Belaúnde-Terry's return to government (1980) coincided with the first manifestations of violence perpetrated by Shining Path. In May of that same year, Peru was preparing to conduct elections. The eyes of the nation were focusing entirely on the development of this process. In this situation, the burning of several electoral urns in the village of Chuschi (a province of Ayacucho) by five masked men belonging to Shining Path went almost unnoticed and was cataloged as an unimportant event.

7. Cynthia McClintock defines Shining Path's project as "a violent change in

government, social structure, and culture . . . a rapid, fundamental, and violent domestic change in the dominant values and myths of a society, in its political institutions, social structure, leadership, and government activities and policies" (40).

8. Rodrigo Franco is the name of a young Aprista militant and president of the state-run company in charge of distributing basic foodstuffs and other goods (Empresa Nacional de Comercialización de Insumos, ENCI) who was murdered by Sendero Luminoso.

9. With a few slogans using maxims such as "honesty, technology and work" and with the notions of authority, order, and stability for "Peru, country with a future" as the goals of his administration, Fujimori led the Peruvian nation along with two unelected agents of power: General Nicolás de Bari Hermoza Ríos, head of the Peruvian Armed Forces, and Vladimiro Montesinos Torres, the elusive figure who handled the increasingly powerful National Intelligence Service (Blondet 13). The relationship and alliance between Fujimori, the Peruvian Armed Forces, and the Intelligence Service consolidated after Fujimori's self-coup in 1992.

10. It must be noted that most agents of the armed forces were not able to understand, let alone speak, the language of the Peruvian Indigenous peoples they encountered in the villages where they were sent to combat the Shining Path insurgents, so it was often impossible for them to correctly distinguish between *senderistas* and civilians.

11. A case that offers an elitist view into this conception of Quechua-speaking Indigenous populations can be found in the report that Mario Vargas Llosa submitted and the research he and other intellectuals conducted on the "massacre of Uchuraccay," in which eight journalists from Lima were executed on January 26, 1983, in the village that bears the same name. The report, drafted on the basis of a few hours of interviews with the inhabitants of the community, concluded that the massacre had been the result of a misunderstanding because the *comuneros* had mistaken journalists for *senderistas*. In his report, as well as in other documents, Vargas Llosa describes the inhabitants of Uchuraccay as "primitive," highlighting the conditions of poverty in which they lived and the violence with which they react when they feel threatened. Notably, Vargas Llosa perceives this violence as an anomaly in our daily lives (those of the "modern" subjects), while he assumes that the inhabitants of Uchuraccay live in an atmosphere of constant violence (*Hatun Willakuy* 50). Likewise, in several of his writings around this event, Vargas Llosa interprets the presence of certain wounds on the bodies of the massacred journalists as magical-religious rituals. For example, he argues that the journalists' ankles were crushed to prevent them from coming back to take revenge on their killers. Similarly, Vargas Llosa perceives magical-religious rituals in the figure of one of the women in the community, who before he and the other researchers left the town, sang and danced a song in a language unintelligible to them. Vargas Llosa describes her as a "small woman," barefoot, almost like a girl but with a wrinkled face, who wore a colorful skirt, a hat with colored ties, and who beat the members of the research commission on the legs with a bunch of plants. The author wonders whether the "woman" was bidding farewell to them with an ancient ritual or whether she was casting a spell on them for belonging to a world foreign to hers, since, as he points out, this "woman" came from a very different Peru to the one he inhabited, an

old and archaic Peru (*Hatun Willakuy* 50–51). This case neatly illustrates how certain sectors of Peruvian society perceive Quechua-speaking Indigenous peoples as archaic, violent, suspicious, alien to Peru, and, therefore, as an obstacle to the modernization of the country. It is therefore not surprising that the final report of the Truth and Reconciliation Commission indicates that 75 percent of the dead and missing persons during the internal armed conflict were native Quechua-speakers or speakers of another Indigenous language.

12. The government of Fernando Belaúnde-Terry adopted the term "terrorist" to refer to members of Shining Path through Legislative Decree 046 of 1981. It refers both to armed actions and to the support of or apology for anyone who "in order to create or maintain a state of fear, alarm or terror in the population or a sector thereof, commits acts that could endanger the life, health or property of any other person" (Decreto Legislativo 046, 1). Due to its general nature, this definition allowed (and still allows) the persecution of anyone who contests the status quo under the pretext of combating *senderista* violence.

13. This culture of fear was difficult to shake. Only when Fujimori began his third term as president of Peru in 2000—a mandate that was possible thanks to the ways in which Fujimori and his allies manipulated the law—was there any social mobilization against the government (Burt, "'Quien habla'" 33).

14. According to the final report of the Truth and Reconciliation Commission, the members of Shining Path kidnapped many women to turn them into sex slaves. They also practiced other forms of sexual violence such as mutilation, on both men and women. We must emphasize what other acts, such as having their hair cut, can mean for women and men. For Andean women, for example, having their hair cut meant an offense to their dignity as women. For Ashaninka women, the fact that members of Shining Path made them leave their homes when they were menstruating represented a humiliation, because according to custom they must sit during the days when they are bleeding (Henríquez Ayin 89–90).

15. Among these novels we can mention *Adiós Ayacucho* (1986), by Julio Ortega; *Lituma en los Andes* (1993), by Mario Vargas Llosa; *Rosa Cuchillo* (1997), by Óscar Colchado; *El cazador ausente* (2000), by Alfredo Pita; *Un beso de invierno* (2001), a short novel by José de Piérola; *Retablo* (2004), by Julián Pérez; *La cacería* (2005), by Gabriel Ruiz Ortega; *Abril rojo* (2006), by Santiago Roncagliolo; *Guerra a la luz de las velas* (2006), a novella by Daniel Alarcón; *La hora azul* (2005) and *La pasajera* (2015), by Alonso Cueto. Moreover, several anthologies addressing this same topic have been published. Among them are Mark R.Cox's anthology, *El cuento peruano en los años de violencia* (2000); *Toda la sangre: Antología de cuentos peruanos sobre la violencia política* (2006), edited by Gustavo Faverón; *Al final de la batalla: Después del conflicto, la violencia y el terror* (2015), by Ana María Vidal Carrasco; and *Incendiar el presente: La narrativa peruana de la violencia política y el archivo (1984–1989)* (2018), by Enrique Cortez.

16. I refer here to the way many of these narratives use the personal experience to address the larger, collective context. Texts like *When Rain Became Floods* (2013), by the ex-soldier, ex-priest, and ex-member of Shining Path, Lurgio Gavilán; and *Los rendidos: Sobre el don de perdonar* (2015), by the historian José Carlos Agüero, the son of two militants of Shining Path who were murdered by members of the Peruvian

Armed Forces, imply a change whereby narrative forms address the wounds and traumas produced by the internal armed conflict.

17. For example, *The Blue Hour* by Alonso Cueto, whose space of enunciation is urban, (post)modern, and Hispanic, tells us the story of Adrian Ormache, a prestigious Peruvian lawyer in one of Lima's wealthiest neighborhoods, who discovers that his father conducted numerous military operations, which included the torture, rape, and murder of many civilians suspected of terrorism during the war against the Shining Path guerrilla organization in the 1980s and 1990s in Peru. Adrian also learns that his father kidnapped and sexually abused Miriam, a young local girl. Motivated by guilt and shame, Adrian decides to offer Miriam financial support, which interrupts and disturbs her life and ends up bringing back memories of her trauma. The novel thus represents Miriam as a passive subject who needs the help of a white man—the son of her abuser—in order to forget and heal.

18. These surgeries were carried out under deception, coercion, or threat toward the woman intervened upon or toward their partners. Some sterilizations were carried out with intimidation and threats to call the police on the women; those who tried to prevent the procedures from being carried out lost access to free health services and were even threatened with detention (Tamayo 41). Similarly, some women were told that should they resist the sterilization procedure the food subsidies provided by the government would be withdrawn (Burt, "Sterilization" 1). Many of the sterilizations were performed in the context of another intervention, such as postpartum, post-abortion, and other reproductive health-care procedures. Similarly, some of these interventions were carried out without the consent of the women, but with the consent of their partners, or were performed even though the women had manifestly refused to consent before surgery. Likewise, in many cases, the women were not duly informed about the irreversible character of the procedures (Tamayo 42). In her testimony, Hilaria Supa, an ex-congresswoman from the Andean region, for example, tells how she was sterilized in a rural clinic she visited to get treatment for a cold. On her visit, Supa received anesthesia and was taken to an operating room where she was sterilized without her consent (quoted in Henríquez Ayin 28). For more information on Supa, see *Threads of My Life: The Story of Hilaria Supa Huamán, a Rural Quechua Woman* (2008).

19. For instance, the film *The Milk of Sorrow* (2006) by Claudia Llosa not only represents the repercussions of the violence of conflict on an individual body but also perpetuates the problematic discourses of transculturation as part of the process of Peruvian modernization. The film presents the protagonist, Fausta, an Andean migrant, as a subject who needs to be de-indianized or transcultured in order to be inserted and integrated into the sociopolitical, economic, and cultural designs of Lima's ruling class.

Epilogue: An Invitation to Opening

Epigraph: Here I purposely include the translation from English to Spanish of Butler's quote in order to signal the necessity of translating queer theory to the Latin American context.

BIBLIOGRAPHY

Acevedo, Claudio, and Eduardo Elgueta. "El discurso homofóbico en la prensa izquierdista durante la Unidad Popular." *Revista IZQUIERDAS2*, no. 3, 2008: 1–12.

Acuña, Hector. "El estigma y la mártir." *Frau Videografía*, 2001–2007.

Acuña, Hector. Entrevista con Alonso Almenara. *El Comercio* Lima, May 24, 2015.

Acuña, Hector. Entrevista con Erika Almenara (June 2011).

Acuña, Hector. *Escenas Catalanas: errancias antropológico-sexuales*. Barcelona: La Máquina, 2020.

Acuña, Hector. "Luchas subalternas mutantes." *El cuerpo es el sujeto*. Galería Weber-Lutgen, 2017, https://serabyecto.lamula.pe/2014/05/16/frau-diamanda-15-anos-de-lucha-subalterna/hectoracuna/.

Acuña, Hector. "Políticas travestis y promiscuas." Dissertation for the Program of Independent Studies (PEI), MACBA, 2018.

Albarracín, M., and J. C. Rincón. "De las víctimas invisibles a las víctimas dignificadas: los retos del enfoque diferencial para la población LGBTI en la Ley de Víctimas." *Revista de Derecho Público* 31 (2013): 1–31.

Anaya, Karen, and Pamelhy Valle. "Desde la Memoria Marginada hacia la Deconstrucción del Estado: Las personas LGBT como víctimas del conflicto armado peruano y los caminos para la no repetición." *Polemos: Portal Jurídico Interdisciplinario*, 2017. http://polemos.pe/desde-la-memoria-marginada-hacia-la-construccion-del-estado-las-personas-lgbt-victimas-del-conflicto-armado-peruano-los-caminos-la-no-repeticion/.

Anzaldúa, Gloria. *Borderlands: The New Mestiza; La Frontera*. San Francisco, CA: Aunt Lute, 2007.

Arendt, Hannah. "The Decline of the Nation-State and the End of the Rights of Man." *The Origins of Totalitarianism* [1951], 267–302. Cleveland: Meridian, 1962.

Arguedas, José María. *Primer Encuentro de Narradores Peruanos, Arequipa, 1965*. Lima: Casa de la Cultura del Perú, 1969.

Arguedas, José María. *Todas las sangres*. Buenos Aires: Editorial Losada, 1964.

Arguedas, José María. *The Fox from Up Above and the Fox from Down Below*. Edited by Julio Ortega. Translated by Frances Horning Barraclough. Pittsburgh, PA: University of Pittsburgh Press, 1990.

Austin, J. L. *How to Do Things with Words*. Cambridge, MA: Harvard University Press, 1962.

Balibar, Etienne. "The Nation Form: History and Ideology." In *Race, Nation, Class: Ambiguous Identities*, edited by Etienne Balibar and Immanuel Wallerstein, translated by Chris Turner 86–106. London: Verso, 1992.

Barr-Melej, Patrick. *Reforming Chile: Cultural Politics, Nationalism, and the Rise of the Middle Class*. Chapel Hill: University of North Carolina Press, 2001.

Barrera, Katerín. "La Loca en el Frente." *Nomadías*, no. 21 (July 2016): 31–41.

Beckman, Ericka. "The Creolization of Imperial Reason: Chilean State Racism in the War of the Pacific." *Journal of Latin American Cultural Studies* 18, no. 1 (2009): 73–90.

Bejel, Emilio. *Gay Cuban Nation*. Chicago: University of Chicago Press, 2001.

Bellatín, Mario. "Tener a la mano lo que no está llamado a existir." *Museo travesti del Perú*. Lima: Institute of Development Studies, 2008.

Benjamin, Walter. "La obra de arte en la época de su reproductibilidad técnica." Translated by Jesús Aguirre. Madrid: Editorial Taurus, 1973.

Berkins, Lohana. "Travestis: una identidad política." *Emisférica* 4, no. 2 (2006). https://hemisphericinstitute.org/en/emisferica-42/4-2-review-essays/lohana-berkins.html.

Berkins, Lohana. "Travestismo, Transsexualidad y Transgeneridad." In *Un cuerpo: mil sexos; Intersexualidades*, edited by Jorge Horacio Raices Montero et al., 85–95. Buenos Aires: Topía, 2015.

Beverley, John. "Theses on Subalternity, Representation, and Politics." *Postcolonial Studies* 1, no. 3 (1998): 305–19.

Bhabha, Homi. *The Location of Culture*. London: Routledge, 1994.

Bianchi, Soledad. "¿La insoportable levedad . . . ? Imágenes y textos, postdictadura y modernidad en Chile." *Documento de Trabajo*, no. 21. Santiago: Universidad Arcis, Centro de Investigaciones, 1997.

Blanco, Fernando. "De los ideales colectivos al sentimentalismo de la primera persona." In *Desdén al infortunio. Sujeto, comunicación y público en la obra de Pedro Lemebel*, edited by Fernando Blanco and Juan Poblete, 71–98. Santiago: Cuarto Propio, 2010.

Blanco, Fernando. "El desliz que desafía otros recorridos: Entrevista con Pedro Lemebel." In *Reinas de otro cielo: Modernidad y autoritarismo en la obra de Pedro Lemebel*, edited by Fernando Blanco, 151–59. Santiago: LOM, 2004.

Blanco, Fernando. "La Frida no envejeció, Yo soy la Frida envejecida: La última performance de Pedro Lemebel." Dossier: Cuerpos que caben en la lengua. *Editorial Pontificia Universidad Javeriana* 21, no. 42 (2017): 40–62.

Blanco, Fernando. "Memorias y desclasificación: la acción directa de la vanguardia estética y los desafíos de la democracia." In *Políticas del amor: derechos sexuales y escrituras disidentes en el cono sur*, edited by Fernando Blanco, Joseph M. Pierce, and Mario Pecheney, 95–113. Santiago: Editorial Cuarto Propio, 2018.

Blanco, Fernando. "Políticas de la ciudadanía sexual y la memoria en la escritura de Pedro Lemebel." *Desde aceras opuestas: literatura/cultura gay y lesbiana en Latinoamérica*, 53–74. Madrid: Iberoamérica, 2006.

Blanco, Fernando, and Juan G. Gelpi. "El desliz que desafía otros recorridos: Interview with Pedro Lemebel." *Nómada* 3 (June 1997): 93–98.

Blanco, Fernando, and Juan Poblete. *Desdén al infortunio: Sujeto, comunicación y público en la obra de Pedro Lemebel.* Santiago: Cuarto Propio, 2010.

Blondet, Cecilia. *El encanto del dictador: Mujeres y política en la década de Fujimori*. Lima: Instituto de Estudios Peruanos, 2002.

Braidotti, Rosi. *Nomadic Subjects: Embodiment and Sexual Difference in Contemporary Feminist Theory*. New York: Columbia University Press, 1994.

Brito, Eugenia, Riet Delsing, Alejandra Farías, and Olga Grau. *Discurso, género y poder: Discursos públicos: Chile 1978–1993*. Santiago: LOM, 2007.

Brunner, José Joaquín. "Campo artístico, escena de avanzada y autoritarismo en Chile." *Arte en Chile desde 1973: Escena de avanzada y sociedad*. Santiago: FLACSO no. 46 (January), 1987.

Buntix, Gustavo, and Susana Torres. "Micromuseo (al fondo hay sitio)." *Museo travesti del Perú*. Lima: Institute of Development Studies, 2008.

Burt, Jo-Marie. "'Quien habla es terrorista': The Political Use of Fear in Fujimori's Peru." *Latin American Research Review* 41, no. 3 (2006): 32–62.

Burt, Jo-Marie. "Sterilization and Its Discontents." *NACLA Report on the Americas* 31, no. 5 (March–April 1998): 5.

Butler, Judith. *Bodies That Matter: On the Discursive Limits of "Sex."* London: Routledge, 1993.

Butler, Judith. *Gender Trouble: Feminism and the Subversion of Identity*. London: Routledge, 1990.

Cabrera, Pilar. "Soy Claudia Rodríguez, activista, travesti, pobre y resentida." *YouTube*, uploaded by Presentes LGBT, February 20, 2017. https://youtu.be/4SZxlVE7cvs.

Camacho García, Gianna. "La realidad de las personas trans en el Perú: seis cosas que debes saber." *FemLATAM. Feminismos Latinoamericanos* (2021). https://femlatam.org/2021/02/03/la-realidad-de-las-personas-trans-en-el-peru-seis-cosas-que-debes-saber/.

Campuzano, Giuseppe. "De engendro fabuloso a performatividad creadora." In *Saturday Night Thriller y otros escritos 1993–2013*, edited by Miguel López, 90–99. Lima: Estruendomudo, 2013.

Campuzano, Giuseppe. "Giuseppe Campuzano y El Museo Travesti del Perú." Interview with Lawrence La Fountain. *emisférica* 6, no. 2 (2010). hemisphericinstitute.org/hemi/es/campuzano-entrevista

Campuzano, Giuseppe. *Museo travesti del Perú*. Lima: Institute of Development Studies, 2008.

Campuzano, Giuseppe. "Reclaiming Travesti Histories." *Sexuality Matters*, special issue of *IDS Bulletin* 37, no. 5 (2006): 34–39.

Campuzano, Giuseppe. "¿Son suficientes dos géneros?" In *Saturday Night Thriller y otros escritos 1993–2013*, edited by Miguel López, 62–65. Lima: Estruendomudo, 2013.

Canaday, Margot. *The Straight State: Sexuality and Citizenship in Twentieth-Century America*. Princeton, NJ: Princeton University Press, 2009.

Cánovas, Rodrigo. "Llamado a la tradición, mirada hacia el futuro o parodia del presente." *Arte en Chile desde 1973: Escena de avanzada y sociedad*. Santiago: FLACSO no. 46 (January 1987).

Carvajal, Fernanda. "La frialdad del éxtasis." *Cuerpo ambulante: Sergio Zevallos en el Grupo Chaclacayo (1982–1994)*. Museo de Arte de Lima, 2004.

Casas, Francisco. "Fotógrafo por encargo." *Fotografías de Mario Vivado: Lo que el sida se llevó: Yeguas del Apocalípsis*, 6–8. Santiago: D21, 2011.

Castillo, Alejandra. "El feminismo no es un humanismo." *Por un feminismo sin mujeres*13–21. Coordinadora Universitaria por la Disidencia Sexual, 2011.

Castillo del, Cristal. Personal interview. February 17, 2021.

Chakrabarty, Dipesh. "Minority Histories, Subaltern Pasts." *Postcolonial Studies* 1, no. 1 (1998): 15–29.

Ciancaglini, Sergio. "Rituales dialogados: Herramientas para una era port-alfabética." *Travesti: Una teoría lo suficientemente buena*, 55–93. Buenos Aires: Muchas Nueces, 2019.

Cieza de León, Pedro. "Crónica del Perú." *Museo travesti del Perú*, i.1a. Lima: Institute of Development Studies, 2008.

Contardo, Óscar. *Raro: Una historia gay de Chile.* Santiago: Planeta, 2011.

Cornejo, Giancarlo. "Las políticas reparativas del movimiento LGBT peruano: Narrativas de afectos queer." *Estudos Feministas* 22, no. 1 (2014): 257–75.

Cornejo Polar, Antonio. "El zorro de arriba y el zorro de abajo: palabra y realidad." In *Los hervores de Chimbote en Los zorros de arriba y los zorros de debajo de José María Arguedas*, edited by Antonio Cornejo Polar et al., 17–76. Chimbote: Río Santa Editores, 2006.

Cornejo Polar, Antonio. *Escribir en el aire: Ensayo sobre la heterogeneidad socio-cultural en las literaturas andinas.* Lima: Editorial Horizonte, 1994.

Cornejo Polar, Antonio. "Hipótesis sobre la narrativa peruana última." *La novela peruana.* Lima: Editorial Horizonte. 1989.

Cornejo Polar, Antonio. *Sobre literatura y crítica latinoamericanas.* Caracas: Universidad Central de Venezuela, 1982.

Cornejo Polar, Antonio. "Sobre literatura y crítica latinoamericanas." *Obras completas de Antonio Cornejo Polar* 6, no. 2 (2013): 9–20.

Cornejo Polar, Antonio. "Un ensayo sobre 'Los zorros' de Arguedas." *El zorro de arriba y el zorro de abajo*, 296–307. Nanterre: Centre de Recherches Latinoaméricaines, 1990.

Cortázar, Julio. "Letter." In *The Fox From Up Above and the Fox From Down Below.* Edited by Julio Ortega, translated by Frances Horning Barraclough. Pittsburgh: University of Pittsburgh Press, 1990.

Cottet Villalobos, Cristián. *Carlos Sánchez: La razón de estar gay.* Santiago: Mosquito Comunicaciones, 2005.

Dajes, Talia. "Staging Terror: Violence and the Aesthetics of Civil War in Contemporary Peru." PhD diss., Ann Arbor: University of Michigan, 2013. deepblue.lib.umich.edu/handle/2027.42/97973.

Declaración de principios del gobierno de Chile. March 1974. es.wikisource.org/wiki/Declaraci%C3%B3n_de_principios_del_gobierno_militar_de_Chile.

Decreto Legislativo No. 046. www.pagina-libre.org/asociacion-peru/Textos/Fondo/Legislacion/DL_046_texto.html.

Degregori, Carlos Iván. *La década de la antipolítica: Auge y huida de Alberto Fujimori y Vladimiro Montesinos (II).* Lima: IEP Instituto de Estudios Peruanos, 2000.

Degregori, Carlos Iván. "The Origins and Logic of the Shining Path: Two Views. In *The Shining Path of Peru*, edited by David Scott Palmer, 51–62. New York: St. Martin's Press, 1994.

Degregori, Carlos Iván, Abelardo Sánchez León et al. *Tiempos de ira y amor: nuevos actores para viejos problemas.* Lima: DESCO, Centro de Estudios y Promoción del Desarrollo, 1990.

Degregori, Carlos Iván, Orin Starn and Robin Kirk, eds. *The Peru Reader: History, Culture, Politics*. Durham, NC: Duke University Press, 1995.

Derrida, Jacques. "Signature, Event, Context." *Glyph*, no. 1 (1992): 172–97.

Devenir, Sofía. *Des-ubicá: Memorias de una dinosauria travesti sudaka*. Santiago: Editorial Gata Kuir, 2017.

Díaz, Barbara, and Valentina Ortega. *Sofía Devenir, una travesti rabiosa*, 2016. YouTube, uploaded by Valentina Ortega, July 26, 2018. www.youtube.com/watch?v=Y6ZuWa3faao.

Diken, Bülent, and Carsten B. Laustsen. *The Culture of Exception: Sociology Facing the Camp*. London: Routledge, 2005.

Disch, Lisa J. "Review of *Being Political: Genealogies of Citizenship* by Engin F. Isin." *Environment and Planning D: Society and Space* 21 (June 2003): 380–82.

Domínguez Ruvalcaba, Héctor. *Latinoamérica Queer: Cuerpo y Política Queer en América Latina*. Translated by Sonia Verjovsky Paul. Ciudad de México: Ariel M.R., 2019.

Domínguez Ruvalcaba, Héctor. *Translating the Queer: Body Politics and Transnational Conversations*. Chicago: University of Chicago Press, 2016.

Donoso, Amelia, and Víctor Hugo Robles. *Sida en Chile: Historias Fragmentadas*. Santiago: Siempreviva Ediciones, 2015.

Donoso, Claudia. "A Brothel Called La Jaula." In *La manzana de Adán*, edited by Paz Errázuriz and Claudia Donoso. Santiago: Fundación AMA, 2015.

Donoso, José. *El obsceno pájaro de la noche*. Santiago: Alfaguara, 2020.

Donoso, José. *Hell Has No Limits*. Translated by Suzanne Jill Levine. Los Angeles: Green Integer, 1999.

Donoso, José. *Historia personal del Boom*. Barcelona: Seix Barral, 1983.

Edwards, Matthew. *Queer Argentina: Movement Towards the Closet in a Global Time*. New York: Palgrave Macmillan, 2016.

Eltit, Diamela. *Réplicas: Escritos sobre literatura, arte y política*. Santiago: Editorial Planeta Chilena, 2016.

Epps, Brad. "Los 'fráxitos' de la disidencia sexual en la época de la globalización neoliberal." In *Eventos del deseo: Sexualidades minoritarias en las culturas/literaturas de España y Latinoamérica a finales del siglo XX*, edited by Dieter Ingenschay, 143–52. Madrid: Iberoamericana, 2018.

Epps, Brad. "Nostalgia de la oscuridad: acción clandestina y amor furtivo en *Tengo miedo torero* de Pedro Lemebel." In *La vida imitada: narrativa, performance y visualidad en Pedro Lemebel*, edited by Fernando Blanco, 109–27. Lewisburg, PA: Bucknell University Press, 2020. 109–27.

Epps, Brad. "Retos y riesgos, pautas y promesas de la teoría *queer*." *Revista Iberoamericana*, no. 225 (2008): 897–920.

Errazuriz, Paz. *La manzana de Adán*. Santiago de Chile: Zona Editorial, 1990.

Espósito, Roberto. *Communitas: The Origin and Destiny of Community*. Translated by Timothy Campbell. Stanford, CA: Stanford University Press, 2010.

Falconí, Diego. *De las cenizas al texto: Literaturas andinas de las disidencias sexuales en el siglo XX*. Havana: Fondo Editorial Casa de las Américas, 2016.

Fernández, Josefina. "Los cuerpos del feminismo." In *Construyéndonos. Cuadernos de lecturas sobre feminismos trans, I*. Edited by Mauro Cabal, 15–26. Mulabi: Espacio Latinoamericano de Sexualidades y derechos, 2008.

Fernández Labbé, Marcos. "Asociales: raza, exclusión y anormalidad en la construcción estatal Chilena, 1920–1960." *Revista de Historia Social y de las Mentalidades*16, no. 2 (2012): 167–94.

Figari, Carlos. "El movimiento LGTB en América Latina: institucionalizaciones oblicuas." In *Movilizaciones, protestas e identidades políticas en la Argentina del bicentenario*, edited by Astor Massetti, Ernesto Villanueva and Marcelo Gómez, 225–40. Buenos Aires: Nueva Trilce, 2010.

Figueroa Díaz, Tamara. *La resistencia de la loca barroca de Pedro Lemebel*. Barcelona: Egales, 2019.

Fiol-Matta, Licia. *A Queer Mother for the Nation: The State and Gabriela Mistral*. Minneapolis: University of Minnesota Press, 2002.

Fischer, Carl. *Queering the Chilean Way: Cultures of Exceptionalism and Sexual Dissidence, 1965–2015*. New York: Palgrave Macmillan, 2016.

Forgues, Ronald. "¿Por qué bailan los zorros?" *El zorro de arriba y el zorro de abajo*, 307–15. Nanterre: Centre de Recherches Latinoaméricaines, 1990.

Foucault, Michel. *The History of Sexuality: The Will to Knowledge, vol. 1*. Translated by Robert Hurley. London: Penguin Books, 1998.

Foucault, Michel. *Society Must Be Defended: Lectures at the Collège de France 1975–1976*. New York: Picador, 2003.

Fornazzari, Alessandro. *Speculative Fictions: Chilean Culture, Economics, and the Neoliberal Transition*. Pittsburgh, PA: University of Pittsburgh Press, 2013.

Fornet, Jorge. "Un escritor que se expone." *Casa de las Américas*, no. 246 (January–March 2007): 67–68.

Franco, Jean. *Cruel Modernity*. Durham, NC: Duke University Press, 2013.

Franco, Jean, Bernardita Llanos, and Héctor Domínguez Ruvalcaba. "Encajes de acero: la libertad bajo vigilancia." *Reinas de otro cielo: Modernidad y autoritarismo en la obra de Pedro Lemebel*, 11–23. Santiago: LOM Ediciones, 2004.

Frazier, Lessie Jo. *Salt in the Sand: Memory, Violence, and the Nation-State in Chile, 1890 to the Present*. Durham, NC: Duke University Press, 2007.

Fuentes, Carlos. *La nueva novela hispanoamericana*. Mexico City: Editorial Joaquín Mortiz, 1969.

González, Lorca Tania. "Me pusieron homosexual: Relatos y fenómenos sociales desde la dictadura." PhD diss., Universidad de Chile, 2015.

González Prada, José. *Free Pages and Other Essays: Anarchist Musings*. Edited by David Sobrevilla. Translated by Frederick H. Fornoff. Oxford: Oxford University Press, 2003.

Gramsci, Antonio. *Selection from the Prison Notebooks*. Edited and translated by Quintin Hoare and Geoffrey Nowell Smith. New York: International, 1971.

Grosz, Elizabeth. *Volatile Bodies: Toward A Corporeal Feminism*. Bloomington: Indiana University Press, 1994.

Guha, Ranajit. Preface. In *Selected Subaltern Studies*, edited by Ranajit Guha and Gayatri Chakravorty Spivak, 35–37. New York: Oxford University Press, 1988.

Haya de la Torre, Victor Raul. *El antiimperialismo y el APRA*. Lima: Fondo Editorial del Congreso del Perú, 2010.

Hatun Willakuy. Versión abreviada del Informe final de la comisión de la verdad y Reconciliación. Lima: Cooperación gráfica Navarrete, 2005.

Halberstam, Jack. *Skin Shows: Gothic Horror and the Technology of Monsters.* Durham, NC: Duke University Press, 1995.

Henríquez Ayin, Narda. *Cuestiones de género y poder en el conflicto armado en el Perú.* Lima: Concytec, 2006.

Horswell, Michael J. *Decolonizing the Sodomite: Queer Tropes of Sexuality in Colonial Andean Culture.* Austin: University of Texas Press, 2005.

Jaime, Martin. *Informe Anual sobre los Derechos Humanos de personas Trans, Lesbianas, Gays y Bisexuales en el Perú 2008.* Lima: Promsex y Red Peruana TLGB, 2008.

Jeftanovic, Andrea. "Cuerpos travestis, perturbando deseos e ideologías." *Políticas y estéticas del cuerpo en América Latina*, 357–80. Bogotá: Universidad de los Andes, 2007.

Kantor, Harry. *The Ideology and Program of the Peruvian Aprista Movement.* Berkeley: University of California Press, 1953.

Klaiber, Jeffrey. "Los cholos y los rotos: Actitudes raciales durante la Guerra del Pacífico." *Histórica* 2, no. 1 (1978): 27–37.

Klarén, Peter. *Modernization, Dislocation, and Aprismo: Origins of the Peruvian Aprista Party, 1870–1932.* Austin: University of Texas Press, 1973.

Klarén, Peter. *Nación y sociedad en la historia del Perú.* Lima: Instituto de Estudios Peruanos, 2004.

Krampack, Federico. "Cuerpos para odiar: la orgía eterna del aprendizaje." *Disidencia Sexual Revista Virtual de Arte y Política Feminista de la CUIDS* (August 2015). disidenciasexualcuds.wordpress.com/2015/08/29/cuerpo-para-odiar-la-orgia-eterna-del-aprendizaje-por-federico-krampack/.

La Fountain-Stokes, Lawrence. Introduction. *Translocas: The Politics of Puerto Rican Drag and Trans Performance.* Ann Arbor: University of Michigan Press, 2021.

La Fountain-Stokes, Lawrence. "Queer Ducks, Puerto Rican Patos, and Jewish-American Feygelekh: Birds and the Cultural Representation of Homosexuality." *Centro Journal* 19, no. 1 (March 2007): 192–229.

La Fountain-Stokes, Lawrence. "Translocas: Migration, Homosexuality, and Transvestism in Recent Puerto Rican Performance." *emisférica* 8, no. 1 (2011). archive.hemisphericinstitute.org/hemi/en/e-misferica-81/lafountain.

Lawrenz, Nina, and Martha Zapata Galindo. Unpublished. Quoted in "Los 'fráxitos' de la disidencia sexual en la época de la globalización neoliberal." In *Eventos del deseo: Sexualidades minoritarias en las culturas/literaturas de España y Latinoamérica a finales del siglo XX*, edited by Dieter Ingenschay, 143–52. Madrid: Iberoamericana, 2018.

Legrás, Horacio. "Subalternity and Negativity." *Disposition/n* 22, no. 49 (2000): 83–102.

Lemebel, Pedro. "El cronista de los márgenes." Entrevista con Andrea Jeftanovic. *Lucero* 11, no. 1 (2000): 74–78.

Lemebel, Pedro. "Es necesario liberar algunas perversiones." Entrevista realizada por Andrés Gómez. *La Tercera*, September 21, 1997.

Lemebel, Pedro. "Manifiesto" (Hablo por mi diferencia). In *A corazón abierto: Geografía literaria de la homosexualidad en Chile.* Edited by Juan Pablo Sutherland. Santiago: Editorial Sudamericana, 2001.

Lemebel, Pedro. *La esquina es mi corazón: crónica urbana.* Santiago: Cuarto Propio, 1995.

Lemebel, Pedro. "La metáfora de la subversión." Entrevista con Elizabeth Neira. *El Mercurio: Artes y Letras.* February 21, 1999. Santiago.

Lemebel, Pedro. *Loco afán: Crónicas de sidario.* Santiago: LOM Ediciones, 1996.

Lemebel, Pedro. "Manifiesto" (Hablo por mi diferencia). In Sutherland, *A corazón abierto*, 35–39.

Lemebel, Pedro. *My Tender Matador.* Translated by Katherine Silver. New York: Grove Press, 2003. (Original: Tengo miedo torero, 2001).

Lenin, Vladimir. "The Dual Power." *Pravda*, April 1917. www.marxists.org/archive/lenin/works/1917/apr/09.htm.

Lewis, Vek. *Crossing Sex and Gender in Latin America.* New York: Palgrave Macmillan, 2010.

Ley 11.625. Título 1. De los Estados Antisociales de las Medidas de seguridad. *Diario oficial de la República de Chile.* October 4, 1954.

Llanos, Bernardita. "Masculinidad, Estado y violencia en la ciudad neoliberal." In *Reinas de otro cielo: Modernidad y autoritarismo en la obra de Pedro Lemebel*, edited by Fernando Blanco, 75–113. Santiago: LOM Ediciones, 2004.

López, Berta. "*Tengo miedo torero* de Pedro Lemebel: ruptura y testimonio." *Estudios Filológicos* 40 (September 2005): 121–29.

Lugones, María. "Colonialidad y género." *Tabula Rasa*, no. 9 (July–December 2008): 73–101.

Macherey, Pierre. *In a Materialist Way: Selected Essays.* Translated by Ted Stolze, edited by Warren Montag. London: Verso, 1988.

Mancilla, Luis Alberto. "Pecado Homosexual. Un Ángel Caído." Santiago: Punto Final, 1996.

Mariátegui, José. *Seven Interpretive Essays on Peruvian Reality.* Translated by Marjory Urquidi. Austin: University of Texas Press, 1971.

Manrique, Nelson. *El tiempo del miedo: la violencia política en el Perú, 1980–1996.* Lima: Fondo Editorial del Congreso del Perú, 2002.

Martínez de la Torre, Ricardo. *Apuntes para una interpretación marxista de historia social del* Perú. Lima: Empresa Editora Peruana, 1947.

McClintock, Cynthia. *Revolutionary Movements in Latin America: El Salvador's FMLN and Peru's Shining Path.* Washington, DC: United States Institute of Peace Press, 1998.

McMurray, George R. *José Donoso.* Boston: Twayne, 1979.

Méndez, Cecilia. "Incas sí, indios no: Notes on Peruvian Creole Nationalism and its Contemporary Crisis." *Journal of Latin American Studies* 28, no 1 (1996): 197–225.

MHOL. "Situación de los Derechos Humanos de Lesbianas, Trans, Gays y Bisexuales en el Perú." *INFORME ANUAL 2005.*

Ministerio de Justicia de Chile. *Código Penal.* November 12, 1874. www.memoriachilena.gob.cl/602/w3-article-92905.html.

Mirassol, María. "In-Between." n.d. www.yorku.ca/aklim/Maria/IN%20between_final.htm.

Misee, Miquel. *Transexualidades, otras miradas posibles.* Madrid: Editorial Egales, 2013.

Mogrovejo, Norma. "Lo queer en América Latina." *Norma Mogrovejo Blogspot*, November 22, 2012. http://normamogrovejo.blogspot.com/2012/11/lo-queer-en-america-latina.html

Monsiváis, Carlos. Introduction. *La esquina es mi corazón: crónica urbana*. Santiago: Cuarto Propio, 1995.

Montalvo Cifuentes, José. "Crímenes de odio durante el conflicto armado interno en el Perú (1980–2000)." *+MEMORIA(S)*, no.1 (2017): 64–65.

Moore, Thomas. "Neither Here nor There." *Parabola* 25, no. 1 (2000): 34–37.

Moraña, Mabel. *Arguedas/Vargas Llosa: Dilemas y Ensamblajes*. Madrid: Iberoamericana Vervuert, 2013.

Moraña, Mabel. *Literatura y cultural nacional en Hispanoamérica (1910–1940)*. Minneapolis: Institute for the Study of Ideologies and Literatures, 1984.

Moreiras, Alberto. *The Exhaustion of Difference: The Politics of Latin American Cultural Studies*. Durham, NC: Duke University Press, 2001.

Moreno, Fernando. "Bordar la Historia desde los bordes: Tengo miedo torero." In *L'ecriture de Pedro Lemebel: Nouvelles pratiques identitaires et scripturales*, edited by María M. Semilla Durán, 119–28. Saint Étiene: Publications de l'Université de Saint-Étienne.

Moreno Turner, Fernando. "La inversión como norma: A propósito de 'El lugar sin límites.'" *Cuadernos hispanoamericanos* 295 (1975): 19–42.

Nancy, Jean-Luc. "Finite History." *The Birth to Presence*, translated by Brian Holmes. Stanford, CA: Stanford University Press, 1993.

Neira, Eloy, and Patricia Ruiz Bravo. "Enfrentados al patrón: Una aproximación al estudio de las masculinidades en el medio rural peruano." In *Estudios culturales: Discursos, poderes, pulsiones*, edited by Santiago López Maguiña, Gonzalo Portocarrero, Rocio Silva Santisteban, and Victor Vich, 211–32. Lima: Red para el desarrollo de las Ciencias Sociales en el Perú.

Newton, Esther. *Mother Camp: Female Impersonators in America*. Chicago: University of Chicago Press, 1979.

Noemi, Daniel. *Leer la pobreza en América Latina: literatura y velocidad*. Santiago: Cuarto Propio, 2004.

Ochoa, Marcia. "Latina/o Transpopulations." In *Latina/o Sexualities: Probing Powers, Passions, Practices and Policies*, edited by Marysol Asencio, 230–42. New Brunswick, NJ: Rutgers University Press, 2009.

Oroz, Rodolfo. *Diccionario de la Lengua Castellana*. Santiago: Editorial Universitaria, 1989.

Ortega, José. *La estética en la narrativa hispanoamericana*. Madrid: Ediciones José Porrúa Turanzas, S.A., 1993.

Ortiz, Fernando. *Cuban Counterpoint: Tobacco and Sugar*. Translated by Harriet de Onís. Durham, NC: Duke University Press, 1995.

Palacios, Nicolás. *Raza Chilena: Libro escrito por un chileno para los chilenos*. Ulan Press, 1918 [2012].

Palverich, Diana. "El cuerpo agredido de la homosexualidad proletaria y Loco afán de Pedro Lemebel." In *Desdén al infortunio: Sujeto, comunicación y público en la obra de Pedro Lemebel*, edited by Fernando Blanco and Juan Poblete, 243–65. Santiago: Cuarto Propio, 2010.

Parada, Silvia. Testimony on CNN Chile. November 25, 2018. https://www.cnnchile.com/pais/la-represion-que-no-importo-las-historias-lgbtiq-en-dictadura-que-chile-jamas-reparo_20181125/.

Pastén, J. Agustín. "Paseo crítico por una crónica testimonial: de La esquina es mi corazón a Adiós Mariquita Linda de Pedro Lemebel." *A Contracorriente* 4 (Winter 2007): 103–42.

Perlongher, Néstor. "Introducción a la poesía neo-barroca cubana y Rioplatense." *Prosa plebeya: ensayos 1980–1992*. Buenos Aires: Colihue, 2008.

Perlongher, Néstor. "La barroquización." *Prosa plebeya: ensayos 1980–1992*, 113–55. Buenos Aires: Colihue, 2008.

Perlongher, Néstor. *La prostitución masculina*. Buenos Aires: Ediciones de la Urraca, 1993.

Pierce, Joseph M. *Argentine Intimacies: Queer Kindship in an Age of Splendor, 1890–1910*. Albany: State University of New York Press, 2019.

Pierce, Joseph M. "I Monster: Embodying Trans and *Travesti* Resistance in Latin America." *Latin American Research Review* 55, no. 2 (2020): 305–21.

Pinochet Le-Brun, Tancredo. *La conquista de Chile en el siglo XX*. Santiago: La ilustración, 1909.

Preciado, Paul B. *An Apartment on Uranus*. Translated by Charlotte Mandell. London: Fitzcarraldo Press, 2019.

Prieto Millán, Soledad. "Perversión y eugenesia a comienzos del siglo XX: La enfermedad venérea y la degeneración como metáfora de la homosexualidad." In *Ficciones políticas del cuerpo: Lecturas universitarias de género, sexualidades críticas y estudios queer*, edited by Juan Pablo Sutherland, 27–44. Santiago: Editorial Universitaria, 2016.

Puar, Jasbir K. *Terrorist Assemblages: Homonationalism in Queer Times*. Durham, NC: Duke University Press, 2007.

Quijano, Aníbal. *Dependencia, urbanización y cambio social en Latinoamérica*. Lima: Mosca Azul Editores, 1977.

Quiroga, José. *Mapa Callejero: Crónicas sobre lo gay desde América Latina*. Buenos Aires: Eterna Cadencia, 2010.

Rama, Ángel. "José María Arguedas transculturador." Prólogo. *Señores e indios*, José María Arguedas, 7–39. Buenos Aires: Calicanto, 1976.

Rama, Ángel. *Writing across Cultures: Narrative Transculturation in Latin America*. Durham, NC: Duke University Press, 2012.

Ramos, Julio. *Divergent Modernities: Culture and Politics in Nineteenth-Century Latin America*. Durham, NC: Duke University Press, 2001.

Rancière, Jacques. *Disagreement: Politics and Philosophy*. Translated by Julie Rose. Minneapolis: University of Minnesota Press, 1999.

Reátegui, Félix. "Las víctimas recuerdan: Notas sobre la práctica social de la memoria." *Justicia Transicional: Manual para América Latina*. Comisión de Amnistía, Ministerio de Justicia. New York: Centro Internacional para la Justicia Transicional, 2009.

Richard, Nelly. "A treinta años del Congreso Internacional de Literatura Femenina Latinoamericana: una conversación con Jorge Díaz." *Abismos temporales: Feminismo, estéticas travestis y teoría* queer, 17–40. Santiago: Metales Pesados, 2018.

Richard, Nelly. *Arte en Chile desde 1973: Escena de avanzada y sociedad.* Santiago: FLACSO no. 46 (January 1987).

Richard, Nelly. "Bordar de pájaros las banderas de la patria libre." *Abismos temporales: Feminismo, estéticas travestis y teoría* queer, 75–89. Santiago: Metales Pesados, 2018. 75-89.

Richard, Nelly. "La crítica de la memoria." *Cuadernos de Literatura, Bogotá* (Colombia) 8, no. 15 (2002): 187–93.

Richard, Nelly. *La insubordinación de los signos (Cambio político, transformaciones culturales y poéticas de la crisis).* Santiago: Editorial Cuarto Propio, 2000.

Richard, Nelly. "Locas, alocadas." *Abismos temporales: Feminismo, estéticas travestis y teoría* queer, 43–55. Santiago, Metales Pesados, 2018.

Richard, Nelly. "Los extravíos de la cita cultural." *Abismos temporales: Feminismo, estéticas travestis y teoría* queer, 201–25. Santiago: Metales Pesados, 2018.

Richard, Nelly. *Margins and Institutions: Art in Chile Since 1973.* Melbourne: Art & Text, 1986.

Richard, Nelly. *Masculine/Femenine. Practices of Difference(s).* Translated by Silvia R. Tandeciarz and Alice A. Nelson. Durham, NC: Duke University Press, 2004.

Richard, Nelly. "Perversiones semánticas y otras." *Abismos temporales: Feminismo, estéticas travestis y teoría* queer, 123–50. Santiago: Metales Pesados, 2018. 123-150.

Richard, Nelly. *Residuos y metáforas: (Ensayos de crítica cultural sobre el Chile de la transición)* Santiago: Editorial Cuarto Propio, 1998.

Risco, Ana María. "El dolor es de los hombres." In *Lemebel oral: 20 años de entrevistas (1994–2014),* edited by Gonzalo León, 31–34. Buenos Aires: Mansalva, 2018.

Rivas, Felipe. "Diga 'queer' con la lengua afuera: Sobre las confusiones del debate latinoamericano. *Por un feminismo sin mujeres,* 59–75. Santiago, Coordinadora Universitaria por la Disidencia Sexual, 2011.

Roach R., Joseph. Introduction. In *Critical Theory and Performance,* edited by Janelle G. Reinelt and Joseph R. Roach, 5–18. University of Michigan Press, 1992.

Roberts, Kenneth. "El neoliberalismo y la transformación del populismo en América Latina: El caso peruano." *Populismo y neopopulismo en América Latina: El problema de la cenicienta,* 245–322. Buenos Aires: Editorial Universitaria de Buenos Aires, 1999.

Robles, Víctor Hugo. *Bandera Hueca: Historia del movimiento homosexual en Chile.* Santiago: Editorial ARCIS/Cuarto Propio, 2008.

Robles, Víctor Hugo. "El grupo Integración: (Una reina en el ropero)." In *Nación Marica: Prácticas Culturales y Crítica Activista,* 19–22. N.p.: Ripio Ediciones, 2009.

Rodríguez, Claudia. *Cuerpos para odiar: sobre nuestras muertes, las travestis, no sabemos escribir.* Santiago: Ají Ediciones, 2018.

Rodríguez, Claudia. *Dramas pobres.* Santiago: Ediciones del Intersticio, 2016.

Rodríguez, Claudia. "Ecofeminismo, decrecimiento y alternativas al desarrollo." *El Desconcierto,* June 2016. ecofeminismobolivia.blogspot.com/2016/06/chile-claudia-rodriguez-para-el-sistema.html

Rodríguez, Claudia. "El arte de re-sentir: Puentes transfronterizos entre lo oral y lo escrito. *Travesti: Una teoría lo suficientemente buena,* 29–44. Buenos Aires, Muchas Nueces, 2019.

Rodríguez, Claudia. LARR-University of Florida Article Award Round Table. Latin American Studies Association International Congress. May 28, 2021. https://www.youtube.com/watch?v=5yH4D70zMGo.

Rodríguez, Claudia. "Se resiste." *Hablo por mi disidencia*. Entrevista con Lars Eddie. SIT Graduate Institute/SIT Study Abroad. Fall 2018.

Rodríguez, Claudia. "Trans andina: Claudia Rodríguez, activista chilena." *La vaca*, April 2019. www.lavaca.org/mu132/trans-andina-claudia-rodriguez-activista-chilena/.

Rodríguez, Ileana. "A New Debate on Subaltern Studies?" *LASA Forum* 33, no. 2 (2002): 14–15.

Rojas Flores, Jorge. *La dictadura de Ibáñez y los sindicatos (1927–1931)*. Santiago: Editorial Universitaria, S.A., 1993.

Ruffinelli, Jorge. "Lemebel después de Lemebel." *Nuevo texto crítico* 22 (2009): 42–43.

Ruiza-Rivas, Tomás. "Museos de Artistas." *Antimuseo*. Mexico City, 2014. www.antimuseo.org.

Salazar, Claudia. *Blood of the Dawn*. Translated by Elizabeth Bryer. Dallas: Deep Vellum, 2016.

Salazar, Gabriel. *Construcción de Estado en Chile (1800–1837)*. Santiago: Sudamericana, 2013.

Salessi, Jorge. *Médicos, Maleantes y Maricas: Higiene, criminología y homosexualidad en la construcción de la nación Argentina*. (Buenos Aires, 1871–1914). Buenos Aires: Estudios Culturales, 1995.

Sarduy, Severo. "The Baroque and the Neobaroque." In *Baroque New Worlds: Representation, Transculturation, Counterconquest*, edited by Lois Parkinson Zamora and Monika Kaup, 30–36. Durham, NC: Duke University Press, 2010.

Sarduy, Severo. "Conversación con Severo Sarduy." Entrevista de Emir Rodríguez Monegal. *Revista de Occidente*. Offprint, no. 93 (December 1970).

Sarduy, Severo. "Escritura/Travestismo." *Escrito sobre un cuerpo: ensayos de crítica*, 72–74. Buenos Aires: Editorial Sudamericana, 1969.

Sarduy, Severo. "Writing/Transvestism." *Review: Literature and Arts of the Americas* 7, no. 9 (1973): 31–33.

Shalá, Noelia. "Prólogo." *Des-ubicá. Memorias de una dinosauria travesti sudaka*. Santiago: Editorial Gata Kuir, 2017.

Shock, Susy. Prólogo. *Travesti: Una teoría lo suficientemente buena*. Buenos Aires: Muchas Nueces, 2019.

Sierra Madero, Abel. *Del otro lado del espejo: La sexualidad en la construcción de la nación cubana*. Havana: Fondo Editorial Casa de las Américas, 2006.

Sifuentes-Jáuregui, Ben. *Transvestism, Masculinity, and Latin American Literature*. New York: Palgrave Macmillan, 2002.

Silva Santisteban, Rocío. *El factor asco: basurización simbólica y discursos autoritarios en el Perú contemporáneo*. Lima: Red para el desarrollo de las ciencias sociales en el Perú, 2008.

Silvano, Santiago. *The Space in Between: Essays on Latin American Culture*. Durham, NC: Duke University Press, 2001.

Spivak, Gayatri. "Can the Subaltern Speak?" In *Marxism and the Interpretation of Culture*, edited by Cary Nelson and Lawrence Grossberg, 272–313. Urbana: University of Illinois Press, 1988.

Spivak, Gayatri Chakravorty. “Subaltern Studies: Deconstructing Historiography.” In *Selected Subaltern Studies*, edited by Ranajit Guha and Gayatri Chakravorty Spivak, 197–221. New York: Oxford University Press, 1998.

Stein, Steve. *Populism in Peru: The Emergence of the Masses and the Politics of Social Control.* Madison: University of Wisconsin Press, 1980.

Stryker, Susan. *Transgender History.* Berkeley, CA: Seal Press, 2008.

Sutherland, Juan Pablo. Introducción. In *A corazón abierto: Geografía literaria de la homosexualidad en Chile*, edited by Juan Pablo Sutherland, 9–32. Santiago: Editorial Sudamericana, 2001.

Sutherland, Juan Pablo. “Recepción crítica y políticas sexuales en las escrituras de la nación.” *Nación Marica: Prácticas Culturales y Crítica Activista*, 65–82. N.p.: Ripio Ediciones, 2009.

Sutherland, Juan Pablo. “Repensarlo todo, Escrituras sin miedo a la nación hegemónica.” *Revista Nomadías*, Universidad de Chile, no. 19 (2015): 207–24.

Tamayo, Giulia. *Reporte de Derechos Humanos sobre la Aplicación de la Anticoncepción Qurúrgica en el Perú. 1996–1998.* Lima: Comité de América Latina y el Caribe para la Defensa de los Derechos de la Mujer, 1999.

Tarapacá / Boletín informativo del Centro “Hijos de Tarapacá.” Santiago: El Centro, 1942.

Tarazona, Emilio. *Accionismo en el Perú (1965–2000): Rastros y fuentes para una primera cronología.* Lima: ICPNA, 2005.

Taylor, Diana. “Opening Remarks.” In *Negotiating Performance: Gender, Sexuality, and Theatricality in Latin/o America*, edited by Diana Taylor and Juan Villegas, 1–16. Durham, NC: Duke University Press, 1994.

Taylor, Diana. *The Archive and the Repertoire: Performing Cultural Memory in the Americas.* Durham, NC: Duke University Press, 2003.

Theidon, Kimberly. *Entre prójimos: el conflicto armado interno y la política de la reconciliación en el Perú.* Lima: Instituto de Estudios Peruanos, 2004.

Tinsman, Heidi. *Partners in Conflict: The Politics of Gender, Sexuality, and Labor in the Chilean Agrarian Reform, 1950–1973.* Durham, NC: Duke University Press, 2002.

Uceda, Ricardo. *Muerte en el Pentagonito: Los cementerios secretos del Ejército peruano.* Lima: Editorial Planeta, 2004.

Valcárcel, Luis E. *Tempestad en los Andes.* Lima: Editorial Universo, 1972.

Vargas Llosa, Mario. *La utopía arcaica: José María Arguedas y las ficciones del indigenismo.* Buenos Aires: Fondo de Cultura Económica, 1996.

Verdesio, Gustavo. “Latin American Subaltern Studies Revisited: Is There Life after the Demise of the Group?” *Dispositio* 25, no. 52 (2005): 5–42.

Vidal-Ortiz, Salvador, and Juliana Martinez. *Travar el saber: Educación de personans trans y travestis en Argentina: relatos en primera persona.* La Plata: Editorial de la Universidad de la Plata, 2018.

Wayar, Marlene. *Travesti: Una teoría lo suficientemente buena.* Buenos Aires: Muchas Nueces, 2019.

Wiese, Patricia. “Reportaje sobre Mujeres y conflicto armado.” *Ideele Televisión*, December 3, 2006. youtube.com/watch?v=4CnbZkCwQ24

Williams, Gareth. "Chimbote and the Shores of Indigenismo: Biopolitics and Bare Life in *El zorro de arriba y el zorro de abajo.*" *Revista de estudios hispánicos* 38, no. 1 (January 2004): 43–68.

Williams, Gareth. *Infrapolitical Passages: Global Turmoil, Narco-Accumulation, and the Post-Sovereign State.* New York: Fordham University Press, 2021.

Williams, Gareth. *The Other Side of the Popular: Neoliberalism and Subalternity in Latin America.* Durham, NC: Duke University Press, 2002.

Williams, Gareth. "The Subalternist Turn in Latin American Postcolonial Studies, or, Thinking in the Wake of What Went Down Yesterday." *Politica Comun* 10 (2016): 1–17.

Wittig, Monique. "The Mark of Gender." *Feminist Issues* 5, no. 2 (1985): 3–12.

INDEX